On Time! On Track! On Target! Managing Your Projects Successfully with Microsoft® Project

Bonnie Biafore

PUBLISHED BY
Microsoft Press
A Division of Microsoft Corporation
One Microsoft Way
Redmond, Washington 98052-6399

Library of Congress Control Number: 2005939169

Printed and bound in the United States of America.

3 4 5 6 7 8 9 QWE 0 9 8 7 6

Distributed in Canada by H.B. Fenn and Company Ltd.

A CIP catalogue record for this book is available from the British Library.

Microsoft Press books are available through booksellers and distributors worldwide. For further information about international editions, contact your local Microsoft Corporation office or contact Microsoft Press International directly at fax (425) 936-7329. Visit our Web site at www.microsoft.com/mspress. Send comments to *mspinput@microsoft.com*.

Microsoft, Active Directory, Excel, Microsoft Press, Outlook, PowerPoint, SharePoint, Visio, and Windows are either registered trademarks or trademarks of Microsoft Corporation in the United States and/or other countries. Other product and company names mentioned herein may be the trademarks of their respective owners.

The example companies, organizations, products, domain names, e-mail addresses, logos, people, places, and events depicted herein are fictitious. No association with any real company, organization, product, domain name, e-mail address, logo, person, place, or event is intended or should be inferred.

This book expresses the author's views and opinions. The information contained in this book is provided without any express, statutory, or implied warranties. Neither the authors, Microsoft Corporation, nor its resellers or distributors will be held liable for any damages caused or alleged to be caused either directly or indirectly by this book.

Acquisitions Editor: Sandra Haynes
Project Editor: Melissa von Tschudi-Sutton
Production: Publishing.com

Body Part No. X11-82258

Contents at a Glance

Part One   Getting a Project Started

Chapter One   Meet Project Management 2

Chapter Two   Selecting and Prioritizing Projects 12

Chapter Three   Obtaining Commitment for a Project 24

Part Two   Planning a Project

Chapter Four   Planning to Achieve Success 42

Chapter Five   What's the Problem? 60

Chapter Six   Visualizing Success: Scope, Objectives, and
                  Deliverables 74

Chapter Seven   Building a Work Breakdown Structure 84

Chapter Eight   Project Resources 104

Chapter Nine   Building a Project Schedule 122

Chapter Ten   Working with a Budget 160

Part Three   Carrying Out a Project

Chapter Eleven   Executing the Project Plan 176

Chapter Twelve   Evaluating Project Performance 184

Chapter Thirteen Managing Project Resources 208

Chapter Fourteen Communicating Information 220

Part Four   Controlling Projects

Chapter Fifteen   Managing Project Changes 256

Chapter Sixteen   Modifying the Project Schedule 266

Chapter Seventeen Balancing the Budget and Other Project Variables . . 288

Chapter Eighteen Managing Risk 296

Part Five   Closing Projects

Chapter Nineteen   Learning Lessons 314

Chapter Twenty   Managing Project Completion 330

Chapter Twenty-One   Archiving Historical Information 340

Table of Contents

Acknowledgments. xv
Introduction xvii
About the CD xxi
    What's on the CD xxi
    Using the CD xxi
    System Requirements xxi
    Support xxii

Part One   **Getting a Project Started**

Chapter One   **Meet Project Management. 2**
    What Is a Project? 3
    What Is Project Management? 4
    The Benefits of Project Management. 7
        Bottom-Line Benefits 7
        Benefits for the Project Team 8
    In Summary 10

Chapter Two   **Selecting and Prioritizing Projects. 12**
    Project Selection and the Project Manager. 13
    Criteria for Selecting Projects 14
        Criteria You Can't Ignore 14
        Linking Projects to Objectives 15
    Prioritizing Projects. 16
        Financial Measures. 17
        Risks and Opportunities. 21
    How a Project Review Board Works 22
    In Summary 23

Chapter Three   **Obtaining Commitment for a Project 24**
    The Project Charter: Publicizing a Project. 25
    Working with Project Stakeholders 28
        Identifying Stakeholders. 29
        Documenting Project Stakeholders. 36

Obtaining and Maintaining Commitment 37

In Summary 40

Part Two **Planning a Project**

Chapter Four **Planning to Achieve Success 42**

What Is Project Planning? 43

   Defining the Problem 43

   Charting the Course 45

   Getting Stakeholder Commitment 45

   Getting Team Members' Buy-In 46

   Pointing the Team in the Right Direction 46

   Tracking Progress 47

Plans Change 47

An Overview of Project Planning 48

   The Project Charter 49

   Project Planning Step by Step 50

   The Components of a Project Plan 50

In Summary 58

Chapter Five **What's the Problem? 60**

The Problem Statement 61

   Identifying the Problem 61

   Adding Constraints to a Problem Statement 63

The Project Mission Statement 64

   Building a Mission Statement 65

   Completing the Project Mission Statement 67

Project Strategy 68

   Identifying Alternatives 68

   Factors for Selecting a Project Strategy 69

   Choosing the Project Strategy 70

In Summary 72

Chapter Six **Visualizing Success: Scope, Objectives, and Deliverables 74**

The Scope Statement 75

   Developing a Scope Statement 77

Preventing Scope Creep 77

Project Objectives 79

Type of Objectives 79

Characteristics of Good Objectives 81

Project Deliverables 82

In Summary 83

Chapter Seven   **Building a Work Breakdown Structure 84**

What's a Work Breakdown Structure? 85

The Benefits of a WBS 88

Building a WBS from the Top Down 89

How to Build a WBS 89

When to Stop Building a WBS 93

Recording a WBS 95

Creating the WBS in Project 96

Modifying the WBS 98

Importing a WBS into Project 99

Detailing Work Packages 101

In Summary 103

Chapter Eight   **Project Resources 104**

The Responsibility Matrix 105

Responsibility Levels 106

Creating a Responsibility Matrix 107

Filtering a Responsibility Matrix in Microsoft Excel 108

The Project Organization Chart 109

Putting a Project Team Together 111

Creating Resources in Project 112

Methods for Adding Resources 113

Resource Information 115

Creating a Resource Pool 119

In Summary 120

Chapter Nine   **Building a Project Schedule 122**

Estimating Effort 123

Estimating Pitfalls and How to Avoid Them 124

Sensible Estimating Practices 127

Statistical Estimating 130

Defining the Sequence of Work **133**

Types of Task Dependencies 133

Identifying the Correct Dependency Type 134

Creating Task Dependencies 135

Automated Dependencies 136

Making Schedules Easy to Maintain 137

Adding Schedule Milestones **140**

Types of Milestones 141

Creating Milestones 143

Refining Task Names **143**

Naming Milestones and Deliverables 144

Unique Task Names 144

Assigning Resources to Tasks **145**

Assigning Resources in the Task Sheet 145

Assigning Resources in the Task Form 147

Using the Assign Resources Dialog Box 148

Building Reality into a Schedule **149**

Accounting for Productivity 149

Managing Part-Time Workers and Multitaskers 151

Scheduling Around Nonworking Time 152

Adjusting Tasks for Resource Efficiency 153

Shortening a Project Schedule **154**

The Fast-Track to an Early Finish .154

Choosing Tasks to Fast-Track 154

Partial Overlaps 155

Running Tasks in Parallel 156

A Crash Course on Project Crashing 156

The Danger in Crashing Projects .157

Time Versus Money 157

In Summary **159**

Chapter Ten **Working with a Budget** **160**

Understanding Capital Budgets **162**

Putting Capital Budgeting into Practice 163

Using a Capital Budgeting Tool 163

Calculating Costs in a Project Schedule............................165
   Specifying Rates for Work Resources in Project...............167
   Entering Rates and Quantities for Material Resources.........169
   Setting a Fixed Cost for a Task 170
Exporting Costs from a Project Schedule 170
   Creating a Filter to Show Only Work Packages 171
   Exporting Costs from a Project Schedule....................172
In Summary 174

Part Three   Carrying Out a Project

Chapter Eleven   Executing the Project Plan 176

A Quick Checklist 177
   Approvals and Commitments 177
   The Project Notebook 178
   Project Baselines...179
A Day in the Life of a Project Manager 181
In Summary 182

Chapter Twelve   Evaluating Project Performance.................. 184

Gathering Data 185
   The Data You Need 185
   Obtaining Time and Status 188
Tracking Schedule Progress.....................................190
   Reviewing Schedule Progress 191
   Tables with Schedule-Related Fields 193
   Filters for Checking Schedule Progress.......................194
Reviewing Cost and Cost Variance 195
   Viewing Cost and Cost Variance..............................195
   Finding Costs That Are Over Budget 197
   Project Cost Reports 198
Earned Value Analysis: Schedule and Cost Performance 199
   Earned Value Status Measures 200
   Analyzing an Earned Value Graph 201
   Earned Value Performance 202
   Earned Value in Microsoft Project 204
In Summary 207

Chapter Thirteen   **Managing Project Resources. 208**

Motivating Project Resources 209
Developing a Team 213
Evaluating People's Performance 215
    Watching for People's Performance 215
    What to Do with Problem People 216
    Reviewing People's Performance Compared to the Plan 217
In Summary 219

Chapter Fourteen   **Communicating Information 220**

Knowledge Is Power 221
The Communication Plan 222
    Who Needs to Know? 223
    What Do You Communicate to Audiences? 225
    What Communication Method Should You Use? 230
    Building a Communication Plan 232
    Creating Communication Reminders 233
Guidelines for Good Communication 235
    What Is Communication? 235
    How to Get Messages Through 237
    Learning to Listen 239
Meetings That Work 240
    Guidelines for Good Meetings 241
    Kickoff Meetings 245
    Project Status Meetings 245
    Management Meetings 247
Project Status Reports 249
Taming E-Mail 251
In Summary 252

Part Four   **Controlling Projects**

Chapter Fifteen   **Managing Project Changes 256**

An Overview of the Change Management Process 257
    What Do You Control with the Change Management
    Process? 258

Managing Change Requests 260

Who Belongs on the Change Review Board? 262

Tracking Changes 262

In Summary 265

Chapter Sixteen   **Modifying the Project Schedule 266**

Simplifying Solution Hunting 267

Displaying Summary Tasks 267

Displaying the Critical Path and Baseline 268

Fast Tracking a Project 269

Overlapping Tasks 270

Running Tasks in Parallel 271

Splitting Long Tasks into Short Ones 273

Scheduling Around Other Tasks 274

Shortening Lag Time 275

Adjusting Resource Allocation 276

Changing Units 276

Adjusting Work Contours 279

Assigning Overtime 280

Substituting Resources 281

Adding Resources to Tasks to Shorten Duration 283

Modifying Baselines 284

Saving Additional Baselines 284

Clearing a Baseline 285

Viewing Multiple Baselines 286

In Summary 287

Chapter Seventeen   **Balancing the Budget and Other Project Variables 288**

Cost, Scope, Quality, and Schedule 289

Balancing Acts 290

Reassigning Resources 290

Optimizing the Schedule 292

Business Decisions 293

In Summary 294

Chapter Eighteen   **Managing Risk** **296**

The Benefits of Managing Risk 297

The Risk-Management Plan 298

     Identifying and Describing Risks 302

     Assessing Risks 304

     Choosing the Risks You'll Manage .305

     Responding to Risks 307

     Setting Up Contingency Funds 309

Tracking Risks 310

In Summary 312

Part Five   **Closing Projects**

Chapter Nineteen   **Learning Lessons** **314**

The Importance of Lessons Learned 315

Collecting Lessons Learned 318

     Meeting Participants and What They Do 319

     Ground Rules 321

Documenting Lessons Learned 325

In Summary 328

Chapter Twenty   **Managing Project Completion** **330**

Project Closeout Reports 331

     Quantitative Results 333

     Qualitative Information 334

Obtaining Customer Acceptance 335

Project Transitions 337

     Transitioning Resources 337

     Handing Off Information 338

Closing Out Contracts 339

In Summary 339

Chapter Twenty-One   **Archiving Historical Information** **340**

Why Chronicle Project History? 341

     Save Documents for Reuse 341

     Save Project Performance for Future Estimates 342

Information to Store about Projects. 343
Ways to Build a Project Archive 345
  Shared Folder. 346
  Shared Workspace 347
Microsoft Enterprise Project Management Software. 347
In Summary 348

Glossary. 351

About the Author 355

Index 357

Acknowledgments

Publishing a book is a project, and each one comes with its share of surprises and challenges. Despite *On Time! On Track! On Target!* being a book about project management, the project team had to wrangle a few issues into submission, and I was fortunate to work with folks with the can-do attitude that every project manager dreams of.

My thanks go to Sandra Haynes, the Microsoft Press acquisitions editor, for convincing me to write this book. The project editor, Melissa von Tschudi-Sutton, was a paragon of tranquility as we revised the schedule and adjusted resources. Curt Philips, the production manager, graciously demonstrated how fast fast-tracking a project can be. And the copy editor, Anne Marie Walker, was gentle yet totally on target with her edits. Andrea Fox polished up the team's work by proofreading the final pages you're reading now. Because you never need information in the order it appears in a book, Rebecca Plunkett made specific tidbits easy to find by creating the index for this book.

A huge round of applause goes to John Pierce for his excellent contributions to the book. He accepted the challenge to write three of the chapters in this book and delivered the scope on time and within budget. What's more, his attention to quality—including writing in a similar style and finding appropriate quotations—is much appreciated.

I also want to thank the reviewers who made sure that I was clear, provided useful information, and most important, didn't make things up. For sharing his uncanny project management sense as well as his sense of humor, I thank my friend, Bob McGannon. I also thank Rozanne Whalen for her thorough technical review and valuable suggestions.

With every book I write, I thank my husband, Pete Speer, for remaining calm in the face of my deadlines. For this book, he was also a readily accessible accidental project manager. He reminded me of what inexperienced project managers need to know and provided diplomatic advice for making the book as useful as possible.

Introduction

If your boss recently breezed past your cubicle and asked you to manage a project, you can blame Tom Peters. Project management has been around for centuries. (After all, how do you think the Pyramids were built?) But Tom Peters's gonzo ravings about the benefits of project management have made many companies sit up and take notice. Starting with his 1999 *Fast Company* article, "The Wow Project," and a steady stream of articles about projects he's written since then, organizations have come to recognize that a lot of the work they do is project-oriented. And when they realize that good project management can save both time and money, that's about the time that people like you receive the call to be a project manager.

You aren't the only one. Membership in the Project Management Institute (PMI), a professional organization for project managers founded in 1969, reached 8,500 in 1990. Its membership topped 100,000 in 2003 only to double (207,066 members) by September 2005. Membership grew 48 percent from September 2004 to September 2005.

If you have little or no formal education in project management, congratulations, you've become an accidental project manager. You probably earned the assignment because you're dependable and good at organizing your work, but you have only a vague idea of what you're supposed to do or what it takes to succeed. To compound the challenge, Microsoft Project can seem like a Japanese puzzle box—getting a handle on one feature leads to another feature that you don't understand.

Even if you know your way around a Gantt chart and can build a decent schedule in Project, chances are nagging problems come up on the projects you manage. That's why project managers are so valuable. Nagging problems *always* come up on projects. By learning more about how to manage projects, you can prevent many problems and you can reduce the impact of many others. For example, scope creep is an all-too-common problem in which one small change to project scope after another sneaks into your plan until you have no chance of meeting your schedule or budget. Setting up a process for managing changes gives the project team the opportunity to say no to changes that aren't that important and to say yes to important changes even if they require a little more time or a little more money.

Although project management includes some techniques that are relatively straightforward, such as defining which task is the predecessor and which is the successor, most of what you do to manage projects is more touchy-feely. Communicating, negotiating, leading, and all other aspects of working with people can consume a lifetime of study, and you'd still have situations that make you stop and think.

The good news is that, as a project manager, you provide a highly valuable service to your organization, and your days will always bring something new and interesting. The bad news is that you're trying to learn new skills while you're overworked—what with trying to corral an untamed project, recovering from mistakes you've made, and trying to learn how to use Project as well. Training would help, but you don't have the time and the training dollars in your organization are probably scarce.

On Time! On Track! On Target! is here to help. This book tackles two broad topics that many project managers need:

■ A practical education in project management

■ How-to instructions for making the most of Project and other Microsoft Office applications to manage projects successfully

On Time! On Track! On Target! isn't some ponderous textbook about project management. It's an easy-to-read guide to managing projects from start to finish. If you're managing projects for the first time, it acts as your mentor by providing practical advice for managing projects more successfully and avoiding the more common project management mistakes. If you're already managing projects, you can jump directly to a chapter to prepare for your next project management task or respond effectively to the latest project situation. The book uses plain English to explain project management tools, techniques, and terminology, so you can learn the lingo as you learn what to do.

Unlike many product-oriented books with chapter after chapter devoted to Project features, no matter how obscure, the primary focus of *On Time! On Track! On Target!* is how to manage projects. However, you will find plenty of instructions for making the most of Microsoft products for project management. You'll learn how to choose the most appropriate feature for the situation you face. And you'll master Project features that are incredibly helpful but also incredibly confusing—until you know their secrets.

The organization of this book follows the PMI methodology and is broken into five parts that correspond to the PMI process groups: initiating, planning, executing, controlling, and closing.

■ *Part One, Getting a Project Started,* corresponds to PMI's initiating process group and describes how to get a project off the ground. The first chapter is an introduction to projects and project management. The other chapters in this part of the book explain how to choose the right projects to perform, gain commitment for your project, and work effectively with *project stakeholders,* people who have a vested interest in the successful outcome of the project. You'll also learn about some of the financial measures that executives use to evaluate projects.

■ *Part Two, Planning a Project,* describes how to define what a project is supposed to accomplish and prepare a plan for achieving those objectives. This part corresponds to PMI's planning process group. The first chapter is an introduction to project planning and explains all the components of a project plan and how they contribute to success. The other chapters in this part of the book explain in detail how to develop different parts of a project plan from the initial problem definition and mission statement to a project schedule and budget. In this part of the book, you'll learn how to use Microsoft Word to author project plan documents, Microsoft Project to build the project schedule, Microsoft Excel to develop a budget and analyze financial measures, and Microsoft Visio to construct project diagrams.

■ *Part Three, Carrying Out a Project,* corresponds to PMI's executing process group and describes what you do when you begin to implement the project plan you developed in Part Two. You'll learn how to evaluate project performance and manage the resources working on your project. Perhaps the most important chapter in the book, Chapter 14, "Communicating Information," not only describes how to build a communication plan for your project, but also offers advice for communicating effectively in writing, in meetings, and via e-mail. You can apply the techniques described in this chapter to every phase of your projects.

■ *Part Four, Controlling Projects,* covers the work you do almost immediately upon beginning to execute a project. This part corresponds to PMI's controlling process group and describes how you manage the changes that are an inevitable part of every project. You'll learn how to control change requests so they don't overwhelm your original schedule and budget. You'll also learn how to modify the project schedule in response to changes, balance the budget with other project performance measures to make good business decisions, and manage risks.

■ *Part Five, Closing Projects,* consists of three short chapters that correspond to PMI's closing process group. Although closing a project doesn't represent much of the time and effort in a project, the work you do is incredibly valuable to future projects. In this part of the book, you'll learn how to collect the lessons that people learned while working on a project, perform the tasks to tie up the loose ends at the end of a project, and store the results of a project for others to refer to in the future.

■ The *Glossary* at the end of the book is a quick reference to the project management terms used in the book.

Chapters in the book describe what project managers do and how these activities help deliver projects successfully. You'll find practical advice about steps to take on large projects and steps that might be omitted for small projects. Many chapters include step-by-step instructions or recommended features for Project and other Microsoft Office applications. In addition, this book includes several helpful features of its own:

■ *Sidebars* provide in-depth discussion of project management techniques.

■ *Best Practices* sidebars describe particularly effective practices used by many project managers to prevent problems or dramatically improve project performance.

■ *Important* tips emphasize tasks that deliver desirable results or activities that can seriously damage project performance.

■ *Tips* highlight shortcuts and other simple but helpful techniques.

■ *Warnings* represent minor problems and how to prevent them.

■ *Notes* provide additional information about topics in the text.

■ *On the CD* identifies content that is available on the companion CD.

About the CD

The companion CD that ships with this book contains many tools and resources to help you get the most out of this book.

What's on the CD

The companion CD includes the following:

- **Documents for a sample project** The *Backyard Remodel Project* folder contains Word documents, Excel workbooks, and Project files for the Backyard Remodel project discussed in the book.

- **Sample project management documents** The *Sample Documents* folder contains samples of typical project management documents constructed with Word, Excel, Visio, and Project.

- **Project management templates** The *Templates* folder contains Word and Excel templates for several types of project management documents.

- **Complete eBook** An electronic version of *On Time! On Track! On Target!* is available in PDF format.

Note Please note that third-party software and links to third-party sites are not under the control of Microsoft Corporation. Microsoft is therefore not responsible for their content, nor should their inclusion on this CD be construed as an endorsement of the product or the site.

Using the CD

To use the companion CD, insert it into your CD-ROM drive; a license agreement should appear automatically. If autorun is not enabled, run StartCD.exe at the root of the CD. After you accept the license agreement, a window appears that enables you to navigate the CD.

System Requirements

The following software is required to open and experiment with some of the sample files included in the companion CD content.

- Microsoft Windows 2000, Microsoft Windows XP, or Microsoft Windows Server 2003
- Microsoft Office Project 2003
- Microsoft Office 2003
- Microsoft Office Visio 2003

Support

Every effort has been made to ensure the accuracy of this book and companion CD content. Microsoft Press provides corrections for books through the Web at the following address:

http://www.microsoft.com/learning/support/

To connect directly to the Microsoft Knowledge Base and enter a query regarding a question or issue that you may have, go to the following address:

http://www.microsoft.com/learning/support/search.asp

If you have comments, questions, or ideas regarding the book or companion CD content, or if you have questions that are not answered by querying the Knowledge Base, please send them to Microsoft Press using either of the following methods:

E-Mail:

mspinput@microsoft.com

Postal Mail:

Microsoft Press
Attn: *On Time! On Track! On Target!* Editor
One Microsoft Way
Redmond, WA 98052-6399

Please note that product support is not offered through the preceding mail addresses. For support information, please visit the Microsoft Product Support Web site at the following address:

http://support.microsoft.com

Part One

Getting a Project Started

In this part

Chapter One   **Meet Project Management**........................ 2
Chapter Two   **Selecting and Prioritizing Projects**................ 12
Chapter Three   **Obtaining Commitment for a Project**.............. 24

Part One:
Getting a Project
Started

On Time! On Track! On Target! Managing Your Projects Successfully with Microsoft Project

Chapter One

Meet Project Management

All white-collar work is project work.

— *Tom Peters*

So you've been asked to manage a project. If you're new to project management, your first question is probably "What's a project?" no doubt followed closely by "How do I manage one?" and finally "How will I know if I did it right?" In this chapter, you'll learn what a project is, the basics of managing one, and why project management is so important.

What Is a Project?

The good news is that you've probably already managed a project without realizing it. You stumble across them every day—at work *and* at home. Besides the projects you work on at the office, some of the honey-dos taped to the refrigerator door at home are probably projects. Here are some examples of both business and personal projects:

- Construct a suspension bridge
- Landscape the backyard
- Launch a new advertising campaign
- Move into a new house
- Migrate data files to a new server
- Throw your spouse a surprise 40th birthday party
- Design a brochure for new services
- Obtain financial aid for your child's college education

What is the common thread between these disparate endeavors?

A project is a one-time job with specific goals, a clear-cut starting and ending date, and—in most cases—a budget.

The most significant characteristic of a project is *uniqueness*. Frank Lloyd Wright's design for the Fallingwater house was a one-of-a kind vision linked to the land on which the house was built and the water that flows past it. The design and construction of Fallingwater was unmistakably a project. Although every project is different, the differences can be subtle. Building a neighborhood of tract houses, each with the same design and the same materials, might seem like the same work over and over. But different construction teams, a record-breaking rainstorm, or a flat lot versus a house built on a cliff transforms each identical house design into a unique undertaking—a project.

Part One:
Getting a Project
Started

On Time! On Track! On Target! Managing Your Projects Successfully with Microsoft Project

---

Important Work that never ends and remains the same day after day is *not* a project. For example, building the walls and rafters for manufactured homes that you ship to their construction sites represents ongoing operations, which requires a very different type of management. Assembling a manufactured home on site is a project.

Dr. Joseph M. Juran defined a project as a problem scheduled for solution. Whether an organization launches a project to solve a problem or fulfill an unmet need, it commits its time, money, and human resources to the project to achieve *specific goals*. Surprisingly, many projects *don't* have clear goals, which is akin to a herd of sheep without a Border collie. There's lots of activity and angst, but very little movement in the right (or even consistent) direction. One of the most important tasks early in the life of a project is determining what the project objectives are and making sure that everyone involved agrees on them. The *scope* of a project is the extent of the work to be done.

Although some projects seem like they never end, a project has a clear-cut *beginning* and a clear-cut *end*. The project objectives help delineate the start and finish of a project. When objectives are well defined, it's easier to figure out how to achieve the objectives and when the project team has achieved them.

One of the reasons that projects need project managers is because projects aren't supposed to last forever or consume every available resource like an organizational black hole. Every project has its constraints—a budget, a small pool of available resources, a short amount of time, or limitations on how to solve the problem.

What Is Project Management?

Projects happen whether they're managed or not. Left unattended, projects seem endless, expend all available resources, and yet still don't deliver what they're supposed to. Some folks assigned to manage projects take great liberties with the guiding statement "Do whatever it takes." They get the project done, but they leave behind a path of destruction and dazed, exhausted workers. So, what is project management and how does it help achieve success?

A project has a set of objectives, a start and end, and a budget. The purpose of project management is to achieve the project objectives on time and within budget. In reality, project management is an ongoing task of balancing the project scope with time, cost, and level of performance and quality. According to the Project Management Institute's Guide to the Project Management Body of Knowledge, project management is divided into five types of processes:

- *Initiating* means officially committing to start a project. Although initiating doesn't consume much time in the life of a project, it's hugely important to success. Stakeholders and management give their support to the project and the project manager, indicating to everyone involved that the project is important. Identifying the potential project stakeholders, unearthing the *real* objectives of the project, and communicating its business benefits all contribute to building the support and buy-in that is crucial for a project to succeed. For example, you might be gung-ho about a fly-fishing vacation in Montana, but bringing that vacation to fruition is tough if your spouse is thinking about a cooking class at the Cordon Bleu. See Chapter 2, "Selecting and Prioritizing Projects," and Chapter 3, "Obtaining Commitment for a Project," for details on how to identify stakeholders and build buy-in for a project.

- *Planning* begins with identifying the problem to solve, the objectives, and the scope of work. But it also includes developing an implementation plan and schedule, which show the work that must be done, who does it, when they do it, and how much it costs. With skill and some luck, the project achieves its objectives within the desired time frame and budget, producing results at the desired level of quality, and without turning the assigned resources into burnt toast. Planning isn't complete without identifying the risks that could interfere with success and how to respond to them.

  Planning up front pays off many times over during the execution of a project. You can either spend some time planning early on or spend far more time putting out fires later. Part Two, "Planning a Project," explains how planning helps a project succeed and describes the components of a project plan.

Tip With the popularity of project management programs, such as Microsoft Project, many people mistakenly consider scheduling a project to be the same as managing a project. When you understand what project management *really* is, you can learn how to apply the features of Microsoft Project to managing projects more effectively.

Part One:
Getting a Project
Started

On Time! On Track! On Target! Managing Your Projects Successfully with Microsoft Project

- *Executing* a project is a project manager's ongoing work, keeping the project team focused on doing the right things at the right time—as outlined in the project plan. Part Three, "Carrying Out a Project," describes project management tasks during execution.

- *Controlling* a project is also ongoing work, but it focuses on monitoring and measuring project performance to see whether the project is on track with its plan. As the inevitable surprises, changes, and occasional disasters arise, the project manager can determine what kind and magnitude of course correction is required to get the project back on track. Part Four, "Controlling Projects," covers how to control a project.

- *Closing* includes officially accepting the project as complete, documenting the final performance and lessons learned, closing any contracts, and releasing the resources to work on other endeavors. Are the exit criteria complete? Does everyone involved agree that the project is a success and have they officially signed off on acceptance? Part Five, "Closing Projects," discusses steps for closing a project.

Planning, scheduling, and controlling sound like activities you can perform in the privacy of your office. But in the real world, project management is mainly about communicating with people (see Chapter 14, "Communicating Information"). *Stakeholders* play a crucial role in the potential success or failure of the project, whether they have a vested interest in the success of the project, work on the project, or are affected by the project in some way. Stakeholders must agree on the problem to be solved, the strategy for the project, and what constitutes success. Moreover, stakeholders can be strong allies or dire enemies, so keeping them informed is one of the most important tasks project managers do.

Communicating with the rest of the project team is equally important. These people perform the work in a project. Team members must understand the work they must do and any work-related constraints. They must also flag problems that arise and collaborate to fix

Best Practices

Capturing lessons learned is an important but often ignored step at the end of a project. The project team meets to document what went well, what did not go well, the reasons for success or failure, and what could be done differently the next time a similar project comes up.

Identifying outcomes that were less than perfect requires a delicate touch. It's important not to point fingers or place blame for problems. The point is to find out how to build on success and prevent problems. Chapter 19, "Learning Lessons," includes some tips on conducting a meeting to collect lessons learned.

Don't let these valuable lessons languish in a filing cabinet. Before you begin the next project, review previous lessons learned to make sure you don't repeat past mistakes.

them. Project managers have to lead, sometimes coax, and occasionally cajole a team of workers to successfully complete a project.

The Benefits of Project Management

Delivering objectives on time and within budget—what more could customers want? These days, customers expect high-quality products and services delivered quickly, with a minimum of fuss, and always for the lowest cost. That's a tall order, but if your company can't fill it, the competition is ready to jump in.

More and more organizations turn to project management to meet these tough requests. With good project management, organizations can deliver what their customers want without burning out the people who make it happen. Contrary to some people's beliefs, project management doesn't make projects take longer or transform organizations into inflexible behemoths. Planning ahead and managing to the plan, organizations can actually become *more* innovative, flexible, productive, and responsive.

Bottom-Line Benefits

The business world cares about money, and that's one reason that project management is growing so popular. By managing projects well, organizations can see all kinds of improvements to their bottom lines:

- **Faster and better return on investment**   Delivering projects on schedule and without cost overruns means that customers achieve a better return on their initial investment and see that return more quickly.

- **Decreased time to market**   With on schedule deliveries, the products or services that projects produce are ready to hit the market when the customer wants them.

- **Increased customer satisfaction**   Project planning identifies what the customer wants. And customers are happier when they get what they want or need.

- **Competitive advantage**   Delivering the right product or service at the right time is one of the best ways to whip the competition. Besides, project management relieves the project team from fighting fires, which means they have the time and energy to develop the best possible product or service.

- **Better support of strategic goals**   Project management keeps people focused on why a project is important and what it's trying to achieve.

Part One:
Getting a Project
Started

On Time! On Track! On Target! Managing Your Projects Successfully with Microsoft Project

Without a project plan, people quickly lose sight of what they're trying to accomplish.

- **Flexibility**   A project plan is a road map of how the project is going to reach its goals. With a plan in place, teams can analyze the effect of changes that arise and develop an alternative more quickly.

- **Increased productivity**   Applying resources effectively and efficiently means that people get their work done more quickly, and when they finish one assignment, they're refreshed and ready to work on something else.

Table 1-1 shows the improvement in financial results that project management initiatives delivered according to research conducted by the Center for Business Practices (*www.cbponline.com*).

Table 1-1   Improved Financial Results Produced by Project Management

Financial Measure	Improvement (%)
Return on investment	88.10
Return on capital	25.45
Economic value added	76.82
Sales growth	34.28
Productivity	61.17

Benefits for the Project Team

Project management sounds like a lot of work—and it is. But the amount of work is nothing compared to what you and your team have to do if you *don't* manage a project. Consider the benefits that project management delivers to the project manager, the project team, and the project itself:

- **Choosing the right things to do**   If you don't know how big your television is, buying an entertainment center to hold it is tough. To succeed, you have to know what the requirements are. A project plan documents project requirements and helps the team deliver what the customer wants—the first time around.

- **Doing the right things**   It's easy to get sidetracked during a project. People come up with better solutions or additional problems to solve, which usually cost more, take longer, and can potentially kill the project with overruns. Rearranging your pantry while preparing food for a dinner party could result in hungry guests.

- **Keeping calm and maintaining consistency** Without a clear-cut plan, team members can get pulled in every direction. The marketing department wants to change the message. The sales team wants a different product to sell. And engineering declares the design unbuildable. Constant change makes it impossible to stick to a schedule and budget, and makes team members cranky. Project management uncovers most of the needs and issues up front. If changes do occur during the project, the project plan makes it easier to adjust the course as well as understand the ramifications of the course adjustment.

- **Knowing where you stand** "It's going pretty well" or "It's not done yet" tend to make management nervous and that often results in constant questioning and an unpleasantly close watch on the project. A project plan lays out where you're going and how you're going to get there. With a plan in place, you can measure how far you've gotten and satisfy anyone's curiosity about project status.

- **Maintaining good communication** People are much happier when they know what's going on. Even bad news is easier to swallow if it's delivered early enough and with a plan for recovering.

- **Preventing problems and fire drills** Project life is much more pleasant when you've identified potential problems up front and have found ways to prevent them or resolve them quickly should they occur.

- **Identifying manageable work loads** Project management breaks down even the most monumental project into smaller, more manageable accomplishments. These pieces are less scary, easier to absorb, and easier to track. In addition, the people working on these pieces aren't frozen into inactivity by what seems like an impossible amount of work in an impossibly short period of time.

The results of the Center for Business Practices survey shown in Table 1-2, on the following page, quantified some of the improvements that project management initiatives provided to projects and their teams.

Part One:
Getting a Project
Started

On Time! On Track! On Target! Managing Your Projects Successfully with Microsoft Project

Table 1-2   Improved Project Results Produced by Project Management

Project Measure	Improvement (%)
Project budget performance	49.96
Project schedule performance	49.23
Resource utilization	50.05
Time to market	43.18
Employee satisfaction	36.00

In Summary

Good project management doesn't have to be costly, complicated, or cumbersome. In short, don't panic. You already know a lot about managing projects. If you've moved to a new home, hosted a family reunion, or remodeled a bathroom, you already know about achieving objectives, sticking to a schedule, working within a budget, and delivering quality. The rest of this book explains how to manage projects more efficiently and effectively, and how to use software tools to do so.

Part One:
Getting a Project
Started

On Time! On Track! On Target! Managing Your Projects Successfully with Microsoft Project

Chapter Two

Selecting and Prioritizing Projects

It's just as unpleasant to get more than you bargain for as to get less.

— *George Bernard Shaw*

Organizations have many projects from which to choose, but they usually don't have the resources to perform them all. So, they must choose. A dart board is expedient, but not the right approach for organizations that care about achieving their objectives. Most organizations quickly realize that they need a process and guidelines for selecting projects if they want to consistently pick the right projects to carry out. The same process works equally well to stop projects that aren't delivering the desired results.

Organizational DNA is as unique as the human variety, which means that each organization uses different criteria to select projects and places different weight on the importance of each criterion. Unfortunately, describing priorities as fluid in some organizations is like calling the Mississippi River a stream. Project managers must learn what drives their organizations and then manage projects to meet those objectives.

This chapter explains why you must understand the process and criteria that your organization uses to select projects. You'll also learn about some of the more common project selection criteria (when organizations do use them) and how to apply them to manage your projects more successfully.

Project Selection and the Project Manager

If you're a project manager and only learn of a project when you're assigned to manage it, project selection criteria might seem of little use to you. To the contrary, project selection criteria and the selection process can affect a project's fortunes at any time during its life cycle.

Like smart investors who monitor their investments to make sure that they're still delivering satisfactory returns with acceptable risk, most organizations evaluate projects as they progress to see whether they're delivering what they promised and still provide more benefit than other contenders. As a project manager, you must manage projects to deliver the results that stakeholders want. And if you can't deliver them all, focus on the results that stakeholders care about most. Although managing to deliver

Best Practices

You say that your organization isn't that organized and you suspect a dart board plays a key role in project selection. Project selection criteria are still important tools in a project manager's toolbox. In fact, if your organization doesn't filter the list of projects it decides to take on, your competition for resources is tougher, because the project portfolio is larger and more fluid.

By making sure that *your* project is aligned with the organization's goals and delivers impressive results in the areas that count, you'll have an easier time obtaining the resources you need— or assistance from management in removing obstacles.

Part One:
Getting a Project
Started

On Time! On Track! On Target! Managing Your Projects Successfully with Microsoft Project

results is covered in Part Four, "Controlling Projects," those potential results are the reason you have a project to manage. Commit those results to your subconscious and make sure everything you do works toward achieving them. You must be able to respond to these business objectives.

Criteria for Selecting Projects

Project selection criteria vary by organization and situation. In a high-tech company, time to market and the number of new features could be the only criteria that matter. For a company that makes medical devices, safety and quality are of ultimate importance, because patients don't want their pacemakers recalled due to design flaws. In addition to helping organizations choose projects, selection criteria help project sponsors and project managers decide whether a project is worth proposing. If a project doesn't meet the selection criteria, the team can bow out before wasting time proposing it to management. This section describes some of the criteria that organizations use to choose projects.

Criteria You Can't Ignore

Some project selection criteria represent automatic go or no-go decisions. Like income tax returns, projects need to satisfy regulatory requirements, such as the Sarbanes-Oxley Act. These projects must move forward if the organization wants to continue in business. Projects such as these move to the head of the project list, particularly if the government sets a deadline for compliance.

At the no-go end of the selection spectrum, an organization's mission, business objectives, and strategies are the most powerful factors in choosing projects. The fastest way to shorten a long list of projects is to ask, "Does this project support our mission and help achieve at least one of our business objectives?" If the answer is no, it's better to choose a project that is more in line with what the organization is trying to achieve. For example, if your company is focusing on improving quality and customer satisfaction, a project to reduce the cost of customer support is probably ill-timed. Table 2-1 on the next page includes types of objectives your project might have to achieve.

Another significant influence is the criteria by which the organization measures the project sponsor's performance. Ask yourself whether a project improves the project sponsor's perceived performance. If the answer is no, the project sponsor could disappear just when you need him most.

Linking Projects to Objectives

Linking a project to organizational objectives and strategies is the best way to show stakeholders the value that a project provides. Business objectives increase team members' commitment. And most important, the link to business objectives is crucial for evaluating change requests that increase or decrease project scope.

By understanding the business objectives that a project is supposed to support, it's much easier to prove the benefit of the project with hard numbers. For example, if your company spends $800,000 each year on support calls, the savings that a project produces is directly related to the number of calls it can eliminate. If an online knowledge base can cut calls in half and costs only $100,000 to implement, management will sit up and take notice.

Important   Projects that conflict with corporate culture and values should not make it through the selection process. If they do, employees begin to doubt that management means what it says. For example, a project to include bonuses for individual achievement in the payroll system is a bad idea for a company that emphasizes teamwork.

Part One:
Getting a Project
Started

On Time! On Track! On Target! Managing Your Projects Successfully with Microsoft Project

Table 2-1 **Types of Objectives**

Categories	Objectives
Sales and Marketing	Increase potential market
	Increase market share
	Reduce time to market
	Extend product life
	Increase customer satisfaction
	Increase quality or safety of products
	Improve reputation
	Decrease price to remain competitive
Production	Improve quality and safety of production process
	Reduce waste
	Decrease installation time
	Use more readily available materials
	Streamline production
Organizational Factors	Satisfy regulatory standards
	Provide value to stockholders
	Improve public perception
	Decrease labor skill level required
	Reduce training required
	Improve communication
	Improve employee morale
	Increase productivity
	Improve working conditions
Financial	Increase revenue
	Decrease costs
	Improve profitability
	Improve consistency of income

Prioritizing Projects

As with regulatory requirements, some projects obtain a priority position more easily than others. But most projects have to jockey for position in an organization's project portfolio. If one business objective far outweighs all others, prioritizing projects could be quite simple. In most cases, additional factors come into play when deciding which of the contenders comes first.

Financial Measures

Many project managers new to their jobs think that project management is mainly about scheduling and tracking progress. But experienced project managers know that project financial measures are crucial for obtaining and maintaining executive support. Financial measures for projects are similar to the measures that investors use to evaluate investment opportunities. Although executives choose from several different project financial measures, they all boil down to which project makes the most of the available money. Considering that you invest an amount of money over a period of time, executives want to know which project provides the best return on that investment. This section introduces the most common financial measures for evaluating projects and explains their pros and cons.

Payback Period

The payback period measures the length of time it takes for a project to pay back what the organization paid to complete the project in the first place. For example, suppose that revamping a production line costs $200,000, but the new and improved production line saves $20,000 each month that it operates. The payback period is the initial investment divided by the payback per period:

Payback period = $200,000 / $20,000 per month, or 10 months

The attraction of the payback period as a project measure is its simplicity and that the data needed to calculate it is reasonably easy to obtain. The measure is easy to understand—even for people who aren't familiar with business finance.

The payback period measure has several disadvantages:

- **Ignores cash flows beyond the payback period** The payback period rewards projects that generate money early on. For example, a project that produces savings more slowly but for a longer period of time would lose in a payback period contest.

- **Assumes cash comes in long enough to pay back the investment** Suppose the product that you build on the revamped production line becomes obsolete before you reach the end of the payback period. Your company doesn't earn some of the savings that the payback period calculation takes into account.

- **Ignores the time value of money** The payback period doesn't take into account the cost of money over time. For example, if you borrow

Part One:
Getting a Project
Started

On Time! On Track! On Target! Managing Your Projects Successfully with Microsoft Project

money to carry out a project, the interest you pay is the cost of money, which increases the longer you owe on the loan. As you'll see in the next section, when the cost of borrowing money is high, this omission can skew the results by significant amounts.

Net Present Value or Discounted Cash Flow

The net present value measure gets its name from the components that go into the calculation:

- **Net**   The calculation takes into account the money invested and the earnings or savings—so the net amount from income minus expenses.

- **Present**   The calculation uses the rate of return that the organization requires from investments to determine today's value for the dollars that the project spends or earns at different times in the future. For instance, a company might specify that projects must provide a 10 percent return on investment.

- **Value**   If the net present value is positive, the investment earns a return greater than the one that the company requires. If the net present value is negative, the project return falls short of the required return.

Important   If a company uses return on investment to prioritize projects, you can be certain that it will also have a minimum return on investment percentage for a project to qualify for funding. Be sure to find out what that minimum is and verify that your projects exceed it.

Net present value requires more information than the payback period measure, but it's still readily available. The big drawback to net present value is the learning curve for people who aren't familiar with this method of financial analysis.

Here's an example of net present value using the revamped production line. The assumptions about the revamped production line are that:

- For simplicity, the company pays for the new production line in a lump sum of $200,000 when the production line begins operation.

- The production line saves $20,000 each month of operation.

- The production line equipment is worth $10,000 (salvage value) at the end of the second year when the production line equipment becomes obsolete and the investment and its returns end.

Most people new to net present value calculations use a chart showing cash inflows and outflows to help calculate the result. Figure 2-1 shows the cash flows for the production line.

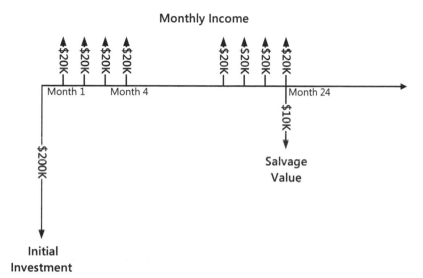

Figure 2-1 A chart of cash inflows and outflows identifies which numbers in the net present value calculation should be positive or negative.

No one in their right mind chooses to calculate net present value without the help of a financial calculator. Microsoft Excel makes short work of net present value calculations with the XNPV function. It accepts the required rate of return, a series of cash flows in or out, and the dates on which they occur. As you can see in Figure 2-2 on the next page, the production line net present value is $243,580, which shows that the project exceeds the 10 percent return the company requires. Money that you spend must be negative and savings or income must be positive.

Tip If you have a regular series of cash flows, you can use the NPV function in Excel. Although you don't have to enter dates for this function, it accepts no more than 29 values, which can crimp calculations based on monthly cash flows. The rate you enter must equal the rate for the period between each cash flow.

Part One:
Getting a Project
Started

On Time! On Track! On Target! Managing Your Projects Successfully with Microsoft Project

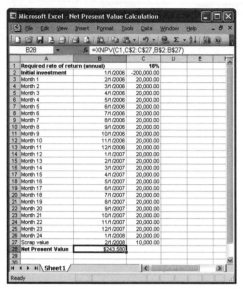

Figure 2-2 The Excel XNPV function calculates the net present value of a series of cash inflows and outflows.

Internal Rate of Return

In finance circles, internal rate of return (IRR) is the annual return that a project delivers, taking into account the time value of money. The IRR is the equivalent of the annual percentage yield (APY) that you earn on a savings account that pays a fixed interest rate (annual percentage rate or APR). If the IRR is greater than the return the organization requires, the project is in good shape. The XIRR function in Excel accepts a series of cash flows in or out, and the dates on which they occur. The spreadsheet in Figure 2-3 shows the calculation of IRR for the revamped production line project using the XIRR function.

As with net present value, the timing of cash flows is important for IRR. The later that cash flows in or cash flows out, the more the cash flows are affected by the time value of money. For example, early income increases the return you earn. However, if you spend money early, you reduce your return more than spending money later on.

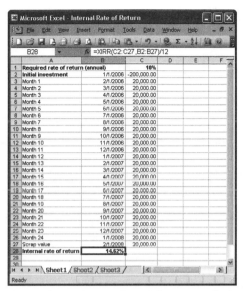

Figure 2-3 The Excel XIRR function calculates the internal rate of return for a project using cash flows and dates.

Risks and Opportunities

Despite great alignment with organizational objectives, some projects still struggle to gain approval because they represent substantial risks. For example, a project that offers outstanding benefits but plans to use untested new technology could be a huge failure if the technology doesn't work. Other projects might not win the top prize for organizational objective alignment, but they provide so much synergy with other projects that they rise a few rungs on the project selection ladder.

As you'll learn in Chapter 18, "Managing Risk," evaluating risks (and opportunities) takes into account the impact should the risk come to pass and the likelihood that it will occur. For example, a project that depends on highly specialized Venetian plasterers who are

The Importance of Stakeholder Support

Alignment with organizational objectives is important for a project because *someone* has to care enough to push for the project to be selected and completed. If a project achieves a business objective, the stakeholder who benefits from that objective is more likely to sponsor the project and fight for it during the selection process.

Of course, stakeholder support is equally important once a project gets under way. Stakeholders can provide resources, eliminate obstacles, and resolve all sorts of problems, as Chapter 3, "Obtaining Commitment for a Project," describes in more detail. Stakeholder support often appears early in the project selection process, when a project review board or a similar entity evaluates the project. The next section describes how a project review board operates.

Part One:
Getting a Project
Started

On Time! On Track! On Target! Managing Your Projects Successfully with Microsoft Project

currently in high demand faces both a major setback if the resources are unavailable and an almost certain probability of a delay.

How a Project Review Board Works

Sponsors and project managers often become attached to their projects. They can lose sight of whether the projects make sense, pick the projects that are the most fun or the least trouble, or refuse to consider whether another project might be better for the entire organization. The solution to this problem is often a project review board, which can be a more objective judge of the merits of potential projects.

A project review board typically comprises high-level executives from every area in an organization. Here's how a project review board usually works:

- **Someone proposes a project**   For the best chance of success, the person who wants his or her project to win a spot in the queue should evaluate the project using the same selection criteria that the project review board applies. And be prepared to answer questions that the board might ask.

- **The project review board analyzes the materials that the person proposing the project submits and asks questions about the proposal**   If the proposal is unclear or incomplete, board members ask questions to clarify what they don't understand.

- **The project review board evaluates the project using the standard project selection criteria**   Because the board includes executives from different areas, the group can identify issues or conflicts between business objectives. For example, if the company is trying to cut costs and increase customer satisfaction, the board could look for the projects that provide the most improvement in customer satisfaction for the least cost.

- **The board approves or rejects the project**   The board communicates its decision to the proposer and explains the reasons for its decision. Telling proposers why a project wasn't chosen not only maintains morale, but also helps them learn what the board looks for in projects.

In Summary

Project managers must understand the project selection and prioritization process. Although a project manager might not influence the initial selection of a project, the selection criteria are useful to ensure that the project obtains the resources it needs and for measuring whether the project is delivering the right results at any point during the life of a project.

Part One:
Getting a Project
Started

On Time! On Track! On Target! Managing Your Projects Successfully with Microsoft Project

Chapter Three

Obtaining Commitment for a Project

Unless commitment is made, there are only promises and hopes . . . but no plans.

— *Peter Drucker*

A project without a team dedicated to making it a success is in trouble from the start. Although a project needs commitment at all levels of an organization, a project sponsor is the executive who is the project's biggest fan, perhaps the person whose performance bonus depends most on the project's outcome. Management support is a boon to a project manager trying to resolve resource shortages, money issues, conflicting priorities, or differences of opinion on project direction.

But the commitment of the people who work on the project day after day is equally important. When team members appreciate the importance of the project, they work harder to meet expectations, stay on schedule, deliver higher quality, and think of creative solutions to problems that arise. In short, they devote themselves to delivering success.

The project charter is often the first visible indication of project commitment. This document is like a backstage pass. It tells everyone involved with a project who the project manager is and the authority that the project manager has for the project.

This chapter begins by explaining what goes into a project charter and how to use one effectively. A project sponsor or customer is the best person to distribute a project charter, so the chapter continues with a description of stakeholders—people who, in some way, are involved with your project, such as sponsors and customers. You'll learn how to identify different types of stakeholders, pinpoint what they expect from a project, and determine how to get them—and keep them—on board.

The Project Charter: Publicizing a Project

If a project makes it through the selection process, it becomes a real project—but only for a finite length of time. Whether a project lasts only a few weeks or several years, it's important that people know up front that the project is under way and why it's important. A project charter is the advance publicity that a project needs.

Unlike executives who hold authority based on their positions in an organization, project managers have authority only between their projects' start and end dates. Because project managers aren't necessarily high in an organization's hierarchy, they must borrow authority from someone else. Project charters come from those people with authority—project customers or sponsors.

Part One:
Getting a Project
Started

On Time! On Track! On Target! Managing Your Projects Successfully with Microsoft Project

Project charters announce to everyone involved who the project managers are, what they are supposed to do, how much authority they have, and who has given them that authority. Project managers have enough to do without convincing people that they can authorize expenditures, approve contracts, or request resources. The project charter does that for them.

Tip If you manage projects in an organization that isn't familiar with project management practices, you might have to ask the project sponsor to prepare a project charter and distribute it. In fact, you can write the project charter yourself and ask the sponsor to sign and send it out.

The good news is that a project charter is a simple document—it's like a project press release. Figure 3-1 shows an example of a project charter.

The sample project charter, *OnTime_Project_Charter.doc*, is available in the *Sample Documents* folder on the companion CD.

Trey Research

Memo

To: Kevin McDowell

From: Zainal Arifin

Date: November 30, 2005

Re: A. Datum Corporation Ubiquitous Computing Project

We have assigned Gretchen Rivas to be the project manager for the Ubiquitous Computing Project. This project is an important and intriguing project for Trey Research and A. Datum Corporation. When complete, the Ubiquitous Computing Project will significantly increase A. Datum Corporation's productivity and quality measures by providing instant and universal access to the company's data and programs.

As project manager, Ms. Rivas is responsible for working with your team to develop a project plan that describes the objectives, deliverables, and implementation plan for the project. She will work with functional managers at Trey Research to assign the appropriate resources to the project. She will also coordinate with you and other managers at A. Datum Corporation to identify the resources needed from your company.

Ms. Rivas will execute the project plan, monitor progress and performance, and take corrective action if necessary. She will communicate assignments to functional managers and the members of the project team. For the duration of the project, Ms. Rivas will prepare and present status reports every two weeks to the Trey Research/A. Datum Corporation project steering committee.

To ensure the success of the project, Ms. Rivas has the authority to manage the project, assign resources, and make financial commitments on behalf of Trey Research. Her authority for the Ubiquitous Computing Project specifically includes:

- Communicating directly with A. Datum Corporation regarding the project.
- Communicating directly with the Trey Research management team regarding the project.
- Making financial decisions relating to the project including procurement, expenditures, and authorizing payments.
- Delegating authority and responsibilities to resources with the approval of the resources' functional managers.
- Negotiating with functional managers and customer contacts for resources.
- Requesting assistance from any member of the steering committee to help resolve issues that arise.

I have the utmost confidence in Ms. Rivas and ask that you support her in achieving the objectives of this project. If you have any questions about her authority or responsibilities, please contact me.

Zainal Arifin

Sponsor for the Ubiquitous Computing Project and Vice President of Engineering

Figure 3-1   A sample project charter.

Here are the typical ingredients for a project charter:

- **Project name**   Brief descriptive names, such as Backyard Remodel Project, are fine.

Note   In the business world, acronyms appear to offer longer names in shorter packages. But spelling them out sometimes takes longer than saying the words they represent. Moreover, acronyms make it harder for people outside the project to know what it's about. For example, the A. Datum Corporation Ubiquitous Computing Project could end up as the ADCUC project. It's a little shorter, but nowhere near as meaningful.

Part One:
Getting a Project
Started

On Time! On Track! On Target! Managing Your Projects Successfully with Microsoft Project

- **Purpose of the project** This can be the mission statement, a one-line summary of what the project is supposed to achieve, or a more thorough description of the business objectives for the project.

- **Project manager** Include a sentence stating that the person named is the project manager for the project and will carry out the responsibilities identified in the charter.

- **Project manager's responsibilities** Including a summary of the work the project manager does in the project helps the audience understand what the project manager needs as well as what project management entails.

- **Project manager's authority** The project charter describes the extent of the project manager's authority and lists specific activities the project manager has authority to perform.

- **A formal announcement of the sponsor's or executive's support** The charter begins the chain of commitment by putting in writing the sponsor's or customer's support for the project and the project manager. In effect, this announcement is like a power of attorney, stating that the project manager is empowered to perform specific tasks under the authority of the sponsor or customer.

Important The choice of the person who signs and distributes the project charter is important. The signature of the company president might look impressive, but that signature can backfire if she asks "What project?" when someone asks her about your work. The project sponsor—the executive or manager who is ultimately responsible for the success of the project and actively supports it—or the project customer are ideal choices to sign and send out the project charter.

Everyone involved in or affected by the project should receive a copy of the project charter. These days, e-mail is the most expedient way to distribute a message. In some corporate cultures, a paper memo carries more weight.

Working with Project Stakeholders

Projects wouldn't get anywhere without people, so much of a project manager's job is working with people. And project stakeholders are the people that project managers work with the most. Project stakeholders get their name because they have a stake in the outcome of the project. Stakeholders include the customers who receive and use the results of a project, departments or vendors that participate in the project, managers who are evaluated on its success, and the employees assigned to work on the project's tasks.

Stakeholders influence a project throughout its life. During planning, they help define project objectives, requirements, and constraints; identify workable strategies; evaluate the project plan and schedule; and provide the funding for the project. After the project gets going, stakeholders do the work, help resolve issues that arise, decide whether changes are necessary, and control or increase the budget. Although the customers and the project sponsor are the most important to please, the sign of true success is a project that makes most, if not all, stakeholders happy.

Stakeholders don't wear "I'm a stakeholder" name tags. Some stakeholders who are incredibly important to the project might not realize they're stakeholders. For example, a marketing department could develop great plans for its new product launch Web site without inviting the Web developers to participate in the requirements session to confirm that new features are feasible.

On the other hand, you're bound to get some folks who claim to be stakeholders but aren't—or who try to influence the project more than their stakeholder roles warrant. For instance, a group might see your project as a way to get its new Web site without having to foot the entire bill. The next thing you know, your project has a host of unnecessary requirements with no additional budget.

Identifying Stakeholders

Your first step in working with stakeholders is to find out who they are and make sure that you have the right ones on your team. The following sections explain the different types of stakeholders, how they contribute to a project, how you can identify them, and how to keep them happy. But if people are vying for stakeholdership and you don't think they should belong, don't be afraid to ask the project sponsor, the project customer, or other stakeholders to help you control who joins the stakeholder group.

Regardless of the role they play or the group to which they belong, stakeholders either contribute something to your project or want something from it. For example, the project sponsor gives you the authority to do your job as project manager and provides support when you ask for it. In return, the sponsor wants a positive outcome.

Part One:
Getting a Project
Started

On Time! On Track! On Target! Managing Your Projects Successfully with Microsoft Project

Project Customer

Project customers make three significant contributions:

1. *Money.* The most important customer contribution is money, because without funding, a project never gets off the ground.

   Surely, whoever pays the bills is your customer. Yes, the person or committee that has final authority over funding is a customer stakeholder. Even the most lavish budgets have their limits and you need to know that limit. But the customer who controls the money usually has other goals besides staying within budget, such as a minimum return on investment (see "Financial Measures," page 17) or positive comparison of benefit to cost (read about the net present value measure; see "Net Present Value or Discounted Cash Flow," page 18).

   To keep a financial customer happy, you must stay on top of the financial performance of your project (see Chapter 17, "Balancing the Budget and Other Project Variables"). At status reporting time, you must be able to explain negative financial results and how you plan to get those measures back on track. If runaway requirements are overwhelming your budget, the financial customer can be a powerful ally to help convince other stakeholders of the need for restraint.

Best Practices

Conflicts arise in the project world and some of the toughest to resolve are from stakeholders that *don't* support your project. Perhaps your project is the best solution for the overall objectives of the organization, but it hurts a few stakeholders' chances to meet their specific performance goals and thus their performance bonuses. Or, it requires one group to radically change the way *it* works to shorten the duration of a business process in which several groups participate.

When a project affects some groups more than others, stakeholders from those groups might push back. Stakeholders also might withhold their support if they don't get the benefits they hoped for from a project. Whether they try to discredit the utility of the selected solution, withhold resources that you need to complete the project, or doggedly drag the project down by raising false issues, these stakeholders do their best to achieve their objectives.

The first step to winning over reluctant stakeholders is to understand their concerns. If you don't know why they are fighting your project, you have little hope of convincing them to play nice. But by understanding their pain points and doubts, you might be able to redirect the project to make them a bit happier. For example, if a group has to change its workflow, you could

Tip In some cases, project sponsors play dual roles as project customers. For example, project sponsors often provide funding for projects that deliver products for external customers. This is also true for many projects that are launched to improve internal corporate processes or functions.

2. *Influence.* Because customers pay for projects, customers usually have a lot of influence over what a project is supposed to accomplish—project objectives, deliverables, and specific requirements.

Unfortunately, the customer who pays the bills often isn't the same one who defines the requirements. At a car dealer, your spouse, who's better at negotiating, might be holding the checkbook, but you're the one who decides whether the car satisfies your commuting requirements.

As you might expect, many people can play the role of the customer who identifies project objectives and requirements. In fact, the difficulty is knowing when to cut off the list of people who tender requirements. Your job is to find out who is authorized to make these kinds of decisions about the project. The project sponsor and the customer who pays the bills are a good place to start, but you'll also have to rely on your own judgment. In addition, the best and most knowledgeable customer representatives can clearly communicate what they want and can prioritize their requests.

reprioritize some of the development work to deliver that group's enhancements first.

Likewise, you can emphasize the benefits your project provides to the entire organization and hope that the stakeholders are magnanimous. Sometimes, you simply don't have any benefits to offer unhappy stakeholders. In that case, you can ask your project sponsor or supporting stakeholders to help you bring the stragglers on board. If performance goals are the issue, you might think that asking the executive team to change compensation plans would be the way to go. Unfortunately, executive teams, project sponsors, and other stakeholders won't always back you up. Compensation plans are complicated and hard to change. Truth be told, in the face of politics and the reality of working with people long after your project ends, executives often choose to maintain their other relationships at your expense.

As a project manager with unwilling and unmoving stakeholders, the best action you can take is to identify the risks that the situation presents (see Chapter 18, "Managing Risk"), develop a workaround plan for those issues, and communicate the risks and options to your entire stakeholder group so it can make an informed decision about what to do. The solutions aren't as straightforward as accounting. There's no one right answer. The risks might never come to fruition. If the risks do arise, your workaround plan might resolve the situation successfully. Unfortunately, project management doesn't always deliver a happy ending. If an unwilling stakeholder damages your project, you might have nothing to do but hope that the team recognizes your best efforts.

Tip For product-oriented projects, you can't include the ultimate customers—the people who buy the products. In these situations, you work with people or groups that represent the end users, such as a usability expert for a Web site or a marketing department with marketing research data.

Part One:
Getting a Project
Started

On Time! On Track! On Target! Managing Your Projects Successfully with Microsoft Project

3. *Approval.* Customers approve deliverables as long as the objectives and requirements have been met.

There's nothing worse than getting to the end of a long project only to find out that the customer isn't satisfied. By working with the customers and other stakeholders to agree on objectives up front, specifying success criteria for a project (described in Chapter 4, "Planning to Achieve Success"), and having stakeholders sign off on scope and deliverables, you'll rarely encounter this kind of disappointment.

Project Sponsor

Projects present a tough organizational problem. They require cooperation between many departments, business units, and companies. But project managers almost never hold positions of authority high enough to oversee all the groups involved. Enter project sponsors—people who *do* have formal authority and are interested in seeing their projects succeed. Project sponsors don't always come from top levels of management. What matters most is that they have enough authority to promote their projects and are willing and capable of taking action when needed.

Signing their names to project charters (see "The Project Charter: Publicizing a Project," page 25) is only the first step in sponsoring projects. The best project sponsors play an active role in the projects they support from beginning to end. Although they appear to sponsor projects, what they *really* do is back the project manager and project team in their efforts. Here are some of the ways that sponsors help:

- *Lend authority* to a project manager by signing and distributing a project charter.

- *Provide guidance* to the project manager about the priority of objectives and performance measures.

- *Review the project plan* and suggest ways to build more support for the project.

- *Advise the project manager* on issues and politics that could harm the project.

- *Regularly review project status* and suggest ways to resolve problems and issues that arise.

- *Maintain the project's priority* and protect its resources within the organization's project portfolio.

■ *Step in to resolve issues* when the project manager's authority doesn't do the job.

Important The project charter doesn't always work. Managers question authority or entrenched bureaucracy makes working across department boundaries almost impossible. Intervention from a project sponsor can break the logjam *and* reiterate the importance of the project.

In return for all this help, the project sponsor wants to see the project succeed. You can win more points with your sponsors by keeping them informed. Good communication is a balancing act (see Chapter 14, "Communicating Information"). Sponsors expect you to manage the project; they don't want you knocking on their doors every five minutes. However, when tough problems arise, they'd rather have you call them in early enough to help instead of finding out after it's too late to do anything.

Tip If your project sponsors aren't as supportive as they could be, they might not know how they can help. Ask your sponsor for the support you want.

Functional Manager

Most companies use a functional organization: managers (called functional or line managers) oversee the performance of a business function, such as accounting, engineering, or marketing. These managers set policies for their domain, are accountable for achieving functional or departmental goals, and supervise the resources that perform the function. The resources for project teams come from these functional groups, so project managers must work with functional managers (with support from project sponsors if necessary) to get the resources they need when they need them.

With a project plan in hand (see Chapter 4), a project manager has a good idea of the skills and characteristics that resources should have. Obtaining those resources—and holding onto them—is one of the most common project management challenges.

Functional managers spend a lot time overseeing their people's schedules—and listening to employees' complaints if they have too much work to do, not enough work to do, work that they aren't trained for, or work that they're overqualified for. They want their employees working on tasks to which they're suited and that are important to the organization's goals.

Part One:
g a Project
Started

On Time! On Track! On Target! Managing Your Projects Successfully with Microsoft Project

A well-planned project schedule and clearly defined work are two ways to win over functional managers. If you demonstrate that your plan assigns the right kinds of resources to tasks and allocates those resources to work a reasonable number of hours each week, functional managers are more likely to fulfill your requests. Planning a project to keep resource workloads consistent is another way to gain functional managers' trust. You won't have to beg for resources to survive workload peaks or apologize for delays or downtime.

Communication is important for working with functional managers. Initially, they want to know what skills you need for your project and any resource constraints, such as cost, timing, or experience. For example, highly specialized resources are usually hard to come by. Tell managers when you need these resources and do whatever you can to maintain the dates for their assignments. If deadlines do slip, notify the managers as soon as possible so both of you can make alternative arrangements.

uilding Relationships with Managers

good relationships with functional managers pay off on project after project. Managing resources effectively is an important first step in building relationships with managers, but there are other ways to earn a manager's trust.

If you have more time than money, work with functional managers to give less-experienced resources a chance to develop their skills. You can pair these people with experts to get work done and help the organization cross-train its people.

After resources are assigned, functional managers respond much like customer stakeholders. The sooner they know about resource problems, the easier it is to solve them. Besides, they can offer solutions you might not think of on your own or find resources that you don't know about.

Warning   Assignments that leave people with little work to do for days on end are a sure way to lose resources to other projects. Another project manager might notice your resources' inactivity or the resources might complain about having nothing to do. Then, when your project needs those resources, they're likely to be unavailable. In the worst case, idle employees could be laid off, not only raising issues for staffing current projects but also disrupting people's lives.

Team Member

The people who do the work for a project are stakeholders, too. They contribute their expertise and time to carrying out the tasks that make up a

project. Team members are a diverse group. In reality, people who act as other types of stakeholders—customers, sponsors, and functional managers—are often team members as well. For example, customers participate in planning and requirements definition, which are project tasks as much as writing the copy for a new marketing brochure or ordering furniture for the new office are. Although team members might make other contributions to projects in other roles, their job as team members is to perform the work that they're assigned. What they expect in return is interesting work, communication, respect, and assignments that don't consume their every waking hour.

During project planning, you gradually develop a picture of the skills you need on your project team and work with functional managers to obtain those resources. As you bring team members on board, you must clearly communicate the work they're supposed to do. To gain their commitment, you must help them understand how their work fits into the big picture of the project.

As the project progresses, it's important to maintain this communication. Team members don't like surprises any more than executives do. Let team members know the work that's up next or notify them if work is delayed or changes have been made.

How Planning Tasks Help Identify Stakeholders

The good news is that the tasks you perform to prepare a project plan go a long way to identify many of the stakeholders. Here is a list of some project plan components and the stakeholders they help identify.

Defining the problem statement and the mission statement usually identify the customer of the project. Who's having a problem that needs to be solved? What is the purpose of the project, and who benefits from the results?

Project objectives and requirements can help identify additional customers and perhaps the project sponsor.

Project strategy, scope, the organization chart, and responsibility assignment matrix (see "The Responsibility Matrix," page 105) identify functional managers and team members. The responsibility matrix can be a great help for weeding out wanna-be customers. If people or groups aren't responsible for a part of the project, they aren't likely to be customers either.

Project Manager

Identifying the project manager is easy. It's you. And this book is all about how you contribute to the success of your projects.

Part One:
Getting a Project
Started

On Time! On Track! On Target! Managing Your Projects Successfully with Microsoft Project

Documenting Project Stakeholders

Who contributes to this project? and Who cares about the project's outcome? are questions that help identify stakeholders, but to work with stakeholders effectively, you need to know more. When you add someone to your list of project stakeholders, make a point of learning the following information about that person:

- **Organization**   At the beginning of a project, you'll need some hints about who works for which company and in which department. Document the stakeholder's organization and department, although you'll eventually have this information memorized.

- **Advisers**   Find out who the stakeholder listens to. If you face delicate negotiations in the future, you can discuss options and fine-tune your approach with advisers before addressing the actual stakeholders.

- **Objectives**   Identify the stakeholder's objectives for the project and list the objectives in order of priority. This ensures that you involve the right people in discussions about a specific objective.

- **Contributions**   List what the stakeholder does for the project. These contributions help you identify who to go to for items such as funding, requirements, and approvals.

In the midst of project execution, you have a million details to remember. Don't count on keeping this information in your head. The form in Figure 3-2 provides one approach for documenting stakeholders.

The stakeholder analysis document shown in Figure 3-2, *OnTime_Stakeholder_Analysis.doc*, is available in the *Sample Documents* folder on the companion CD.

Stakeholder Analysis

Name	Organization	Advisers	Project Support
Wolfgang Peterson	A. Datum Mgt	CFO Engineering manager	Supports project

Represents	Objectives	Obj. Priority	Contributions
Customer	Increase quality	1	
Customer	Increase productivity	2	
Customer	Increase share price	3	
Customer	Increase market share	4	
Customer			Funds project
Customer			Approves project plan
Customer			Authorizes major changes

Figure 3-2   Keep track of stakeholders, what they want, and how they can help.

Obtaining and Maintaining Commitment

*The quality of a person's life is in direct proportion to their com-
mitment to excellence, regardless of their chosen field of
endeavor.*

— *Vincent T. Lombardi*

Projects depend on people to complete them, which means that building
commitment to a project doesn't require specialized project management
skills. All it takes is good people skills. Of course, people skills are far more

Part One:
Getting a Project
Started

On Time! On Track! On Target! Managing Your Projects Successfully with Microsoft Project

art than science and take time to master. This section introduces a few of the more effective ways to get people on board.

- **Know what stakeholders expect** There are few things as delightful as receiving something that you didn't realize you needed, whether it's dual-control heated seats in your car or an easy-to-navigate Web page. As project manager, the more you understand about what your stakeholders need—as well as what they want—the better equipped you are to meet and exceed their expectations.

  Keep in mind, understanding stakeholders' expectations doesn't mean delivering *everything* they ask for. You have to help stakeholders balance conflicting objectives like the list of requirements and the time and budget that's available. In some cases, your job is to explain to stakeholders why they won't get what they *want*—but they will get what they *need*.

- **Promote your project** Face it. If you liked selling, you'd be a salesperson. The reality is that you have to do some promotion as a project manager. When you understand the importance of a project, you have to help other people understand its benefits as well. You must reassure the customers that the project delivers what they need. You must convince managers that their resources are vital to the project. And you must show the project team how the project benefits each member.

- **Make people feel important** This chapter shows how every person involved in a project is important to its success. The best way to gain people's commitment is to help them see the importance of what they do. For example, testing has been an afterthought in many a software project. But the *test lead,* the job title of the person responsible for supervising and leading the testing of a software application, is one of the most influential people on a software project—the end users' advocate. The test lead makes sure that the software project requirements are measurable and realistic. The test plan documents what the software is supposed to do and how to measure success. And thorough testing finds defects that would otherwise frustrate end users and sap their productivity.

- **Keep people informed** No one likes surprises. Tell people what they need to know, and when they need to know it. Remind team members about what's due now and what's coming up next week. Notify stakeholders if plans change or issues arise.

■ **Be honest** As a project manager, you should prefer to be honest than to be liked. Always saying yes makes you popular initially. Eventually, stakeholders catch on. Unfortunately, it's much harder to regain trust than it is to lose it.

Projects are a balancing act between scope, time, cost, and quality. Instead of trying to please everyone, work to get stakeholders to agree on project objectives up front and then focus on achieving those objectives.

Tip Being honest doesn't mean being rude. If you must tell team members something they might not want to hear, give them a way to save face. For example, if a team member forgets an important aspect of his deliverable, say something like, "This requirement was at the end of the list, so you might have missed it. However, it's very important to the customer. Can you revise your work by tomorrow to include it?"

Some of your stakeholders are powerful people, but you are the project manager and you know more about the project than anyone else. It's up to you to manage stakeholders' expectations and help them make the right decisions. If something doesn't make sense, raise a red flag. If objectives are unattainable or in conflict, point them out and help people agree on what's important. Ask for help if you need it, but also help stakeholders find solutions to problems. Most important, keep people informed and keep everyone moving toward the project goals.

Best Practices

The authority conferred upon a project manager by the project sponsor is incredibly important, but you can't manufacture the clout that you need to manage a project. You have to earn it. This power or influence comes from several sources:

■ *Expertise in managing projects* is necessary to do your job well. It also helps you convey confidence, which builds confidence and commitment in the rest of the team.

■ *Technical or professional expertise* related to the project builds your credibility with the specialists working on the project. Without this expertise, team members might view you as a paper pusher—or worse, try to hoodwink you on project matters.

■ *The ability to make good decisions* goes a long way to earn people's trust and respect. Although some people will disagree with your decisions, they're more likely to support you if they see that you solicit input, evaluate the input you receive, and then make decisions that do the most good.

■ *Leadership* is a valuable skill, but is especially important in project management, when you must influence a lot of people without built-in power.

Part One:
Getting a Project
Started

On Time! On Track! On Target! Managing Your Projects Successfully with Microsoft Project

In Summary

Projects are truly collaborative efforts. Their success depends on commitment from many people in many groups. Commitment begins with a sponsor and the publication of a project charter, which announces a project and your authority to manage it. Some stakeholders participate in planning a project, but the commitment from all types of stakeholders is equally important, from the customer who pays for the project to the people who do the work. The most effective way to gain commitment from this diverse group is with good people skills—tools that no project manager should be without.

Part Two

Planning a Project

In this part

Chapter Four   **Planning to Achieve Success** **42**

Chapter Five   **What's the Problem?** **60**

Chapter Six   **Visualizing Success: Scope, Objectives, and Deliverables** **74**

Chapter Seven   **Building a Work Breakdown Structure** **84**

Chapter Eight   **Project Resources** **104**

Chapter Nine   **Building a Project Schedule** **122**

Chapter Ten   **Working with a Budget** **160**

Part Two:
Planning a
Project

On Time! On Track! On Target! Managing Your Projects Successfully with Microsoft Project

Chapter Four

Planning to Achieve Success

You've got to be very careful if you don't know where you're going, because you might not get there.

— *Yogi Berra*

Maybe action movies are to blame for making people want to jump in and *do* something instead of planning first. Because of competition and the overall fast pace of business, the "Just keep driving and I'll get out the map" mentality is quite common. Time, money, and resources are always in short supply while the list of project goals seems to grow longer. That combination is an almost irresistible goad to action.

Many project managers—and the executives that oversee them—look at the mountain of work and think they don't have time for planning. The truth is, the tighter the time and the tougher the constraints, the more important a plan becomes. Planning ahead is the only way you can do the right things *and* get them right the first time.

What Is Project Planning?

No doubt you've heard the theory of putting enough monkeys in front of typewriters pounding the keys at random to eventually produce the works of Shakespeare. Take that theory another step and you might think that you don't need a plan, because you'll eventually get the project right. Unfortunately, with limited resources, a project plan is essential if you want to complete your project successfully on the first try.

In essence, project planning is a combination of defining the problem you're trying to solve and determining the right way to solve it. That brief description can be deceiving, because there's a lot to planning a project. The rest of this chapter introduces the concepts of project planning, and Chapters 5 through 10 describe the steps in detail.

Defining the Problem

Identifying the problem that you're trying to solve sometimes turns out to be harder than you'd think. In fact, there are almost always several obstacles to overcome to get to the heart of the problem.

One obstacle is that most people are good at solving problems, which means they like to start the solving part as quickly as possible. Without carefully defining the problem, you end up with plenty of solutions—most likely to the wrong problem. A project team can work as smoothly as a Swiss watch, but if it's working toward the wrong objectives, the project will fail.

Part Two:
**Planning a
Project**

On Time! On Track! On Target! Managing Your Projects Successfully with Microsoft Project

Another obstacle is that people often don't know what they want or have trouble describing what they want in words. Unfortunately, they're good at recognizing what they *don't* want, so the words you don't want to hear come all too easily. Getting people to think about the problem instead of its symptoms isn't easy, but it's essential if you want your project to succeed. Chapter 5, "Defining a Project," discusses how to define problems.

Furthermore, different people often have different wants, which sometimes conflict with one another. Like the blind men touching different parts of an elephant and describing the animal in turn as a wall, a tree, a fan, a rope, a snake, and a spear; projects look different depending on people's perspectives. Spending time defining the problem synchronizes the different views to unmask the true project—what everyone involved recognizes as success.

Not soliciting input or feedback during the planning stage from the people who implement the plan is asking for trouble. Without buy-in, they're likely to say, "You want what done by when?" when they finally see the plan you've developed—sometimes, with good reason. People who don't perform the work are often prone to underestimating how long it will take or may forget chunks of work that must be done.

If you don't know where you're going, you can't tell how close you are to getting there. During project execution, a project plan tells you where you're supposed to be. By comparing your plan to where you really are, you can figure out whether the project is off course and how to get it back on track.

Project planning isn't all that different from other types of planning. The same questions that newspaper reporters ask to uncover a story—Who, What, When, Where, Why, and How—work equally well to plan a project.

Charting the Course

If you've ever booked an airline ticket online, you know that there are dozens of ways to get between point A and point B. Part of planning a project is evaluating different approaches and strategies to achieve project objectives.

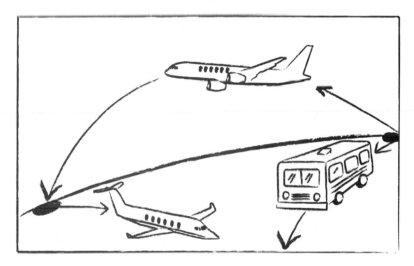

Each option has its pros and cons, so the project team must weigh the choices and pick the one it thinks has the best chance of success. For example, the price for a flight that connects through Chicago might be right, but you must decide whether the risk of a missed connection is worth it.

Getting Stakeholder Commitment

A project plan is a helpful tool for communicating the proposed approach to others and getting everyone on board. Project managers never have the authority to make *every* decision on a project, so they must rely on the support of management, key stakeholders, and executive sponsors to help them get the resources they need and to remove obstacles that get in the way of progress.

Part Two:
Planning a
Project

On Time! On Track! On Target! Managing Your Projects Successfully with Microsoft Project

To give their support, stakeholders must feel comfortable that their needs are met and that the approach is feasible. An earnestly delivered "Trust me. It'll work." doesn't convince these folks. By documenting the project goals and the plan for achieving them, you give stakeholders the chance to evaluate the proposed project. A project plan that communicates why the project is important and how you plan to make it a success is essential to obtain—and maintain—stakeholders' support.

Hold a Meeting to Sign Off on a Project Plan

Although it's tempting to circulate a project plan and request that stakeholders sign off on the plan, don't do it. The copies of the plan are likely to sit in stakeholders' inboxes only to be signed at the last minute without a thorough review. Later, you'll pay the price as people realize that the plan doesn't address their needs the way they expected.

A better approach is to schedule a sign-off meeting and distribute the project plan in advance. Ideally, stakeholders read the plan before coming to the meeting. However, as project manager, you should present the plan at the meeting, highlighting potential problems or conflicts.

Don't take head nodding as a sufficient sign that the plan is okay. Encourage questions—the harder, the better. To get the ball rolling, ask a few tough questions of your own.

If the project begins to go awry, you may have to turn to stakeholders to approve more money, more time, scope changes, or other items to help get the project back on track. If you've earned their trust with a good project plan, it's easier to keep their commitment when times are tough.

Getting Team Members' Buy-In

Buy-in from stakeholders isn't the only commitment you need. Team members who do the work during the execution phase have to be on board as well. Understanding the benefits of a project and their part in it helps team members take ownership, not only for their part but for the success of the project as a whole.

Pointing the Team in the Right Direction

Project teams are far more productive when they know what they're supposed to do and how they're supposed to do it. A project plan helps team members see where they're headed and stay focused on the destination.

Communicating the plan to team members does more than jump start project success: it helps them make good decisions during the course of their day-to-day work. And that's good news for the project manager who otherwise works nonstop answering team members' questions and making constant course corrections.

Tracking Progress

Important Progress isn't progress if you're headed in the wrong direction, no matter how fast you're going. In *The 7 Habits of Highly Effective People*, Stephen Covey tells of a group hacking their way through the jungle. One member of the group climbs a tree and calls down to her teammates, "Hey! We're in the wrong part of the jungle." The reply shouted back is "Shut up! We're making good progress!"

A project plan maps out your destination and how you're going to get there. Only then can you gauge how far you've gone and the true progress you've made.

Plans Change

Dwight D. Eisenhower once said that planning is everything but plans are worthless. Huh? The reason Eisenhower considered plans worthless is because they change as soon as they are complete, if not sooner. Projects rarely unfold exactly the way you planned. Yet, project managers still plan, because the *act* of planning uncovers so much valuable information.

So, go ahead, plan, and document your results in a project plan. It doesn't have to stay the same. In fact, changes are a sign that a plan is being used.

Part Two:
Planning a
Project

On Time! On Track! On Target! Managing Your Projects Successfully with Microsoft Project

Note Planning up front is important for two reasons. You figure out ahead of time how to achieve the project objectives while averting disasters. But more important, once a project starts, it's time to guide the project in the direction you set.

An Overview of Project Planning

- **Why are we undertaking this project?** Helps define the problem to be solved (see "The Problem Statement," page 61).

- **What are we going to do?** Helps identify the project objectives (see "Project Objectives," page 52) and scope of work (see "The Scope Statement," page 75).

- **How are we going to do it?** Is the project strategy (see "Project Strategy," page 68).

- **When will we start and when must we finish?** Sets the project schedule (see Chapter 9, "Building a Project Schedule").

- **How much is it going to cost? or How much do we have to spend?** Defines the project budget (see Chapter 10, "Working with a Budget").

- **Who is going to do the work?** Identifies the project organization and resources (see "Putting a Project Team Together," page 111).

- **How good must the results be?** Defines the quality objectives (see "Project Objectives," page 79).

Obtaining Time to Plan

Regardless of how obvious the importance of planning is to project managers, management sometimes is adamant that work begin immediately. Giving in to management's demands may seem like the right career choice at the time, but it's only a temporary solution. When the project fails, as it's likely to do without a plan, your career is even more at risk.

Take the time to explain how planning helps ensure project success. Projects that your management wouldn't dream of performing without planning can be influential—for example, preparing the business plan for the next round of venture capital, planning for the acquisition of another company, or figuring out the best way to exercise executive stock options. If all else fails, negotiate a shorter amount of time for planning—it's better than nothing.

After you've fought for planning time, be sure to collect project performance measures and lessons learned when the project is complete. By demonstrating how your hard-won project planning led to project success, it will be easier to obtain planning time for the next project.

Answering these questions takes some time and effort, which is the task for Chapters 5 through 10. When you've obtained your answers, you can build a detailed road map—the project plan.

The Project Charter

Before a project manager can delve into project planning in earnest, the project sponsor publishes a project charter to announce the project and, more important, to identify the authority and responsibilities of the project manager assigned to the project.

Most managers in a hierarchical organization get their power from their position in the pyramid. If they change positions, they inherit the power of the new position. But project managers' authority is fleeting—it lasts only as long as the projects to which they are assigned. Formal acknowledgement of the project manager's authority is key. Otherwise, the project manager could run into resistance from functional managers who question their authority to request resources or spend money.

Tip Keep a copy of the project charter close at hand. Hanging a framed copy on the wall isn't out of the question. As phone calls come in or people stop by your office with questions, referring them to the project charter is an effective way of communicating your authority.

Project charters come in several forms, from simple statements of the project manager's authority for a project to detailed documents that can pass as actual project plans. At a minimum, a project charter should include:

- The name and business purpose of the project
- The name of the project manager assigned to the project
- The extent of the project manager's authority to manage the project
- A brief summary of the project

See the file *OnTime_Project_Charter.doc* in the *Sample Documents* folder on the companion CD for one example of a project charter.

The project sponsor establishes the project manager's authority by signing the project charter and distributing it to everyone involved in the new project. Publication doesn't have to be a formal affair. These days, the project charter is often delivered via e-mail.

Part Two:
Planning a
Project

On Time! On Track! On Target! Managing Your Projects Successfully with Microsoft Project

> **Tip** Although the project sponsor is the official author of the project charter and distributes it to stakeholders, in many cases, the project manager prepares the project charter for the sponsor's signature.

Project Planning Step by Step

Project planning is a series of steps that help identify the problem to solve and the best way to solve it. Figure 4-1 shows the steps to planning a project. The rest of this section introduces the parts of a project plan, which are the results of these steps.

The Components of a Project Plan

As you learned in the previous section, project planning includes a number of steps, but eventually the result is a tangible deliverable—the project plan. This section introduces the components of a project plan and explains why they're important.

> The companion CD includes an example of a complete project plan, *OnTime_Project_Plan.doc*, in the *Sample Documents* folder.

Problem Statement

A problem statement documents the problem—not the symptoms or someone's premature hunch about a solution. See Chapter 5 to learn about defining problems and developing problem statements.

Here's an example of the right way and the wrong way to define a problem:

- **Right** We can't enjoy our backyard because there is a large mud hole in the middle of it.
- **Wrong** We need a two-level wooden deck in the backyard.

> See the *Sample Documents* folder on the companion CD for an example of a problem statement, *OnTime_Problem_Statement.doc*.

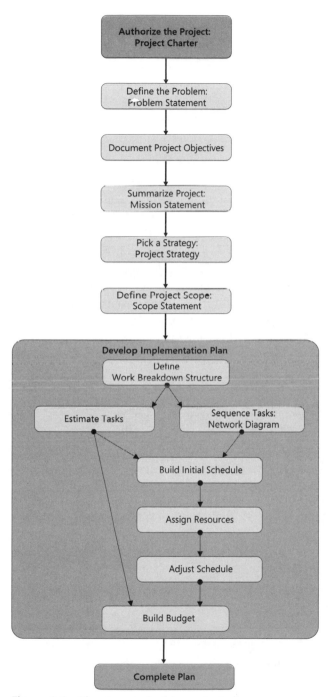

Figure 4-1   The steps to build a project plan.

Part Two:
Planning a
Project

On Time! On Track! On Target! Managing Your Projects Successfully with Microsoft Project

Project Mission Statement

What project manager wouldn't want her team to be on a mission? A project mission statement summarizes the purpose and the goals of the project, which help foster the project team's commitment. As a project progresses, team members can consult the mission statement to decide whether their decisions and activities contribute to the success of the project. Chapter 5 discusses how to build a project mission statement.

Project Strategy

Most problems have more than one solution, but some solutions are more appropriate than others. A project team must evaluate different solutions based on project objectives to decide which one is best. For example, when remodeling a backyard, a multilevel swing set with a slide and monkey bars may be the envy of the neighborhood kids, but this solution doesn't give parents much to do. And hiring a landscape contractor to do a radical make-over of the entire backyard probably costs more than your project sponsor (you) wants to pay. The project plan includes the selected strategy so that stakeholders can decide whether it fits with business objectives and other initiatives. Chapter 5 describes how to identify possible solutions and the criteria to use to evaluate them.

Project Objectives

Project objectives come in several flavors: business, financial, technical, and quality. For example, the components of the backyard remodel should be durable enough to withstand the abuse of three energetic children and two excitable dogs, be easy to maintain, and cost no more than $5,000.

Project objectives are more specific than the project mission statement, but they too prevent misunderstandings about what should be done and help team members focus on what is important. Chapter 6, "Visualizing Success: Scope, Objectives, and Deliverables," describes the different types of objectives that often appear on project plans and explains how to identify and document project objectives.

Scope Statement

The scope statement tells the project customers (internal and external) what they will receive at the end of the project. Unlike some of the other parts of a project plan, the project scope not only states what *is* within the boundaries of the project, but also what *is not*. Table 4-1 provides an example of a simple scope statement.

Table 4-1   One Example of Project Scope

Project Scope	Not in Scope
Design a wooden deck and patio.	A swimming pool or water feature is out of scope for this project.
Purchase all materials and provide all equipment needed to construct the deck and patio.	Design and construction does not include planting any trees, shrubbery, flowers, or grass. The homeowners will handle this task.
Construct the deck and patio.	
Stain and seal the completed deck and patio.	
Clean up the area and remove all construction trash.	

Deliverables and Success Criteria

Some deliverables are easy to identify. A tangible result like a patio ready for a party is a deliverable, but so is a soil analysis or a completed building inspection. Initially, the deliverables you identify correspond to the overall output of the project: a new product, an enhanced service, a remodeled backyard. As you develop the work breakdown structure (see "Building a WBS from the Top Down," page 89) you identify intermediate deliverables, because each work package and summary task contributes something to the final project. For instance, intermediate deliverables for a backyard remodel might include a design, blueprints, building permits, the delivery of construction materials, a poured foundation, a completed patio, and a signed building inspection certificate. Chapter 6 discusses different types of deliverables and other contractual requirements.

Best Practices

A good scope statement is your best protection against *scope creep*, the insidious oozing expansion of what a project includes. Scope creep usually appears in the guise of questions like, "Could you do this for me? It won't take long." And before you know it, your project is late and over budget.

Without a clear description of project scope, change control is impossible and scope creep is practically guaranteed.

Part Two:
**Planning a
Project**

On Time! On Track! On Target! Managing Your Projects Successfully with Microsoft Project

Deliverables help define the scope of a project and identify all the work required to complete the project. As you include deliverables in a project plan, double-check that you have tasks and estimates for producing those results. For example, the effort required to produce documentation is sometimes overlooked. If the government is the client and thousand-page reports are key deliverables, forgetting to schedule documentation work spells failure regardless of how successful you are with other project deliverables.

Tip   The purpose, scope, and deliverables for a project are often bundled into a document called a *statement of work*. This brief synopsis of a project is often included in legal contracts.

Each deliverable and milestone in a project should stipulate criteria that help project managers and stakeholders determine whether the work to date has been completed successfully. You don't have to take a sledgehammer to the concrete foundation to see if it's set. Success criteria might be the receipt of an inspection report from a building inspector.

Many projects include progress payments triggered by the delivery of specific results. Don't let project payments be held hostage because stakeholders can't decide whether a deliverable is complete. Clear success criteria keep projects and payments flowing smoothly.

Project Assumptions

Assumptions can be dangerous because people don't realize they're making them. After you document assumptions, they lose their menace. Suppose you receive two bids from high-school kids for mowing your lawn; Kid A's bid is half the price of Kid B's bid. The difference is easy to understand when you know that Kid A assumes that you're providing the lawn mower, gas, and garbage bags.

Caution   Inspect the assumptions you gather for disguised risks. For example, if Kid A assumes that the weather will always be good on the weekends when she doesn't have school, there's a risk that the lawn will go unmowed during monsoon season.

Throughout the planning process, you must strive to uncover as yet unspoken assumptions. When you identify assumptions, add them to the project plan. In some cases, you can document assumptions about what will be done in the project scope or project objectives.

Work Breakdown Structure

A work breakdown structure is the key to a project plan. You must break the work of a project down into manageable tasks and subtasks before you can build a project schedule, assign resources, or track performance. Chopping work up into smaller chunks helps team members understand the work to which they're assigned. These lowest level subtasks are called *work packages*. After you start implementing your plan, you also track progress based on the completed tasks.

Constructing a work breakdown structure isn't always easy, because you can usually break down projects into subtasks in different ways, even if the work is the same. Chapter 7, "Building a Work Breakdown Structure," discusses techniques for developing a work breakdown structure.

Project Schedule

A project schedule is the timeline for a project. You put the work packages (and their estimated durations) from the work breakdown structure in the sequence in which they must be performed to figure out when the project will finish. Chapter 9 describes how to transform a work breakdown structure into a schedule.

Part Two:
**Planning a
Project**

On Time! On Track! On Target! Managing Your Projects Successfully with Microsoft Project

During project execution, project managers compare actual performance to the baseline project schedule to see whether work is on time or running late. Although finish dates for tasks indicate whether the tasks are on schedule, milestones in a schedule are another way to track progress. Milestones based on project deliverables are easy to evaluate; if the deliverable success criteria has been met, the milestone is complete. On the other hand, if the project is falling behind, you can make course corrections before the project becomes unmanageable.

Project Organization and Resources

Getting the right resources for a project makes a big difference. Working with fewer resources than you planned for or assigning people with less experience can delay the schedule. But people, equipment, and materials are almost always in short supply, so compromises are always a probability. The project plan doesn't just list resource names or generic skill sets. If you can delineate the skill sets you need, when, and for how long, it's easier to obtain resources or negotiate alternatives if the resources you want are unavailable. Chapter 8, "Project Resources," discusses project organization and resources.

The number of resources needed for different skill sets or the hours that resources are assigned each day is crucial for staffing decisions. Functional managers can evaluate resource requirements to determine whether the current staff can handle the project, some overtime will cover the gap, or hiring temporary or permanent staff is necessary.

Budget

Don't expect to hear that money is no object. Even if a project is launched to improve customer satisfaction, you can count on financial folks to calculate return on investment or the break-even date. Whether someone tells you how much money you have to work with or you have the luxury of calculating how much the project will cost, you do have to build a budget and then track performance against it. Chapter 10 discusses budgeting and cost estimating

The level of detail that you include in a project plan depends on what stakeholders want to see. For example, a fixed-bid project might include only the fixed price for the entire project. However, behind the scenes, a detailed budget accounts for all the project costs, from labor to rental equipment to profit margin.

Risk Management Plan

Things do go wrong. Although some people enjoy putting out fires, you don't want them on your project team. The more sensible approach to managing project risk is to identify potential risks ahead of time and plan for how you'll handle them. Chapter 18, "Managing Risk," discusses risk management.

A risk management plan begins with what could go wrong—the concrete supplier might go out of business, the bonus that the homeowner hoped to use to pay for the project might be cut in half, or a buried power line might require a change in design. You estimate their impact and likelihood. For most projects, a risk management plan covers possible approaches for the risks with significant impact and reasonable likelihood.

But risk management doesn't stop with planning. Throughout the life of a project, you must monitor the risks you've identified and watch for new risks that may arise.

Communication Plan

Whenever people work together, communication is an essential ingredient for success. Truth be told, the lion's share of a project manager's job is communication. A communication plan (Chapter 14, "Communicating Information") describes how you're going to keep the people involved with a project informed. Communication strategies may be simple or sophisticated and can range from a weekly status report to a collaborative Web site. At their core, communication plans answer the following questions:

- Who needs to know?
- What do they need to know?
- When do they need to know it?

Quality Plan

Examples abound showing that it's easier, faster, and cheaper to do things right the first time than to do them over. A quality plan begins with the quality objectives for the project, whether they come from the organization's quality policies or customer requirements. The plan then describes the quality assurance and control strategies and activities used to achieve the quality objectives of the project.

Part Two:
Planning a
Project

On Time! On Track! On Target! Managing Your Projects Successfully with Microsoft Project

Change Control Plan

Change is a given during the life of a project, whether it's a bonus you decide to contribute to your backyard budget or three weeks of rainy days that prevent the construction trucks from getting to your job site. With the rest of your project plan complete, you have a foundation for controlling change in a project. Project scope, deliverables, requirements, and pretty much the rest of your project plan sets the baseline. After stakeholders approve the plan, you need change management to manage the changes to that baseline.

A change management plan (see Chapter 15, "Managing Project Changes") describes the process for managing changes. The sophistication of change management depends on the size and complexity of the project. A small project might rely on a spreadsheet and e-mail for change management. Mammoth projects might require change boards (committees of people who agree on changes) and different categories of changes. But change management boils down to a few steps:

- Recording change requests

- Evaluating cost, schedule, and quality impact for change requests

- Deciding the fate of change requests (accepting, rejecting, or requesting modifications)

- Accepting change requests and updating project documents to reflect the change

In Summary

The amount of planning you need depends on the project you're managing. A few hours of planning are sufficient for a small dinner party for some friends, but the first moon landing required years of it.

Depending on the characteristics of your project, you might not need every project plan component presented in this chapter. As you're planning your project, consider each component and how it might help your project succeed. For small projects, a sentence or two might be enough to describe your communication plan or other sections. In the chapters that follow, you'll learn how to build each section of a project plan for projects large and small.

Part Two:
Planning a
Project

On Time! On Track! On Target! Managing Your Projects Successfully with Microsoft Project

Chapter Five

What's the Problem?

A project is a problem scheduled for solution.

— *J.M. Juran*

Organizations don't undertake projects for the fun of it. Usually, projects come about because an organization has a problem it wants to solve, a business objective to achieve, or an opportunity to cash in on.

People *love* to solve problems—so much so, that they sometimes come up with solutions to problems that aren't particularly troublesome. As they do with diseases, people often notice the symptoms first and only with analysis and diagnosis do they identify the underlying issue. Digging deeper to identify what a project is supposed to solve or achieve is crucial to success. As antibiotics won't help a person who has the flu, the best solution to the wrong problem will ultimately fail.

This chapter discusses how to identify problems, business objectives, and opportunities, and describe them in a problem statement. It also introduces a project mission statement—a brief but inspiring summary of the purpose of the project to obtain and maintain commitment to your project. With the problem diagnosed and documented, you can finally unleash your project team to begin the task of finding a solution. The project strategy is the approach selected to solve the problem.

The Problem Statement

The problem to solve or the business objective to achieve drives all other aspects of a project, as shown in Figure 5-1 on the next page. Without the right problem or objective, you're not likely to select the right solution or strategy. And without the right solution, the best project plan and highest quality deliverables won't make stakeholders happy. If you've given an infant a bottle filled with water instead of formula, you know how disappointing the wrong deliverables can be. In a project plan, the problem statement is a concise definition of the problem to solve or the business objective to achieve.

Identifying the Problem

To pinpoint problems, you're better off putting on your investigative reporter's hat. Why turns out to be one of the best questions for identifying a problem or business objective. If you ask someone to describe a problem, you're likely to get a solution instead. But if you ask stakeholders *why* the organization should perform the project, *why* something is a problem, or *why* a solution is needed, you're more likely to hear the problem (or some aspect of it.)

Part Two:
Planning a
Project

On Time! On Track! On Target! Managing Your Projects Successfully with Microsoft Project

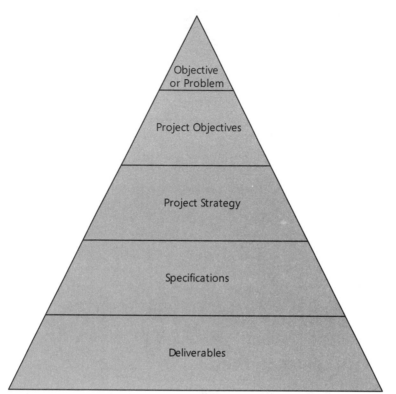

Figure 5-1   The problem or business objective drives all other aspects of the project.

Best Practices

Although people often describe problems by providing solutions, you can sometimes reverse engineer those solutions to find the real problem or business objective. Once again, the question why comes to your rescue. Simply ask your stakeholders why they need the solution they've suggested.

Suppose your boss asks you to manage a project to create a centralized corporate database. If you ask why the company needs a centralized database, you might learn that groups can't obtain the data they need, data contain duplicate or inconsistent records, data aren't backed up properly, and so on. Those answers are all problems that a project can solve. However, a centralized corporate database isn't the only—or necessarily the best—way to solve them.

Asking why a problem is a problem is a powerful tool for unearthing business objectives. For example, why is poor access to data a problem? Perhaps support staff can't respond to customer requests. Why is that a problem? Well, the organization needs more support people, which increase costs, and frustrated customers take their business elsewhere. A few rounds of "Why is that a problem?" helps you discover that the business objective is to reduce costs and improve customer service.

For example, consider the backyard remodel project. If you ask for the problem, different family members might say the backyard needs a deck, a patio, a swimming pool, or a swing set. The question "Why do you want to make over the backyard?" might deliver an answer, such as, "We can't do anything in the backyard because there's a big mud hole."

Adding Constraints to a Problem Statement

Solutions usually have no place in problem statements. But what if your organization has already made decisions that constrain the solutions you can use? You can include significant constraints in the problem statement (in addition to the assumptions section of the project plan) to ensure that project strategies take those constraints into account. The following problem statement includes a definition of the problem and the constraints on its solution:

Our corporate data is stored in several places, resulting in groups being unable to access the data they need to do their jobs, some data being skipped by the organization's backup procedure, and duplicate or inconsistent information between different databases. These problems reduce our productivity, the quality of our service, and the quality of the data that we deliver to our customers. This project will help us provide better products and services to our customers by resolving these problems using hardware and software that the organization already owns.

Part Two:
Planning a
Project

On Time! On Track! On Target! Managing Your Projects Successfully with Microsoft Project

> **Note** Although the symptoms and solutions that you gather from stake-
> holders usually don't appear in the problem statement, they're valuable
> components of your project plan. People's perceptions of the problem
> often end up as other project objectives (see "Project Objectives," page 79),
> and these objectives help you decide which solution is best when you select
> a project strategy (see "Project Strategy," page 68).

The Project Mission Statement

*Vision without a task is only a dream. A task without a vision is
but drudgery. But vision with a task is a dream fulfilled.*

— *Willie Stone*

A problem statement identifies where you are, which is an important first step. The project mission statement states where you want to be—the purpose and the goals of the project. Like a game of tug-of-war, a project team won't get very far when people pull in different directions. The project mission statement conveys the vision of a project to the team, building commitment and aligning everyone to achieve the same goal.

Projects compete for money and resources, and not every project gets the okay to proceed. By communicating why the project is important, a project mission statement also reaffirms stakeholders' reasons for initiating the project.

> *"Would you tell me, please, which way I ought to walk from here?"*
>
> *"That depends a good deal on where you want to get to," said the Cat.*
>
> *"I don't much care where–" said Alice.*
>
> *"Then it doesn't matter which way you walk," said the Cat.*

Working with Stakeholders

Producing a problem statement, project mission statement, project objectives, and strategy takes time because stakeholders must agree on the goals before the project begins. As introduced in Part One of this book, stakeholders often have conflicting goals and expectations. As project manager, you have the unenviable job of helping stakeholders reach agreement on what the project will achieve.

Whether you meet with stakeholders individually or in meetings, you must document all the goals, objectives, and expectations stakeholders have, and then work with stakeholders to determine what the project should accomplish.

One additional challenge is that stakeholders might pressure you to skip the time-consuming process of reaching agreement in order to get the work started. It's the project manager's job to keep them focused on one of their most important duties—to set the vision and direction of the project.

"–so long as I get somewhere," Alice added as an explanation.

"Oh, you're sure to do that," said the Cat, "if you only walk long enough."

— *Lewis Carroll, Alice's Adventures in Wonderland*

As a project progresses, team members do work and make decisions. A project mission statement helps them decide whether what they are doing is moving the project in the right direction—preventing wrong turns or dead ends. And, should the going get tough, a mission statement helps boost morale by reminding everyone why the work they do is important.

Important Many organizations make the mistake of writing a project mission statement only to forget it in the throes of day-to-day activity. Keep the mission statement in people's minds by printing it on a certificate or laminated card that team members can pin to their cubicles or office walls. If the mission statement is brief, add it to the cover page of project documents.

Building a Mission Statement

A project mission statement should be short and inspiring, much like persuasive advertisements. Someone reading a good project mission statement knows what the project is trying to accomplish and why it's important. Truly great project mission statements make people long to be a part of the project team.

Despite its power, a project mission statement answers only a few simple questions:

- Who's the customer?
- What are we trying to accomplish?
- Why is it important?
- What approach are we going to take?

As you might expect, good project mission statements aren't easy to write. You must first work with stakeholders to unearth the factors that are most influential to the success of the project—what must the project deliver to make its customers happy? Then you must transform that information into a few sentences that inform and inspire people.

Part Two:
Planning a
Project

On Time! On Track! On Target! Managing Your Projects Successfully with Microsoft Project

Who's the Customer?

Because mission statements are short, they focus on the needs of the customer. Projects have plenty of stakeholders (see "Identifying Stakeholders," page 29), but customers take center stage for the project mission statement. Whether you work on a mission statement by yourself on a small project or hold brainstorming sessions with all stakeholders, start by identifying the customer or customers who ultimately decide whether the project is a success. For example:

- If you're trying to improve corporate data management to increase productivity, the project customers could be the management team.

- If the project is supposed to improve customer service, the project customers are the organization's external customers.

- If the project is supposed to streamline business processes to alleviate overtime and employee frustration, the customers are some of the organization's employees.

What Are We Trying to Accomplish and Why Is It Important?

After you've identified the customers for the project, the next step is to target what the customers want and why. Of course, you've probably heard—or even said—"I want it all." Customers do want a lot of things, but the mission statement focuses on only the most important.

To build a mission statement, you work with stakeholders to distill the problems, objectives, and opportunities to the results that the customers want most from the project as shown here. Opinions will differ. Customers sometimes disagree. Meetings to reach consensus on this crucial statement can last a day or longer.

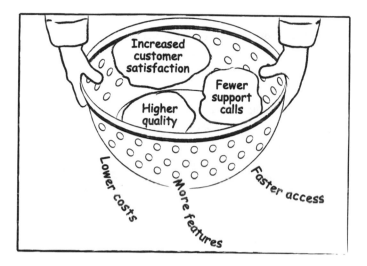

What Approach Are We Going to Take?

A project mission statement includes, *at a very high level*, the approach or strategy for the project. Therefore, building a project mission statement is an iterative process. You hone it as you collect more information about the project. During your initial information gathering interviews and meetings, you identify the customers and other stakeholders for the project (see Chapter 3, "Obtaining Commitment for a Project") and what will make them happy. An initial mission statement that answers the first three questions (Who's the customer? What are we trying to accomplish? Why is it important?) helps the team identify the project strategy. With the project objectives defined and the project strategy chosen, you can complete the mission statement.

Completing the Project Mission Statement

Although you leave the mission statement meeting with stakeholders with a draft of a mission statement, chances are this draft needs some editing to strengthen the message and instill the inspirational tone you desire. The process is like writing an introduction for someone you greatly admire, the toast you'd give at your best friend's wedding, or the eulogy you hope someone would one day give for you.

If you aren't a speech writer or wordsmith, don't panic. Nowhere is it written that the project manager must craft the final mission statement. Quite often, you can spot a willing and able writer from e-mails or documents you receive from stakeholders. Ask the ones who send you clear and concise

Part Two:
Planning a
Project

On Time! On Track! On Target! Managing Your Projects Successfully with Microsoft Project

messages if they're willing to work on the mission statement. Or, engage a technical writer, who's experienced in taking complex information and turning it into understandable prose.

Here's an example of a project mission statement:

The mission of the data management project is to delight our external customers and earn their loyalty with new services targeted to their industries while providing faster response to sales and customer service requests. Our project will achieve this by increasing the flexibility of our databases and improving the quality of our data with better synchronization between databases.

Project Strategy

If you don't know where you're going, you will probably end up somewhere else.

— *Laurence J. Peter*

High school seniors grouse about the SAT tests they take for college and don't realize that questions with only one correct answer are some of the easiest problems they'll deal with in real life. Projects almost always solve open-ended problems—which have more than one correct answer. Fortunately for project managers and their teams, some answers are more appropriate than others. By evaluating alternatives in light of the project mission and project objectives (see Chapter 6, "Visualizing Success: Scope, Objectives, and Deliverables") a project team can determine which solution is best. Once you've selected a solution, the project strategy is where you document your choice in the project plan.

Strategic planning for projects is similar to strategic planning in other areas of business. You must know where you want to go to make good strategic planning decisions. A backyard that invites the family to spend quality time together leads to a much different design than one dedicated to winning the local gardening competition. You can't wait too long to strategize, or customers and stakeholders might have already made decisions that limit your options. If the kids found the brochure for the multistation slide/swing/sandbox, your hopes for a prize-winning iris garden could be dashed.

Identifying Alternatives

Potential solutions arrive uninvited as you try to identify the problem that the project is supposed to solve. These solutions are just guesses, because people presented them without knowing the problem, objectives, or project mission. Once you know what the project is supposed to accomplish, a few brainstorming sessions with stakeholders can reveal more suitable solutions to consider.

For example, consider the backyard remodeling project. A mud hole that prevents the family from enjoying the outdoors is the problem. The mission is to remodel the backyard so that the family can spend more time together but also pursue their unique definitions of fun. A family meeting to discuss the project could begin with each person's idea of a fun backyard: a garden, a horseshoe pit, swings, and a tree house. But some family brainstorming might lead to a solution that incorporates a common area for the entire family along with backyard niches for each family member.

Factors for Selecting a Project Strategy

The project strategy that stakeholders select must satisfy a gauntlet of conditions. The winning strategy must satisfy the primary business objectives and most of the other project objectives, but there are other tests to pass as well. Here are some factors to consider when evaluating project strategies:

- **Is the strategy feasible?** Feasibility is important if you're considering a solution that's unusual or untried. Large projects often include feasibility studies to validate that the strategy will work before committing too many dollars and resources to a particular approach.

- **Does the strategy satisfy the project objectives?** Without an implementation plan, you don't have details about a strategy's deliverables, cost, schedule, or quality. Stakeholders must make educated guesses about how well a strategy satisfies the objectives.

A Quick Guide to Brainstorming

Brainstorming is one of the best ways to extract creative ideas from a group of people. Chaotic can be the descriptor of choice as people throw ideas out at random, but some rules increase the effectiveness of the technique.

- Clearly communicate the purpose of the brainstorming session so that the participants understand the goal of the session—for instance, to identify potential strategies for the project at hand.

- Set a time limit to focus brainstorming activity.

- Assign someone to facilitate the discussion. A facilitator welcomes all ideas and prevents criticism of others' ideas regardless of how wacky they seem at first, which in turn makes everyone more comfortable about participating. The facilitator also records all the suggestions on a flip chart or white board, so that participants can view them.

- When time is up, the group can categorize, merge, and refine the ideas into a list of options for further study.

Part Two:
Planning a
Project

On Time! On Track! On Target! Managing Your Projects Successfully with Microsoft Project

> **Note**   As you'll see in the next section, emphasizing must-have objectives helps the team weed out strategies that fail the crucial tests. Prioritizing project objectives helps the team focus on what's important. For example, a new database application could satisfy the technical objectives for the database management project but blast the budget out of the water.

- **Are the risks acceptable?**   Every strategy has its risks. An informal risk analysis of all the possible strategies helps stakeholders eliminate dangerously precarious solutions. For example, stakeholders don't want to buy a product from a new software company that could go out of business.

- **Does the strategy fit the organization's culture?**   If the organization has always written its own applications, a strategy that uses outside vendors is unlikely to succeed. Similarly, senior management that swears by technology might dismiss solutions that focus on process improvement. Cultural and psychological factors are not only tough to quantify but also tough to overcome. If stakeholders decide on a strategy that doesn't fit the organization's norms, success requires strong commitment from management, the project sponsor, and stakeholders.

Choosing the Project Strategy

Choosing a project strategy is a qualitative process. No one has enough information to make precise comparisons or judgments and many criteria are subjective. A decision matrix, like the one shown in Figure 5-2, helps organize the objectives and other criteria, and can be as qualitative or as quantitative as you want.

	Weighting	Extend current system	Develop data warehouse	New ERP system	Process improvement	Data warehouse and process
Existing software and hardware	Req	Y	Y	N	Y	Y
Less than $800K	Req	Y	Y	N	Y	Y
Synchronize data	Req	N	Y	Y	Y	Y
Customize reports	3	5	4		2	4
Flexibility	3	2	5		4	5
Reduces data errors	3	2	4		4	5
Improved backups	2	2	4		4	5
Complete by 4th qtr	1	2	3		3	4
Total		62	95		86	101

Figure 5-2 A decision matrix helps you evaluate solutions using project objectives and other criteria.

Here's one way to use a decision matrix to evaluate alternatives:

1. Fill in the column headings with the strategies you've identified.

   Include one column for a weighting factor. If you use numbers such as 1, 2, and 3 for low, medium, and high importance, you can calculate weighted results to emphasize solutions that meet the most important criteria.

2. Add project objectives that must be met to the top rows of the matrix. If an alternative doesn't satisfy any of these make-or-break objectives, you can skip filling in the rest of that alternative's boxes.

3. Prioritize the other project objectives and criteria. If none of the solutions satisfy all of the objectives, you can focus on the more important criteria.

4. Rate how well an alternative satisfies each criterion. You can use numbers or Yes and No. If you want to score the alternatives, assign a value

Part Two:
Planning a
Project

On Time! On Track! On Target! Managing Your Projects Successfully with Microsoft Project

to Yes. For example, in Figure 5-2, each Yes answer earns 15 points. The following table demonstrates how to calculate the score for the data warehouse and process improvement strategies.

Criteria	Points
Existing software and hardware	15 for Yes
Less than $800K	15 for Yes
Synchronize data	15 for Yes
Customize reports	$3 \times 4 = 12$
Flexibility	$3 \times 5 = 15$
Reduces data errors	$3 \times 5 = 15$
Improved backups	$2 \times 5 = 10$
Complete by 4th qtr	$1 \times 4 = 4$
Total	101

Important   If you do use numbers and calculations to rate strategies, the results are merely approximate ratings. For example, results of 85 and 87 are too close to call. Look instead for strategies whose ratings are significantly higher than the others, such as the data warehouse and process improvement strategies in Figure 5-2.

In Summary

The problem statement, project mission statement, and project strategy are the guiding lights for a project. The problem statement and project mission statement tell the team what the project is supposed to do and why. The project strategy is the how.

In the next chapter, you'll learn how to identify all of the project objectives, which contribute to the selection of the project strategy. You'll also learn about the other components of the statement of work: the scope, deliverables, contractual requirements, and success criteria.

Part Two:
Planning a
Project

On Time! On Track! On Target! Managing Your Projects Successfully with Microsoft Project

Chapter Six

Visualizing Success: Scope, Objectives, and Deliverables

I don't know the key to success, but the key to failure is trying to please everybody.

— *Bill Cosby*

The previous chapter introduced the problem statement, project mission statement, and project strategy: three different views that represent why the project is important and what it is supposed to accomplish. Those descriptions view the project from 25,000 feet; they're good for identifying where you started and your destination.

This chapter starts the descent into the details of a project. The scope statement, project objectives, and deliverables are a closer look at the project's planned accomplishments. The scope statement identifies what the project's going to do—and what it isn't. Project objectives describe all the smaller goals that form the overarching mission. Deliverables are the results provided during the life of the project.

The Scope Statement

Project scope drives the rest of a project's implementation plan. The schedule, delivery date, resources required, and budget all derive from what the project will and won't do. If the scope changes, one or more of the plan's values must change as well.

Several components of a project plan define the scope of a project:

- *Deliverables* indicate what customers will receive.

- *Work breakdown structure* defines the work that the team will perform.

- *Requirements and specifications* demarcate features of the finished project.

- *Scope statement* is more like a fence that defines the boundaries of the project, as Figure 6-1 on the next page illustrates. It describes what's in bounds and out of bounds based on the project plan as it currently stands. Keeping the project team focused on within bounds activities helps keep the schedule and budget in bounds as well.

Telling the project's customers what they're going to get and what they aren't helps eliminate unpleasant surprises for everyone. If you commission a sailboat designer in San Diego to build a custom sailboat, it's important to know whether the price and schedule include delivering the boat to your marina in Baltimore. If the designer calls you to pick up the boat and you thought the boat would be delivered, that phone call isn't fun for either one of you. Moreover, you'll view the project as a failure, even though the sailboat is everything you wanted—except for the delivery snafu.

Part Two:
Planning a
Project

On Time! On Track! On Target! Managing Your Projects Successfully with Microsoft Project

Backyard Remodel Scope Statement

This scope statement identifies the work that will be performed for the backyard remodel project. The project team will evaluate any work not specified in this scope through the change management process.

Included Scope

The backyard remodel project will include the following work and deliverables:

- Identify the code requirements for the construction, obtain required permits, and ensure that all inspections are performed

- Design the deck and patio, including lighting and landscaping; and produce detailed design drawings

- Excavate for foundation and regrade yard for landscaping design

- Provide materials for in-scope construction

- Construct deck and patio, railing and stairs, and install wiring and lighting

- Remove construction trash

Excluded Scope

- Install walkways

- Plant shrubs, trees, flowers, and sod

- Seal, stain, and paint deck and patio

Figure 6-1   A sample scope statement for the backyard remodel project.

A clear scope statement makes it easy to spot changes that expand the project. For customers, a scope statement that contains inclusions and exclusions helps the customers decide whether the project is worth the price. For the project team, the scope statement makes it easier (although not pain free) to discuss with customers the effects of additional requests on the project plan.

Developing a Scope Statement

The scope statement is a bit of a balancing act. It's mainly a high-level view of what the project will do so the customer knows what to expect when the project is complete. But the scope statement must also describe the project clearly enough so you can determine whether work is beyond the boundaries of the project.

The CD includes a sample scope statement, *Backyard Remodel Scope Statement.doc*, in the *Backyard Remodel Project* folder.

Because the specifics of what the project does appear in other sections of the project plan, the scope statement summarizes the extent of the work. Figure 6-1 shows an example of a scope statement for the backyard remodel project. For example, the family has decided to take responsibility for the landscaping and the final finishes on the deck and patio to save some money. However, the included scope specifically includes grading the yard for the landscaping because the family doesn't own a grader.

Preventing Scope Creep

If you thought the movie *The Blob* was scary, you already know why scope creep is the bane of project management. Without a clear scope statement, little bits of work and "Oh, would you add just this one thing" requests insidiously bloat the project scope until your budget, time, and resources are exhausted. Each request often sounds so simple that you don't see the harm in saying yes. But all the small changes can add up and doom the project.

Best Practices

Assumptions are one of the pitfalls of project scope. The customer just assumes that a task is part of the project, whereas the project team assumes just the opposite. As long as the assumptions go unspoken, trouble lies ahead.

You can unearth conflicting assumptions by asking everyone involved to visualize project success. For example, ask the project customers, stakeholders, and members of the project team, "What results do you see when you think of this project as a success?" Write down everything they say. Don't be afraid to ask if there's anything else—more than once. The goal is to collect the assumptions that people haven't thought to voice. If the vision of success turns out to be much too large for the budget and resource pool, you can negotiate the project scope with the team instead of with lawyers.

Scan the definitions of success for conflicting views. Work with the team to resolve the differences. If the scope statement expands or contracts, evaluate whether you have to revise the rest of the project plan to support those changes.

Part Two:
Planning a
Project

On Time! On Track! On Target! Managing Your Projects Successfully with Microsoft Project

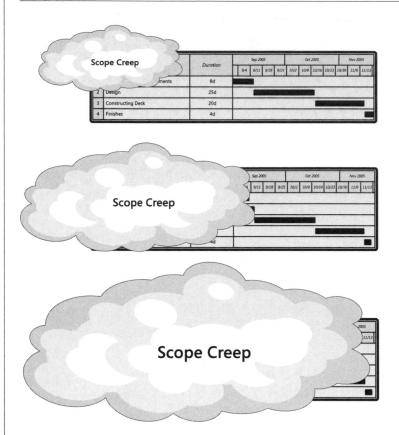

Fortunately, you *can* protect a project against scope creep and still give customers and stakeholders what they ask for. That's where the change management process comes in (see "An Overview of the Change Management Process," page 257). If someone asks for a feature or a change that isn't in the project scope, funnel it to the change management process. If customers or stakeholders decide that the change is worth the additional time and cost, you can add it to your original plan.

Caution   Scope creep comes in another form that's harder to prevent, because it's your project team that does the creeping—often without your knowledge. Engineers and other technical types are known for their perfectionism. Set the bar and they'll try to raise it. The problem that arises is that the implementation plan is based on the project objectives, but project team members are using up time and money to do more.

Your best defenses against this type of scope creep are clarity and vigilance. Begin by emphasizing what's in scope and the importance of meeting the project objectives. Then, if you notice that tasks are starting to run long, talk to team members to find out why. If team members talk directly to customers and stakeholders, be sure to ask if changes or additional requests are an issue. Gently remind team members that the objectives in the project plan should be their focus.

Project Objectives

As you gather information about a project, you're bound to learn about other expectations for the endeavor. The project mission statement summarizes what the project is supposed to do, but project objectives are specific criteria for project success. The list of project objectives answers the simple but all-powerful question, "How will we know that we've succeeded?" Just like the scope statement, a list of objectives prevents misunderstandings and helps people focus on what's expected.

The usual project management suspects are obvious contenders: on time, within budget, fulfilling the scope, and delivering the deliverables. But specific objectives for each project are unique. For example, a project to upgrade a financial institution's systems could include an objective of no interruption to market trading. The backyard remodel project might have an objective to keep as many of the existing trees as possible.

As you identify objectives, find out how important each objective is to the ultimate success of the project. If you must trim the list of objectives later to meet the budget, schedule, or resource constraints, you can turn to the list to decide which objectives stay or go.

Important　The project plan represents a balance between scope, cost, schedule, and quality. As you develop the project plan, you might have to adjust your project objectives to maintain that balance given project constraints. If objectives change *after* the project plan is approved, be sure to revisit the entire project plan to rebalance its scope, cost, schedule, and quality.

Type of Objectives

Objectives come in a variety of flavors. Because different teams within the overall project team often focus on specific types of objectives, project plans usually group objectives by type. Here are some of the types of objectives that projects must satisfy:

■　*Business* objectives can cover a lot of ground, from tactical objectives like reducing the time that customers spend on hold or increasing

Part Two:
**Planning a
Project**

On Time! On Track! On Target! Managing Your Projects Successfully with Microsoft Project

membership renewals to strategic objectives like expanding into a new market or reducing the time to market.

■ *Financial* objectives deal with either budgets or the measures that organizations use to evaluate their performance. Some examples of financial objectives include achieving a specific return on investment, staying within budget, increasing revenue or profit, or cutting costs.

■ *Performance* is another broad category of objectives. Meeting deadlines and sticking to the schedule, satisfying requirements, and conforming to specifications all fit in the performance bucket. For example, the backyard remodel project could have schedule objectives to not start excavation until the kids are back in school but to complete the concrete work in October before the ground freezes.

Tip   Objective types aren't always black and white. For some projects, a performance objective could also be a business objective. For example, consider a project to develop a new accounting system. A performance objective to complete the system by October is the same as the business objective to complete the system to provide two months of overlap before the new fiscal year.

■ *Technical* objectives relate to technical issues, such as whether to use technology and which kind. For example, some projects might apply the newest technology, whereas others that must meet stringent up-time requirements might choose tried and true products. If the product that a project produces must work in less-developed areas, the project might include an objective to use readily available technology that is dependable or easy to repair without specialized tools.

■ *Quality* objectives represent how good the results must be. For example, the number of product returns should be less than a specific number; customer satisfaction ratings from surveys should increase to a specific level; or the number of service calls should decrease by a specific percentage.

Important   Government regulations and legal issues grow more significant every day. Don't forget about objectives such as conforming to regulations or reducing the company's exposure to lawsuits.

Characteristics of Good Objectives

Good objectives make it easy for everyone to agree that the objectives have or haven't been met. Choosing objectives that are realistic helps keep the project on track, and the project team won't throw in the towel because the objectives are unattainable. Here are characteristics to consider as you define objectives:

- *Specific objectives* clearly state what the project is supposed to achieve. If objectives are unclear or vague, team members won't know whether they are doing the right thing, or worse, customers tell you when you deliver that the project doesn't meet their expectations. An objective requiring that the new deck and patio should be easy to maintain could lead to disagreement over the definition of easy to maintain. A more specific objective would be the new deck and patio require less than one weekend of maintenance each year with an annual cost of less than $300.

- *Measurable or verifiable objectives* are ideal, because there's no question whether the project met them. For example, specifying the program is easy to use turns out to be darned difficult to prove. Restate objectives with measurable or confirmable results whenever possible. For example, the program achieves 95% ratings for ease of use in user surveys.

- *Achievable objectives* not only ensure that the project can succeed, but they also maintain the morale of the project team. There's nothing wrong with setting challenging objectives to urge everyone to extend themselves. But unrealistic or downright impossible objectives simply sap people's desire to even try.

Best Practices

You can't please everyone all of the time. Chances are good that the initial list of project objectives is more than the budget, timetable, and what available resources can handle. Suppose you hire an architect to design your dream home. You happily ask for this and that until you get the construction bids from builders. And suddenly, the separate his and hers master bathrooms go from a requirement to nice to have.

The initial project plan should contain the objectives you gather during your research unless some of them are clearly out of the question. But don't be surprised if you revisit the objectives during subsequent project phases as the feasibility of your strategy and better estimates become known.

Part Two:
Planning a
Project

On Time! On Track! On Target! Managing Your Projects Successfully with Microsoft Project

Note If the project has constraints on budget, schedule, and resources (and what project doesn't?), the objectives should be achievable given those constraints. For example, if a project must be completed by the end of the year, it's unrealistic to set an objective that states that the assigned resources work on the project only after they've finished their regular duties.

Project Deliverables

Projects typically deliver something in the end, whether it's a new service, a streamlined process, or a wireless GPS child collar that'll notify parents when kids wander from the yard. The final deliverable—that last milestone that triggers the big payment or celebration—is great for keeping the team focused on the ultimate project goal. But projects contain interim deliverables that represent tangible results throughout the life of the project. For example, the final deliverable for the backyard remodel is a completed deck and patio, but blueprints for the construction crew are essential to the success of the project.

Interim deliverables aren't necessarily for the project customer. The construction blueprints, for example, are important for obtaining permits and bids, and for the contractor who builds the deck. But the homeowner might never see them. Furthermore, project management also generates interim deliverables, such as the project plan, status reports, and updated risk reviews.

Interim deliverables provide milestones that give project team members a tangible target to achieve. If you assign someone to analyze your product return business process, months could go by with no sign of completion. Alternatively, consider a deliverable of a study with recommendations for improving the business process. The people assigned to the task have a better idea of what they are supposed to deliver.

Here are some examples of deliverables for the backyard remodel project:

- Project requirements
- Initial design
- Final design and drawing set
- Construction permit
- Foundation complete
- Foundation inspection approved
- Framing complete

- Framing inspection approved
- Deck complete
- Final inspection approved
- Occupancy certificate

Tip   Interim deliverables also give you a way to measure progress during the project. In fact, many project managers try to define deliverables that occur at the same frequency as status reports, so they can judge the progress that's been made since the last report.

Deliverables aren't always as concrete as concrete foundations. But deliverables have one thing in common: you can tell whether they've been delivered. As the preceding list indicates, the list of requirements for a project is a deliverable. Similarly, the description of the target audience for a book is a deliverable as well. If a deliverable is a tangible result, you can pick it up or look at it. A deliverable such as a new service isn't something you can touch. The true deliverable in this case is that the new service is available for customers to use.

Projects for the government and some other organizations, such as foundations, include contractual requirements that can delay payments or trigger penalties. If your project includes contractual requirements, such as documentation or financial reports, be sure to include those items in your list of deliverables.

In Summary

The scope statement, project objectives, and deliverables all help define what the successful completion of a project looks like. The scope statement differentiates between the results the project will achieve and those it won't. Project objectives are the specific measures of success that everyone can review to see if the project accomplished its goals. And deliverables are the results that you can see, touch, or otherwise evaluate—as signs of progress during the course of the project and as an indication that the project has finally reached its goal.

The next chapter begins the detailed work of building an implementation plan for a project. You'll learn how to identify and break down the work required to complete the project into manageable pieces that you can assign to project resources.

Part Two:
Planning a
Project

On Time! On Track! On Target! Managing Your Projects Successfully with Microsoft Project

Chapter Seven

Building a Work Breakdown Structure

The work was like peeling an onion. The outer skin came off with difficulty . . . but in no time you'd be down to its innards, tears streaming from your eyes as more and more beautiful reductions became possible.

— *Edward Blishen*

The division of labor for dinner could be you microwaving a couple of frozen dinners while your spouse gets out the plates, forks, and napkins. But the surprise party for your parents' 40th wedding anniversary is another story. You want the party to be amazing—like their marriage—so you don't want to forget anything. The best way to make sure everything gets done is to break the project down into small, manageable pieces. You could divide the work into planning the party, buying the supplies, preparing the food, and decorating the backyard. Or you could keep track of the work that you've hired the caterer, bartender, florist, and tent wrangler to do.

Regardless of the way you break down the work, the important point is that smaller servings of work help the project manager (or party host in this example) keep track of what's been done and what's on deck, and also helps everyone working on the project perform their parts successfully. A *work breakdown structure* (WBS) is the tool that project managers use to divide a project into tasks called *work packages*. But a WBS helps everyone involved see the scope and organization of the work in one easy-to-read chart.

This chapter describes a WBS and how it helps you plan and manage a project. You'll learn how to build one that effectively communicates the work to be done. This chapter also explains methods for decomposing work into properly sized portions as well as techniques for getting your WBS into Microsoft Project, so you can begin building a project schedule (see Chapter 9, "Building a Project Schedule").

What's a Work Breakdown Structure?

A WBS is a simple though aptly named component of project planning. It shows the work in a project broken down into progressively smaller tasks. The tasks at the lowest level represent work you can assign to team members to perform.

A WBS is project management's answer to the proverbial question, "How do you eat an elephant?" The answer is "One bite at a time." In essence, a WBS details the bites—the list of tasks you must perform to complete a project. You use the work packages in the WBS to estimate the time and resources each deliverable takes (see "Estimating Effort," page 123), identify the types of resources you need (see Chapter 8, "Project Resources"), and link the

Part Two:
Planning a
Project

On Time! On Track! On Target! Managing Your Projects Successfully with Microsoft Project

work packages (tasks) to create the project schedule (see "Defining the Sequence of Work," page 133).

A WBS contains two kinds of tasks: summary tasks and work packages. As you can see in Figure 7-1 and Figure 7-2, differentiating the two is easy:

- *Work packages* are the lowest-level tasks that represent actual work that people perform, like dig holes, pour footings, and install decking.

- *Summary tasks* comprise the remaining tasks, which summarize several work packages or several lower-level summary tasks. For example, a summary task called Preparing Lumber, shown in the WBS in Figure 7-2, could include work packages of Cut Lumber, Treat Lumber, and Pre-Drill Holes in Lumber. But the Preparing Lumber summary task is also a part of a higher-level summary task called Constructing Deck.

You can show a WBS either as a diagram or as an outline. A WBS diagram looks like an inverted tree, starting with the project summary task at the top and ending with the work packages at the bottom, as Figure 7-1 illustrates.

A WBS in outline form shows the same information as a WBS diagram, but it takes up a lot less space. If you've built a list of tasks in the Task Sheet view in Project, the WBS outline shown in Figure 7-2 is an old friend. Each level in the outline is indented a bit more to the right. The first column in Figure 7-2 shows another component of a WBS—the *WBS code*. Following an outline-oriented numbering scheme, WBS codes show the level of the hierarchy to which tasks belong as well as which lower-level tasks belong to higher-level (parent) summary tasks.

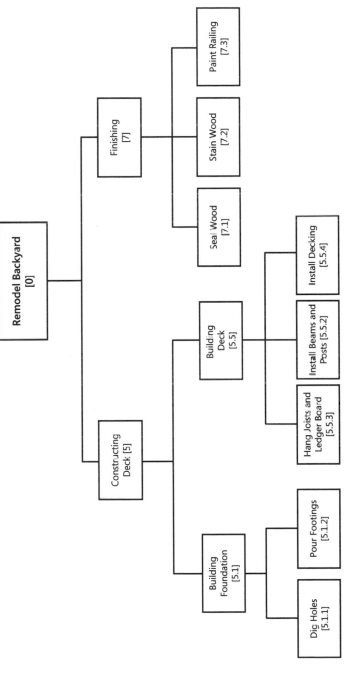

Figure 7-1   A WBS diagram shows the hierarchy of project tasks from the overall project at the top to work packages at the bottom.

Part Two:
Planning a
Project

On Time! On Track! On Target! Managing Your Projects Successfully with Microsoft Project

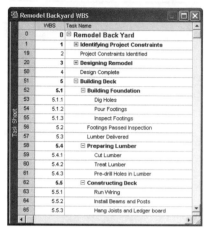

Figure 7-2   A WBS outline indents tasks at each level of the hierarchy to show summary tasks and work packages in a compact space..

The Project file for the WBS shown in Figure 7-2 is *Backyard Remodel WBS.mpp* in the *Backyard Remodel Project* folder on the companion CD.

The Benefits of a WBS

If you try to perform a project with only a vague direction, like "Remodel the backyard," chances are good that you'll forget to complete an important task, or the workers won't understand exactly what they're supposed to do. Part of the power of a WBS is that it presents project work in portions that people can handle. But more than that, a WBS does the following:

- **Helps stakeholders visualize the scope of the project**   A WBS provides an overview of the project, which stakeholders can review at any level of detail they want.

- **Shows the work defined by the scope statement in more detail**   A scope statement (see "The Scope Statement," page 75) is only a high-level view of the boundaries of a project. A WBS exposes the detailed tasks that comprise the overall project scope.

- **Helps people understand their work assignments**   Team members appreciate clear instructions about what they are supposed to deliver. A work package communicates the extent of an assignment. The relationship of the work package to the rest of the WBS increases workers' commitment by showing how their efforts contribute to success.

■ **Exposes additional work to be done**   Project deliverables that don't have corresponding work packages or summary tasks in the WBS are a warning that you haven't yet identified all the work that the project requires.

■ **Improves the accuracy of a project schedule and estimated costs** With smaller tasks, team members can better estimate the level of effort and the materials and equipment needed.

■ **Provides a foundation for measuring progress**   Once you begin executing the project, work packages and summary tasks are either in progress or complete. By breaking work into smaller components, you have more points at which you can accurately measure progress.

Building a WBS from the Top Down

Constructing a WBS can be a challenge, because you can often break down projects in different ways, even if the work you ultimately perform is the same. You can tame WBS creation by applying the same divide-and-conquer technique that the WBS itself represents.

How to Build a WBS

You can create a WBS more easily and more accurately with a few simple steps. The procedure boils down to starting at the top and working your way down, and then fine-tuning and verifying the WBS by working your way back up to the top.

Step One: Identify High-Level Tasks Using Project Deliverables and the Scope Statement

Because project deliverables (see "Project Deliverables," page 82) document the tangible results that a project is supposed to provide, you start your WBS by creating high-level tasks for every project deliverable you've identified. For example, if a deck in the backyard is one project deliverable, create a high-level task for constructing that deck.

You break down high-level tasks by detailing intermediate deliverables. For example, a construction permit and blueprints aren't end results for the backyard project, but you need tasks in the WBS to produce them.

Part Two:
Planning a
Project

On Time! On Track! On Target! Managing Your Projects Successfully with Microsoft Project

> **Tip** Don't worry about organizing tasks into top-level and lower-level
> tasks at this point. Later on you'll review your WBS to see if a different
> arrangement of summary tasks and work packages makes more sense.

A scope statement (see Figure 6-1, page 76) is another high-level view of
what a project is supposed to do. Compare the scope statement to the tasks
you've already added to the WBS. If an item in the scope statement isn't yet
present in your WBS, add a task for it now. For example, the scope statement in Figure 6-1 includes "Design the deck and patio, including lighting
and landscaping; and produce detailed design drawings." This one scope
item identifies several project tasks:

- A summary task for the design phase of the project
- A task for designing the deck
- A task for designing the patio
- A task for designing lighting and landscaping
- A task to produce detailed design drawings

Figure 7-3 shows a high-level WBS created by reviewing deliverables and
the scope statement for the backyard remodel project.

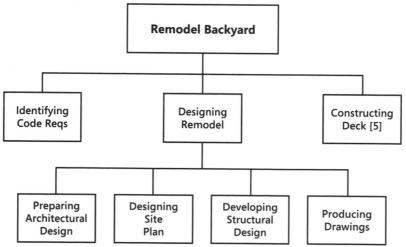

Figure 7-3 Project deliverables and the scope statement can provide ideas for
the high-level tasks in a WBS.

Step Two: Fill In the Remaining Levels of Tasks That Make Up the Work in the Top-Level Tasks

For small projects, this step might be as simple as adding a few more tasks under each high-level task. But for most projects, filling in the rest of a WBS quickly becomes an assignment that requires more hours—and expertise—than the project manager possesses.

The basic approach for identifying tasks at the next level is to ask what deliverables and tasks are needed to complete the summary task (sometimes called the parent task). Consider the top-level task Designing Remodel. What is involved in designing a new backyard? An architectural design, a site plan, engineering drawings for the structure, construction permits, and the approval of the client are all deliverables for the overall design. Add tasks to produce each of these deliverables.

Consider the high-level task Designing Backyard Remodel. Here is the initial decomposition:

- **Preparing Architectural Design**
  The design includes a deck, which means that the project needs an architectural design.

- **Designing Site Plan**   The project includes a design for landscaping the yard, although performing the landscaping is out of project scope.

- **Developing Structural Design**   Building a safe deck requires a structural design for the wood framing and foundation.

Good Task Names

Task names that effectively communicate work are like poetry. They make their point in only a few well-chosen words. Every task name includes the desired result and the action that produces it. The deliverable is the noun in each task name, such as Site Plan. The action to produce the deliverable is the verb. For example, Identify Top 5 Risks clearly states the action and the desired result.

Weak task names reduce the effectiveness of a WBS. Task names without a verb leave the work to be performed in doubt. For example, a task name like Deck doesn't indicate whether the task is to design a deck, build it, or buy a new deck of cards for the Friday night poker game.

Vague verbs aren't much better. A task to analyze risks could go on forever, if you assign it to the worrywart on your team. Action verbs, such as identify or prioritize, communicate work more clearly.

Some project managers prefer to differentiate summary tasks from work packages by name. Because summary tasks represent ongoing activity, you can name summary tasks using the "ing" form of a verb (called a gerund if you want to impress your friends) and work packages with the present tense of the verb. For example, the design summary task might be Developing Structural Design, whereas one of the work packages is Select Components.

Part Two:
Planning a
Project

On Time! On Track! On Target! Managing Your Projects Successfully with Microsoft Project

- **Preparing Final Drawing Set**   A set of drawings is required to show the client the design and to obtain a building permit.

- **Obtaining Building Permit**   The building permit is essential to begin construction.

Tip   Very large projects typically require a dozen or more levels to break down work into small enough pieces. In fact, the higher WBS levels often represent projects in their own right, each contributing major deliverables to the parent project—like the booster rockets, computers, communication system, and lunar module in the early space program. If vendors or subcontractors perform these subprojects, you can ask them to develop the WBS for their part of the project.

In large projects, you might find it more convenient to use only nouns or major deliverables for the higher-level WBS summary tasks. When you get to the lower levels, switch back to verb-noun task names.

Best Practices

Working initially in small teams is one of the best ways to build a WBS. If you have too many people involved at the beginning, you'll be herding cats: redefining work packages, changing approaches, rearranging summary tasks, yet rarely making visible progress.

Put together a small group of people familiar with the entire project and knowledgeable in at least one of its aspects. This team can build the top two or three levels of the WBS. For instance, the managers from each department or company involved in the project can focus on the big picture tasks at the top. By the time you reach the third or fourth level of the WBS, you'll need people with specific expertise to identify the work packages that are required. Assign these lower-level summary tasks to small groups of people, such as the structural engineering team that knows all the steps to preparing a structural design. See "Creating the WBS in Project" on page 96 for tips on how to incorporate tasks from other teams into your project-wide WBS.

Don't forget to include the project management tasks that you perform in the WBS. Although many project management tasks continue from project beginning to end, you need tasks to track the work you do.

Step Three: Revise the Structure of the WBS

You can decompose most projects in more than one way. For example, one project manager might break a project into phases, such as planning, design, construction, and cleanup; whereas another might prefer to focus on completed products, such as houses, streets, and neighborhoods.

The groupings you use depend on your organization, the project objectives, and how you want to track progress. For example, breaking down work into construction phases makes it easy to track the work for different types of workers, such as carpenters, plumbers, painters, and landscapers. For massive construction projects like building an airport, different companies are usually responsible for major deliverables. In situations such as this, you might break down the work into the subprojects that each vendor delivers: the terminal building, the runway, the baggage handling system, the parking garages, and final integration.

Revising the structure of the WBS provides a great opportunity to assemble the people who contributed to the construction of the WBS. True, you'll have to play traffic cop to facilitate the meeting, but the interactions between experts and stakeholders can produce a more effective WBS and build more commitment to the project at the same time. In addition, the questions and discussions that people ask of each other help identify missing work packages.

> **Note**   Regardless of the structure you choose for higher levels of a WBS, the work packages remain the same.

Step Four: Verify the Structure of the WBS

The whole point of choosing a particular structure for a WBS is communication. The WBS is meant to help team members understand their assignments and help you track progress. After you've revised the WBS, check that each summary task is important to at least one stakeholder. If not, you can safely move its work packages to another location in the WBS. For example, if a project includes a significant quantity of documentation and the technical writing group manages documentation deliverables, a summary task called Producing Product Documentation makes sense. For a smaller project with one technical writer who works directly with the development team, you might include a work package for writing the users' guide within the summary task for developing the program.

When to Stop Building a WBS

Work packages are like bowls of porridge in the fairy tale about Goldilocks and the Three Bears. Work packages that are too big or too small are unacceptable—you want work packages that are just the right size. Large work packages make it difficult to get an accurate picture of progress. The team lead could reassure you that everything is on track for weeks only to ask for a two-month extension at the last minute. Work packages that are too small

Part Two:
Planning a
Project

On Time! On Track! On Target! Managing Your Projects Successfully with Microsoft Project

waste valuable time due to micromanagement. But how can you tell that a work package is just right?

Here are a few guidelines for building a WBS to the right level of detail:

- **To help track progress** Break down work to match your reporting periods (for instance, weekly or every other week). If you limit work packages to the length of your reporting period, work packages will be complete within two status-reporting periods. Many project managers like to break down work into packages that take between 8 and 80 hours (at least 1 day to no more than 2 work weeks).

- **To improve estimates** Break work into portions that you can accurately estimate. For instance, you may have no idea how long it will take to build a house, but you do know that you'll need two days to tile the kitchen floor. After you've estimated the work packages, you can add up all your estimates to obtain totals for the whole project.

- **To limit the detail to what you can manage** Decompose project work only to the level of detail that you can and want to manage.

When Tiny Tasks Are Okay

Although tracking tasks that take less than a day would overwhelm most projects with excessive supervision and near paralysis from nonstop status reporting, short tasks have their purposes. Consider a television nightly news show. In 30 minutes, the show hands off the limelight from the anchor to reporters in the field, the weatherperson, the sportscaster, and several commercial interruptions. Complex projects that must finish within very short time frames require a detailed execution plan, and work packages of very short duration are the answer. For example, installing software programs in a production environment with limited downtime is one example where short duration tasks are necessary. Besides identifying the intricacies of teamwork, short duration work packages quickly highlight delays.

Of course, a lot of planning goes into a television news show and that planning isn't broken into minute-long segments. For projects with some complexity, only a small number of tasks will be short in duration.

Tip Most people can remember and work on up to five tasks without forgetting something. Even the most agile jugglers can rarely handle more than eight tasks regardless of the help they get. To maintain focus on the work, limit your WBS to no more than eight levels. If the size of the project requires more than eight levels to reach the right amount of detail or duration, consider breaking the project into subprojects. The top-level project can have five to eight levels in its WBS, and each subproject can have its own multilevel WBS.

Recording a WBS

You can choose from several techniques for assembling the summary tasks and work packages for a WBS, depending on your work environment, the size of your team, and the programs you prefer to use. Low-tech methods like sticky notes on a whiteboard to high-tech methods like using an LCD projector to show tasks as you build them in a Microsoft Office application can work equally well. Here are some methods to consider for your WBS deconstruction sessions.

■ **Sticky notes**   Although sticky notes are low-tech, they're great for capturing tasks as your team shouts them out in rapid-fire fashion. Sticky notes are easy to move around as you search for the ideal structure for your project. Every team member can have a pad of sticky notes, so no one person is stranded as stenographer.

You can use sticky flip chart pages to act as summary tasks. When you assign a work package to a particular summary task, place the small sticky note on the big sticky page containing that summary task.

Caution   Adhesive is the primary downside to the sticky note approach—specifically, its tendency to grow less sticky with time. Ideally, you should transfer the results of a sticky note session to Project or another program before you leave the meeting room. If you must transport your large sticky pages, fold and carry them very carefully so the WBS doesn't get rearranged during the journey back to your office.

■ **Microsoft Project**   You can build a WBS in the Microsoft Office application that you prefer. Capturing the WBS directly in Project saves you the step of transferring the WBS from another program when it's time to build the project schedule.

In Project, the Task Sheet pane on the left side of the Gantt Chart view is perfect for building an outline of your tasks. (On the View menu, click Gantt Chart to display the Gantt Chart view.) In the Task Sheet pane, you indent and outdent tasks to represent summary tasks and work packages (see "Creating the WBS in Project," page 96). And you can move individual tasks or groups of tasks around as you rearrange the WBS structure (see "Modifying the WBS," page 98).

Part Two:
Planning a
Project

On Time! On Track! On Target! Managing Your Projects Successfully with Microsoft Project

Tip If you build a WBS in Project, you can transform it into a hier-archical diagram using the Visio WBS Chart Wizard (if you use Microsoft Project 2003 and Microsoft Visio 2000 or later). In Project, display the Analysis toolbar by choosing View, pointing to Toolbars, and then choosing Analysis. On the Analysis toolbar, click Visio WBS Chart Wizard. To create a chart of all tasks, simply choose Launch Wizard.

If you want to create a WBS of only some tasks, on the Analysis tool-bar, click Apply Task Selection View. For every task you want to include in the diagram, type Yes in the cell in the Include in WBS Chart? column. After you've selected all the tasks you want, on the Analysis toolbar, choose Launch Wizard.

■ **Microsoft Word** Outlining in Microsoft Word (on the View menu, choose Outline) is a great solution for teams that aren't familiar with Project. It's easy to indent, outdent, insert, move, or delete tasks; most team members are familiar with the program. With a few intermediate steps, you can readily import into Project a WBS that you built in Word (see "Importing a WBS into Project," page 99).

Tip Although Visio includes project management templates, it isn't the best tool if you expect some frenzied rearrangement of the WBS during your capture sessions.

Creating the WBS in Project

Regardless of the method you choose to capture work packages and sum-mary tasks, ultimately, you want your WBS in Project so you can turn it into a schedule. But before you can use Project task dependencies to link tasks to build a schedule (see "Defining the Sequence of Work," page 133), you need those tasks in Project at the correct level of the WBS. If you capture work on a white board or with sticky notes, you can type the tasks directly into Project.

For all but the smallest projects, transferring handwritten tasks into Project represents a marathon of typing names and indenting tasks. When the right steps in the right order become second nature, you'll shorten the drudgery and reduce the mistakes that you make as well. The following steps make short work of transcribing tasks from paper to Project:

1. Enter all the top-level summary tasks at the same time. Because these tasks sit at the top level of the outline in the Task Sheet pane, all you have to do is type the name in the Task Name field and then press the Down Arrow to move to the next task. Project keeps the next task at the same level as the previous one. If you need some inspiration for tasks to use, refer to the WBS in Figure 7-2.

2. Enter the subordinate tasks for a summary task. This step works the same in every level of the WBS you're working on. Repeat this step for each summary task in your WBS. That is, add second-level summary tasks to each first-level task; add third-level summary tasks to the second-level tasks; and so on. When you've added the work package tasks to the lowest-level summary tasks, you're done. Here are the steps for adding subordinate tasks to their summary task:

   a. Insert a blank row below the summary task by clicking the Task Name cell immediately *below* the summary task to which you want to add tasks.

   b. Press Insert as many times as needed to create blank rows for each subordinate task. For example, if the Building Foundation summary task has three work packages, insert three blank rows.

   c. The insertion point appears in the Task Name cell for the first blank task below the summary task, so you can type the name for the first subordinate task.

   d. Press Enter to save the name.

   e. Select the task you just created and, on the Formatting toolbar, click the Indent button (shown in Figure 7-4 on the next page) to indent the task one level in the outline (and thus the WBS).

   f. After the first subordinate task is indented, you can add all the remaining subordinate tasks at the same level by pressing the Down Arrow and typing the task names.

Part Two:
Planning a
Project

On Time! On Track! On Target! Managing Your Projects Successfully with Microsoft Project

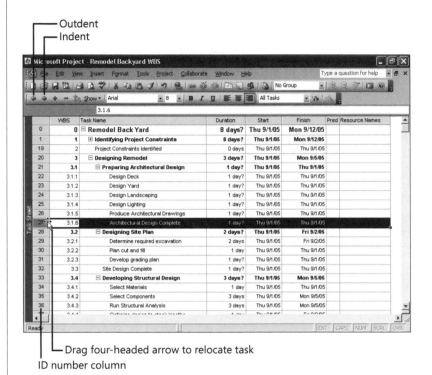

Figure 7-4   You can move tasks up and down in the Task Sheet or indent them to change their level in the WBS.

Modifying the WBS

After you finish transcribing your summary tasks and work packages into Project, take a few minutes to scan the outline. If you spot misplaced tasks or tasks at the wrong level, use the following techniques to move tasks to their correct locations:

- **Make a task into a subtask**   Select the task. On the Formatting toolbar, click Indent, shown in Figure 7-4. When you indent a task, the task above it becomes its summary task.

- **Move a subtask to a higher level**   Select the task. On the Formatting toolbar, click Outdent, shown in Figure 7-4.

- **Relocate a task to another summary task**   Click the ID cell (the column containing the number immediately to the left of the Task Sheet and shown in Figure 7-4) for the task you want to move. Project selects the entire task row and the pointer turns into a four-headed arrow. Drag the task to the new position in the outline. Project sets the task to the same level as the task above it. Indent or outdent the task if necessary.

Importing a WBS into Project

Project can import tab-delimited and comma-delimited files, which means you can transfer task names from almost any other program. For example, if a team puts together part of the WBS as a Word outline, you can save the outline as a text file. Opening the text file in Project automatically starts the Import Wizard to help you import the tasks into a Project file.

Ideally, you want tasks to import into Project at the correct WBS level. You can accomplish this feat by adding outline level numbers to the text file *before* you import it. Figure 7-5 shows an example of a text file with WBS levels added. A task name followed by ",1" indicates a top-level task; a task name followed by ",3" indicates a task at the third level.

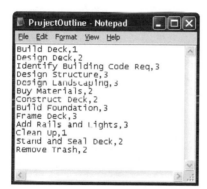

Figure 7-5   To indicate the level of tasks in the WBS, type a comma and the level number after the task name.

Here are the steps for importing your WBS text file into Project.

1. In Project, on the File menu, click Open.

2. In the Open dialog box, choose All Files from the Files Of Type drop-down list and double-click the name of the WBS text file you want to import.

3. When the Import Wizard starts, step through the pages and choose the following settings:

   Map option

   On the first Import Wizard – Map page, the wizard automatically selects the New Map option, which is what you want.

Part Two:
Planning a
Project

On Time! On Track! On Target! Managing Your Projects Successfully with Microsoft Project

Import mode option

> Accept the default selection of the As A New Project option.

Tasks

> On the Import Wizard – Map Options page, select the Tasks
> check box to import the tasks.

Import Includes Headers

> Clear the Import Includes Headers check box.

Text Delimiter

> From the Text Delimiter drop-down list, choose the comma (,).

Task Mapping

> On the Import Wizard – Task Mapping page, map the values in
> the text file to Project fields. For the first column in the import
> file (Text File Field 1), choose the Name field as the Microsoft
> Office Project Field. For the second column in the import file,
> choose the Outline Level field, as shown in Figure 7-6. After you
> map the fields, Project shows how it will import the first set of
> values from your text file, so it's easy to choose the correct fields.

4. Click Finish to import the text file. Project automatically assigns WBS
   sequence numbers to your tasks, which you can see in the WBS field
   visible in Figure 7-4.

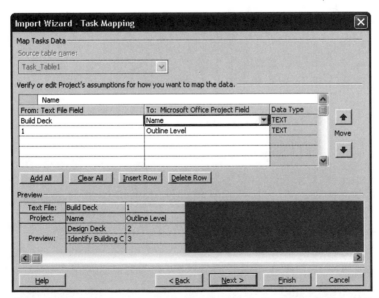

Figure 7-6 Map the columns in the text file to the Name field and Outline Level
fields in Project.

Detailing Work Packages

If you ask your teenage son to clean his room, the results might not be what you had in mind. You can improve your chances that your son will meet your expectations by specifying that cleaning a room includes hanging up clothes, making the bed, vacuuming the carpet, dusting the furniture, and neatening the papers on his desk. Similarly, a brief work package name in a WBS isn't enough to tell team members about the project work they're supposed to perform. Creating documents that describe work packages in more detail helps the team members assigned to the tasks do their work correctly and completely.

A work package document identifies the work to perform, how to tell that the task is complete, and how to tell if it was done correctly. If the details of work are documented elsewhere, a work package can be quite simple. For example, blueprints describe exactly how to frame a building or where to run wires. The work package can briefly describe the extent of the work, such as Frame First Floor Walls, but reference the blueprints or specifications for details.

Sometimes, work packages do require more detail. If work isn't described elsewhere or the person assigned to the task is new, you should make the work package more specific. Creating a checklist of the subtasks that comprise a work package can guide junior team members through the work, but checklists also help more experienced workers to remember all the steps. For example, the work package for installing a new server in Figure 7-7 on the next page includes a checklist of tasks to perform, a completion state, and reference documents that the assigned resource could turn to should questions arise.

Fast Access to Work Packages

As the project manager, you can keep work package documents close at hand by adding a hyperlink from the task in the Project schedule to the work package document. To create a hyperlink in a Project task, do the following:

1. In Project, select the task you want to link to a work package document.

2. Choose Insert and then choose Hyperlink.

3. In the Insert Hyperlink dialog box, in the Link To pane, verify that Existing File Or Web Page is selected.

4. Navigate to the folder that holds the work package document and double-click the name of the work package file.

After you create a hyperlink, in the Indicators cell of the Task Sheet, you'll see a hyperlink icon, which looks like the earth with one link of chain. (If the Indicators column isn't visible, right-click the Task Sheet and choose Insert Column on the shortcut menu. From the Field Name drop-down list, choose Indicators, and click OK.)

Part Two:
Planning a
Project

On Time! On Track! On Target! Managing Your Projects Successfully with Microsoft Project

WBS #:   5.1.2

Work package: **Install Exchange Server**

Package owner: **Karina Agerby**

Owner org: **IT**

Participants: **Toby Nixon**

Description:

Install Exchange Server in test environment:

- Install operating system
- Identify OS patches required
- Load OS patches
- Install Exchange Server software
- Load Exchange Server patches
- Create e-mail entries
- Test connection to network with test e-mail

Completion state: **Exchange Server is connected to the network and can send and
receive e-mail .**

Reference docs: **IT Naming Standards**

                     Server Architecture

Figure 7-7   Work package documents provide the detail that team members
need to complete their tasks successfully.

The companion CD includes a Microsoft Word template for a work package, *Work Package.dot* in the *Templates* folder.

In Summary

A WBS is the list of tasks the project team must perform to complete a project. It is the foundation for estimating work, choosing resources, building a project schedule, and eventually tracking progress. Small teams of people can tackle different areas of a WBS. A management team might work on the high-level WBS, whereas teams of experts might flesh out the lower levels and work packages. Regardless of how you develop a WBS, you can choose from several methods for getting the WBS into Project so it's ready for the next planning steps.

Part Two:
Planning a
Project

On Time! On Track! On Target! Managing Your Projects Successfully with Microsoft Project

Chapter Eight
Project Resources

*Leadership is the art of getting someone else to do something
you want done because he wants to do it.*

— *Dwight Eisenhower*

Projects are a lot like stage plays. People have their roles to play and if some-one forgets the lines, an awkward silence descends over the entire produc-tion. What's more, unless improvised conversations are part of the entertainment, the playwright, director, and producer might be unhappy about actors making up dialogue as they go. As a project manager, you must set the stage for your project, ensuring that team members know the parts they play and who is responsible for what.

In this chapter, you'll learn about the responsibility matrix and project orga-nization chart—two documents that line up the participants for your project. The first identifies the groups that participate and the level of responsibility that they carry. The second shows the reporting structure for team mem-bers within the project team as well as to the organizations beyond the boundaries of the project.

But you won't get very far until you actually put together teams of people who do the project work. This chapter also discusses approaches for build-ing a team of resources to perform tasks and then describes how to add those resources to a Microsoft Project file so you can assign them to tasks.

The Responsibility Matrix

The purpose of the responsibility matrix (sometimes called the responsibil-ity assignment matrix) is to state, with no room for misunderstanding, who is responsible for different parts of a project and who has authority to make or approve decisions. Projects can suffer when too many groups consider an activity as their responsibility, such as when ancillary groups try to add their requirements to an already overburdened project. They suffer as much, if not more, when *no one* accepts responsibility for activities. The responsibility matrix dramatically improves project communication, not only by identifying who's in charge and who's doing the work, but also groups that need to be consulted and those who merely need to know what's been decided.

The responsibility matrix *isn't* a detailed document of every person assigned to a project, so you can put it together early in your project plan-ning process, long before you identify the specific resources for your team or allocate them to tasks. Here are a few of the benefits that the responsibil-ity matrix provides:

■ **Resolve conflicts over who's responsible**   Reviewing the responsibility matrix with stakeholders during project planning can identify areas of the project that have multiple groups who think they're in charge. By

Part Two:
Planning a
Project

On Time! On Track! On Target! Managing Your Projects Successfully with Microsoft Project

working through disagreements at the beginning of a project, before tensions rise and people have delineated their turf, you can resolve those conflicts *before* someone has to make an important decision.

- **Identify orphaned areas of the project**   If you hear someone say "I thought *you* were going to do that," who knows how many tasks have been dropped for work that groups consider someone else's responsibility? If the responsibility matrix shows that no one is responsible for doing the laundry, the project environment could get ugly—and smelly.

- **Clarify interaction between stakeholder groups**   Projects often require complex interaction between groups, each of which contributes to deliver the solution. The responsibility matrix outlines the interactions between groups within the project team as well as between the project team and groups outside of the project, which is especially helpful in today's business world, with outsourcing, partnering, subcontracting, and other arrangements between organizations.

   For example, the telephone menu systems that you can talk to rely on a telephone network, voice recognition software, a software application for the menus of commands and the behavior they initiate, business systems that provide rules about situations like returns, and database servers that contain customer records. It's easy to end up with confusion about who does what when calls from customers who want to talk to customer service consistently get cut off. The responsibility matrix might show that the technical support group is responsible for troubleshooting problems and consulting other technical groups if necessary to resolve the issue.

Responsibility Levels

The responsibility matrix shows four levels of responsibility, from those who need to be notified when something happens to those who have the final say. However, the four levels are usually abbreviated to the acronym RICA:

- *R* indicates that a group is *responsible* for completing the work in a section of the project. For example, a high school junior who's applying to colleges is responsible for filling out the college application forms (regardless of how much he wishes his friends who write well would author his college essays).

- *I* stands for *inform*, which means that the group merely needs information about the task, such as the postal service, which needs to know where the student's mail gets forwarded when he's at college.

- *C* indicates that the group is *consulted* about decisions in a section of the project. The group participates in discussions about a decision or direction but isn't ultimately accountable. For example, a guidance counselor or relatives who attended the colleges in question can help the student decide if the schools are a good fit, but beyond that, they don't have any authority in the decision.

- *A* stands for *accountable*. A group that is accountable can make decisions about the section of the project, approve deliverables or other group's decisions, and can delegate groups to do the work. For example, the parents are accountable for their contribution to the cost of college. They can set the amount of money they can provide to pay for college, and if funds are limited, they might also be accountable for choosing a school that they can afford. Each college is accountable for deciding whether the student passes its entrance criteria.

Creating a Responsibility Matrix

The aptly named responsibility matrix is a two-dimensional matrix that links stakeholder groups in the columns with major sections of the project in rows, as shown in the example in Figure 8-1. In the cell at the intersection of a stakeholder group and a section of the project, you add the levels of responsibility that the group has over that part of the project.

A	B	C	D	E	F	G
	Student	Parents	College	High School	Relatives	Postal Service
Obtain school records	R,A			C		
Complete applications	R,A			C	C	
Copy financial records		R,A				
Complete financial aid applications	R,C	R,A	I			
Accept student	I		R,A			
Choose college	R,A	C,A	I	I	I	I

Figure 8-1 Because a responsibility matrix is like a spreadsheet with stakeholders in columns and project sections in rows, Microsoft Excel is a great tool for building one.

Part Two:
Planning a
Project

On Time! On Track! On Target! Managing Your Projects Successfully with Microsoft Project

The responsibility matrix, *OnTime_Responsibility_Matrix.xls*, shown in Figure 8-1, is available in the *Sample Documents* folder on the companion CD.

Here are some guidelines for choosing the stakeholders and project sections that you add as column headers and row labels:

- **Major sections or activities**   In the cells in the first column of the matrix, list the *major* sections of the project. The responsibility matrix is not where you identify who is responsible for each task in a project. For example, the items that you list in the project scope statement often correspond to the sections of the project that appear in the responsibility matrix.

- **Stakeholder groups**   In the cells in the first row of the spreadsheet, list the key stakeholder groups for the project. You don't add individual names, in part because you might not know them yet, and more important, because those assignments are made later when you build the project schedule. The only time you might add someone's name to the responsibility matrix is when that person alone completes a significant part of the project or is the only person who makes a decision.

With the stakeholders and project sections identified, you can start filling in the cells in the middle. Stakeholders can play more than one role, so a cell shows every responsibility that a stakeholder group has for that section of the project. For example, a college is responsible for evaluating the student's application and has the final authority to decide whether to accept the student.

Filtering a Responsibility Matrix in Microsoft Excel

If you manage a large project with many groups and project parts, the Filter feature in Excel can show only the project sections related to a specific stakeholder group. Here are the steps for filtering the responsibility matrix for choosing a college to show only tasks that the parents are responsible for working on in some way:

1.   Open the *OnTime_Responsibility_Matrix.xls* worksheet with Excel.

2.   On the Data menu, point to Filter, and then choose AutoFilter. Small buttons with arrows appear in the cells in the first row of the worksheet.

3. Click the button in the Parents column to display that column's Filter list.

4. On the menu, choose Custom.

5. In the Custom AutoFilter dialog box, in the first list box, which specifies the test, choose Contains. In the second list box, which specifies the value, type **R**.

6. Click OK to apply the filter. Figure 8-2 shows the custom filter and the results it provides.

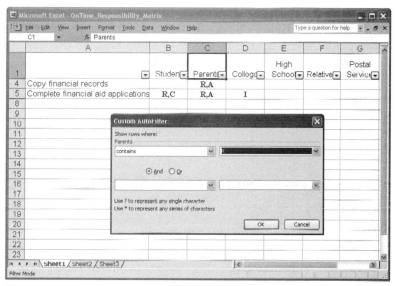

Figure 8-2 In Excel, you can filter the responsibility matrix to show only the parts of a project with which a stakeholder group is involved.

The Project Organization Chart

In addition to identifying the groups that are involved with the project, project team members also need to know the chain of command for the project. If a question arises or a decision is needed, who do team members go to? And if someone wants to escalate a problem that is taking too long to resolve, who should be called next? Most organizations use organization charts to document who reports to whom; similarly, projects rely on organization charts to show the reporting structure for people involved with a project.

Part Two:
Planning a
Project

On Time! On Track! On Target! Managing Your Projects Successfully with Microsoft Project

Project organization charts often show additional relationships besides the chain of command within the project. If you're managing a project that delivers a product to an external customer, the project organization chart shows some of the reporting structure within the customer's organization. For example, if the Director of Accounting who sponsored the project must report progress and performance to the Chief Financial Officer, who, in turn, reports to the Board of Directors, the project organization chart shows those reporting lines as well. Similarly, in organizations that use functional departments, people report not only to someone on the project, but also to their functional managers.

Project organization charts are almost identical to regular organization charts, so you can use the organization chart template in Microsoft Visio to document the project chain of command. To create a project organization chart in Visio, on the File menu, point to New, point to Organization Chart, and then choose Organization Chart on the submenu. Visio creates a blank drawing and displays the Organization Chart stencil. You can drag and drop shapes onto the drawing to create the chart, as shown in the sample organization chart in Figure 8-3.

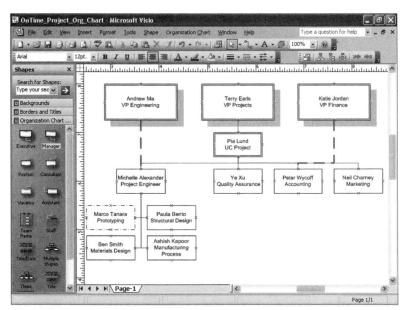

Figure 8-3 The Organization Chart template and stencil provide everything you need to build a project organization chart, including dashed connectors to indicate reporting outside the project.

The project organization chart, *OnTime_Project_Org_Chart.vsd*, shown in Figure 8-3, is available in the *Sample Documents* folder on the companion CD.

If you have information about the project organization in another program such as Excel, Microsoft Access, or a Microsoft Exchange Server directory, you can import names and titles from those programs into your Visio diagram. On the Organization Chart menu, choose Import Organization Data and follow the steps in the wizard.

Putting a Project Team Together

As you identify the work that must be performed to complete project tasks and document it in work packages (see "Detailing Work Packages," page 101), you can identify the skills needed by the resources who do that work. Initially, you identify resources simply by their skills: backhoe operator, copy editor, or senior Java programmer with financial background.

Obtaining resources that have the right skills or characteristics is usually a challenge. Some resources are simply scarce, such as a consultant who is an expert in physical and computer security issues who is also fluent in German, Italian, and Japanese. Other resources might be more plentiful but still hard to obtain because every project uses them, such as a backhoe operator for construction projects.

As temporary endeavors, projects don't have resources of their own. Most of the time, you obtain the people who perform project work from functional managers,

Best Practices

When you first build your project schedule, you won't know how many resources you need. As you craft work packages into a sequence of tasks and assign resources to those tasks, you develop a preliminary plan of how many resources you need with different types of skills.

However, if the schedule that results is too long or too costly, you have to revise the schedule. To shorten the schedule, you might add resources to some of the tasks (see "A Crash Course on Project Crashing," page 156). To reduce costs, you might replace resources with less expensive ones. The reality is that putting your project team together is an iterative process that begins with your initial schedule and continues until the project finishes.

through vendors, partners, and sometimes from the project customer. Although it's tempting to ask for people you know are right for the job or you've worked with before, the better approach is to provide functional managers or other resource managers with work packages and assignment information. With the work package, the time frame, and any constraints

Part Two:
Planning a
Project

On Time! On Track! On Target! Managing Your Projects Successfully with Microsoft Project

such as cost, the managers can determine the best people for the assignments. And the side benefit is that you build relationships with those managers as someone who lets them do their jobs, not a prima donna who shows up demanding this and insisting on that.

After you successfully acquire resources for a project, the next challenge is keeping those resources assigned to your tasks. Assigning people to work 12-hour days and weekends not only increases overtime costs, but it leads to burnout, errors, rework, and employee turnover—none of which are characteristics of a successful project. Conversely, assignments that leave people idle for days on end are open invitations to lose those resources to other projects. Then, when you need those people, they might still be working on their other assignments, or in the worst case, laid off.

Assigning resources effectively is the antidote to all these problems. As you'll learn in Chapter 9, "Building a Project Schedule," estimating work accurately and assigning the resources you need based on their true availability produces a more realistic schedule. Fine-tuning the schedule to maintain more consistent workloads helps keep resources available and simplifies managing who should be doing what.

Optimizing resource allocation provides additional benefits that simplify project management in the long run. Functional managers will be more likely to assign their best resources when they have good information about assignments and confidence that the schedule is realistic. Team members are more likely to willingly accept assignments on projects that won't consume their every waking hour.

Creating Resources in Project

Before you can assign resources to tasks in Project, you must tell Project about those resources. You can start by specifying a few key fields, such as the resource name, whether the resource is a work or material resource, and rate or cost. But Project includes many additional fields that you can use to fine-tune resource assignments, such as work resources' availability and codes that indicate the skills they possess. Unsurprisingly, Project provides several methods for entering information about resources. In this section, you'll learn about adding resources manually and ways to create resources from information you have stored elsewhere. This section also describes the information you can store about resources in Project. Finally, you'll learn how to create a resource pool to hold resources that you share among several projects.

Methods for Adding Resources

For projects with only a few resources, the Resource Sheet view in Project displays a table with the most commonly used fields for resources. However, if you work with dozens or hundreds of resources and store the information you need in another program, it's much easier to import data into Project.

Adding Resources Manually

In Project, the Resource Sheet view helps you make quick work of entering resource information. You can type or choose values in cells and use the pointer or keyboard shortcuts to navigate to the cells you want. As you can see in the Base Calendar cell for the project manager in Figure 8-4, some fields, such as Type, Accrue At, and Base Calendar include lists to simplify data entry.

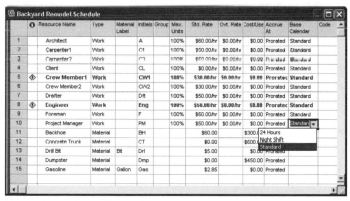

Figure 8-4   Press the Tab key to move to the next cell in a row. Or, to skip several cells, click the cell in which you want to enter a value.

To display the Resource Sheet, use one of the following methods:

- On the View menu, choose Resource Sheet.

- In the View bar, click the Resource Sheet icon.

Part Two:
Planning a
Project

On Time! On Track! On Target! Managing Your Projects Successfully with Microsoft Project

■ On the View menu, choose More Views. In the More Views dialog box, double-click Resource Sheet.

Tip   If you are adding only work resources, you can speed up your data entry a little more with a table that includes only the fields for work resources. With the Resource Sheet visible, on the View menu, point to Table: Entry, and then choose More Tables. In the More Tables dialog box, double-click Entry – Work Resources to display a table that includes fields such as Max. Units and Std. Rate. If you are adding only material resources, choose the Entry – Material Resources table to display material resource–specific fields, such as Material Label. See "Resource Information," page 115, to learn more about the fields for resources.

Importing Resources

As you might expect, you can import resource information into Project as you can task information. Project accepts data from Access databases, Excel workbooks, XML files, and delimited text files. But you can also import resources directly from an Address Book, if Project is installed on the same computer as Microsoft Exchange.

For example, to import resources from an Address Book, on the Insert menu, point to New Resource From, and then choose Address Book. If your organization uses Active Directory to store information, when you point to New Resource From, choose Active Directory to import resources from that repository.

Excel provides the Microsoft Project Plan Import Export Template, which includes columns that map directly to Project resource fields. Here are the steps for creating and importing an Excel workbook of resource information:

1. In Excel, on the File menu, choose New.

2. In the New Workbook task pane, click On My Computer.

3. In the Templates dialog box, click the Spreadsheet Solutions tab, and then double-click Microsoft Project Plan Import Export Template. Excel creates a new workbook with columns that correspond to the most commonly used Project resource fields.

4. At the bottom of the Excel window, click the Resource_Table tab.

5. Enter resource information into the appropriate cells and then save the file when you're done. For example, use the resources shown in Figure 8-4 to experiment with the template.

6. To import the resources from the Excel workbook, in Project, open your Project file.

7. On the File menu, choose Open and navigate to the folder that contains the Excel workbooks with your resource information.

8. In the Files Of Type list, choose Microsoft Excel Workbooks.

9. Double-click the file name for the Excel workbook. The Import Wizard appears.

10. On the Welcome To The Project Import Wizard page, click Next. On the next page, select Project Excel Template and click Next.

11. On the Import Wizard – Import Mode page, select Append The Data To The Active Project and click Finish. Project imports the resources to your Resource Sheet.

Resource Information

To create a resource in Project, the only field you must fill in is Resource Name. Project automatically sets the Type field to Work, which represents a resource that contributes time to a project, such as a person or equipment you rent by the day. It also fills in the Initials field with the first letter of the resource's name and sets the Std. Rate to $0.00. If you don't track project costs, you're ready to assign the resource to tasks. However, if you want to get the most out of Project, you probably want to fill in other resource fields. Figure 8-5 on the next page shows the Resource Information dialog box, which includes all the fields you can set up for a resource, not just the ones visible in the Resource Sheet. This section describes the most popular resource fields you can use and what they do.

Basic Information

The two most important resource fields are Resource Name and Type. Here are some guidelines for filling them in:

■ **Resource Name** If you are adding a resource that represents a job or skill set, fill in Resource Name with the job name, such as Carpenter. To add a real person, fill in the field using the format "Last Name, First Name." Project then displays people sorted by their last names, which makes it easier to find the people you want.

Part Two:
Planning a
Project

On Time! On Track! On Target! Managing Your Projects Successfully with Microsoft Project

- **Type**   Project includes work resources and material resources. Work resources are those that contribute time to a project, such as people and equipment that you rent by the hour or day. When you create a work resource, Project automatically adds "/hr" to the value you type in the Std. Rate field. Material resources are physical resources that a project consumes, such as gasoline or lumber. When you set the Type field to Material, the value in the Std. Rate field is simply a dollar value.

- **Material Label**   For material resources, enter the units that the material comes in. For example, for gasoline, the Material Label might be Gallon.

- **Initials**   If you display the resources assigned to tasks in Gantt Chart view, full resource names take up a lot of space, particularly for tasks with several assigned resources. By typing initials or abbreviations in the Initials field, you can display compact resource identification on taskbars.

- **Max. Units**   For a work resource, the Max. Units field specifies the percentage of a workday that the resource is available. As described in "Building Reality into a Schedule" on page 149, you can enter a value, such as 75%, if you want to reflect the amount of time a resource works on project work in each workday.

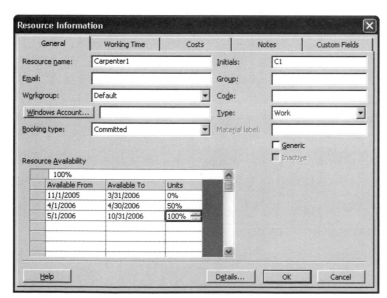

Figure 8-5   If you don't see a resource field that you want to fill in, double-click a resource row in the Resource Sheet view to open the Resource Information dialog box.

Cost Information

If you track project costs, you can define the pay rates or costs for work and material resources. See "Calculating Costs in a Project Schedule" on page 165 for step-by-step instructions for adding costs to resources. Here is a summary of cost fields you can specify:

- *Std. Rate* is the pay rate for a work resource or the cost per unit of measure for a material resource. For example, a work resource's pay rate of $50 per hour appears as $50.00/hr. For a material resource, type the price per unit, such as $2.85 for a gallon of gasoline, and then in the Material Label cell, type the unit of measure, such as Gallon.

- *Ovt. Rate* is the pay rate when a resource works longer than the standard workday. Some companies don't pay overtime at all, which means that the value in Ovt. Rate is $0.00. Whether you pay the same hourly rate for overtime hours or a premium rate, type the pay rate per hour in this field.

- *Cost/Use* represents a fee that you pay each time you use a resource. For example, if you pay $450 each time you fill up a dumpster, add that cost in the Cost/Use field.

- *Accrue At* tells Project when the project incurs a cost. Start represents a cost that occurs at the start of a task, such as the lumber that you pay for when it's delivered. End represents a cost that occurs at the end of a task, such as a consultant's fee that you pay only after the consultant's work is complete. Prorated shows the cost spread out over the duration of the task, which is typical for the labor costs associated with the people who work on tasks.

Tip   In the Resource Information dialog box, you can create up to five *different* rates for a resource, which is helpful for resources whose costs differ depending on the type of work or to reflect increases in wages that will take effect at some point in a project's schedule. See "Specifying Rates for Work Resources in Project" on page 167 for more information.

Categorizing Resources

Project offers two fields for categorizing resources. The Group field, which is visible in the Resource Sheet view, is useful if you want to sort, group, or filter tasks based on the department to which resources belong.

Part Two:
Planning a
Project

On Time! On Track! On Target! Managing Your Projects Successfully with Microsoft Project

Outline Code fields (Project includes Outline Code1 through Outline Code10), on the other hand, offer you the ability to build a hierarchy, for instance, to reflect the organizational structure of your company or the skill sets of the resources. For example, you could set up Outline Code1 to represent the reporting structure within your organization, such as Pres.Eng.Struct to represent the structural engineering department. To use an outline code to represent skills, you might set up Outline Code2 with one value like IT-Sys-UNIX to represent UNIX system administrators.

To set up outline codes for resources, on the Tools menu, point to Customize, and then choose Fields. In the Customize Fields dialog box, click the Custom Outline Codes tab to view and configure the outline codes you can define. In addition to specifying whether the outline levels include letters or numbers, you can specify how many characters or digits each level can contain and the separators between the levels. You can also specify valid entries at each level to limit codes to the ones that you define.

You can apply a custom outline code to a resource in the Resource Information dialog box. To do so, click the Custom Fields tab. Resource outline codes that you've set up will appear on the screen, as illustrated in Figure 8-6. In the Value cell, type the code for the resource.

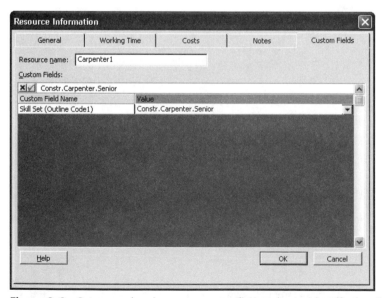

Figure 8-6   Set up and assign resource outline codes to identify the skill set or reporting structure for a resource.

Resource Availability

Project provides two ways to specify when resources are available. In the Resource Sheet, you can choose a resource calendar in the Base Calendar field to specify working and nonworking time. For example, the Standard calendar as initially defined in Project shows working time from 8:00 A.M. to 12:00 P.M. and from 1:00 P.M. to 5:00 P.M. Mondays through Fridays. If resources work a different schedule, such as the night shift, you can assign another calendar, either a built-in calendar like Night Shift or one that you customize, for instance, with Monday through Saturday as working days.

In the Resource Information dialog box, click the Working Time tab to specify working and nonworking time for only the current resource. For example, you can block out a resource's vacation as nonworking time.

The Resource Information dialog box contains one additional way to specify availability. On the General tab, the Resource Availability section enables you to specify the percentage of time that a resource is available over time. For example, if your construction workers are available 50 percent of the time between April 1 and April 30, 100 percent of the time between May 1 and October 31, and unavailable from November 1 through March 31, you can fill in rows of the Resource Availability table, as illustrated in Figure 8-5.

Creating a Resource Pool

If your organization runs several projects at once, all of which share the same pool of resources, setting up resources in individual project files isn't the way to go. By setting up a resource pool of shared resources and linking it to all your projects, you can see who's available and who is already fully committed.

You create a resource pool just as you do a regular project schedule. On the Standard toolbar, click New. Project creates a new blank project. Display the Resource Sheet and enter your resources or import them. If you have resources in an existing Project file, you can copy them from that file into your new file for the resource pool. (In the Resource Sheet, select all the resources and press Ctrl+C. In the new Project file, in the Resource Sheet view, press Ctrl+V.)

To link a project to your resource pool, do the following:

1. Open the resource pool Project file.
2. Open the project schedule Project file.

Part Two:
Planning a
Project

On Time! On Track! On Target! Managing Your Projects Successfully with Microsoft Project

3. On the Tools menu, point to Resource Sharing, and then choose Share Resources.

4. In the Share Resources dialog box, select the Use Resources option.

5. In the From list, select the Project file that represents your resource pool, as demonstrated in Figure 8-7.

6. Click OK.

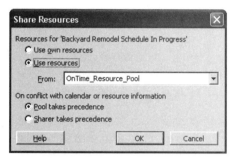

Figure 8-7 Assign a resource pool to your project files when you share resources with other projects.

A sample resource pool, *OnTime_Resource_Pool.mpp*, is available in the *Sample Documents* folder on the companion CD.

In Summary

During project planning, you create the responsibility matrix to identify which groups are involved in different parts of the project, the level to which each group is involved, and, most important, who has the final say for that part. Then, when you begin building your project schedule, you'll also begin to identify the resource you need to perform the work. The project organization chart is like a regular organization chart except that it shows who people report to both within the project environment and in their respective companies.

But to finalize a schedule in Project, you must assign resources to tasks, which means you must add resources to Project. You can specify resources in Project in several ways, depending on whether you have existing resource information and where you store it. You can also fill in only the basic information or specify resources in great detail.

Part Two:
Planning a
Project

On Time! On Track! On Target! Managing Your Projects Successfully with Microsoft Project

Chapter Nine

Building a Project Schedule

Time flies. It's up to you to be the navigator.

— Robert Orben

When you build a WBS (see Chapter 7, "Building a Work Breakdown Structure"), you define the work the project team must do. After you've put your project team together (see Chapter 8, "Project Resources"), you know who you have to work on project tasks. To build a project schedule, you need a few more pieces of information: how much time each task is likely to take, the order in which the work must occur, and exactly who does the work.

Estimates of the time that tasks should take can make or break a project. Underestimating and overestimating are both dangerous, but no one can predict the future with complete confidence or accuracy. Putting project tasks in the right order can be surprisingly easy or maddeningly difficult. For example, unless you're working in unusual gravitational conditions, building a foundation has to finish before you can build anything on top of it. In this chapter, you'll learn about estimation pitfalls to avoid and ways to improve your predictions. This chapter also describes the options you can choose for building a sequence of tasks and when to use each one. In addition, you'll learn to use Microsoft Project features to build a schedule that's accurate and easy to maintain.

Until you assign resources to tasks, you don't know when tasks might start or end. You can define the duration of tasks first and then assign the resources you need to complete the work in that time frame. Or you can assign the resources that are available to determine how long tasks will take. Either way, those resource assignments complete your initial schedule.

This chapter shows you how to assign resources in Project regardless of whether you start with durations or hours of effort. It also identifies common misconceptions about resource assignments that can lead to unrealistic schedules—and how you can apply Project features to bring your schedule back to reality. After you assign resources and balance their workloads, chances are stakeholders will tell you that the project has to be finished faster. You'll learn two common techniques for shortening project schedules and how to apply them using Microsoft programs.

Estimating Effort

Estimating how long a project will take and how much it will cost amounts to guessing, because you don't know what's going to happen in the future. Yet, decisions about whether projects make sense financially and which of those projects to run depend on good estimates, so you have to estimate project performance as best as you can.

Part Two:
Planning a
Project

On Time! On Track! On Target! Managing Your Projects Successfully with Microsoft Project

The purpose of project estimates is not to make your job difficult or to taunt project teams with unreachable targets. As you learned in Chapter 2, "Selecting and Prioritizing Projects," cost estimates and the resulting financial measures are the basis for many business decisions. The old adage, "Time is money," is true. The estimates of time and effort for a project are the basis for many project costs. By developing as realistic estimates as you can, you not only improve your chances of project success but also support the overall financial performance of your organization.

Estimating Pitfalls and How to Avoid Them

Perhaps the most important aspect of estimating is setting realistic stakeholder expectations, which wouldn't be difficult if everyone waited patiently until you finished your analysis and deemed your estimate complete. The problem is that stakeholders, executives, and managers seem to ask for estimates before you know enough to prepare them. The following sections describe the most common estimating pitfalls and how you can circumvent them.

Beware the Ballpark Estimate

You're riding the elevator to your office on Monday morning, looking forward to your first cup of coffee and semiconsciousness, when the project sponsor steps on, smiles, and casually asks, "How's the project schedule shaping up? Any idea when you expect the project to finish?" You hesitate, knowing that the answer you give will either help or haunt you to the last day of the project.

Ballpark estimates are almost always too soon (for the finish date) and too low (for resources and costs). Without your planning documents, you can easily forget a few big tasks or hundreds of small details that make up a complete project. Unfortunately, stakeholders tend to remember the estimates that you provide under friendly pressure.

The best ballpark estimate is one you don't give. Responses such as, "We haven't finished our analysis yet, but I should be able to answer your question in (fill in the amount of time)," often do the trick. What the questioners won't admit is that they're just fishing. They don't expect you to give them an answer, but if you do, they're happy to hold you to it.

If you feel as if you must give a ballpark estimate, consider the risk you're taking and do what you would for other risks in a project—give yourself contingency funds. Similar to the premium pricing that businesses request to offer a fixed-price bid, a ballpark estimate should be your most conservative estimate multiplied by a safety factor. Try multiplying by four—you'll probably still be too soon and too low, but at least closer to reality.

Estimating Work on Estimated Scope

Estimating the length of construction for a house without knowing whether it's an ice-fishing hut or a trophy home is risky business. Project objectives, scope, requirements, and product specifications all contribute to the accuracy of estimates, so you have to finish a fair amount of planning before you get to any kind of estimate accuracy. At the same time, organizations don't want to spend too much time on a project that is going to take too long and cost too much. The most common solution to this problem is a series of progressively more accurate estimates (see "Approaches for Estimating," page 129).

The Danger of Excessively Low Estimates

You might be tempted to give stakeholders the numbers you think they want to hear, but low estimates are a setup for bad business decisions. Suppose you're buying a car and the salesperson gives you an estimate of your monthly payment based on the purchase price and the loan interest rate the dealer offers. You sign all the papers only to discover that the car costs $5,000 more after the dealer adds the extra charges for an engine and tires. What's more, your monthly payment has jumped from $550 to $725 because the dealer considers you a credit risk and has upped your interest rate. With a better estimate, you could make a better decision about buying the car—or at least trying another dealer.

Low estimates undermine organizations' financial processes. The first casualty is return on investment or ROI (see "Financial Measures," page 17), which is the percentage return that a project delivers on the money invested in it. Shorter estimated schedules equate to lower estimated costs, and thus, a more attractive ROI. For example, suppose your company requires an ROI of at least 15 percent. A low estimate might make a project appear to meet the required 15 percent ROI, but when the project is over, the ROI ends up with a single-digit return. The company didn't earn the profit it expected from its investment in the project. Even worse, the investment could have been put to better use on a different project with a better and more likely ROI.

Part Two:
Planning a
Project

On Time! On Track! On Target! Managing Your Projects Successfully with Microsoft Project

> **Important**   Optimistic estimates with tight schedules and tiny budgets
> can make project teams miserable. Team members work hard to meet tar-
> gets that, in reality, are unattainable, which damages morale and the will to
> succeed. As the project manager, you spend time trying to get projects
> back on track—when it was the estimates that were off track. And status
> meetings with stakeholders aren't much fun when projects are behind
> schedule and over budget, even if an unrealistic estimate is to blame.

High Estimates Hurt, Too

Excessively conservative estimates are no better than optimistic ones. First
of all, high estimates have a nasty habit of coming true. Whether team members take more time to increase quality, work at a more leisurely pace, or
stakeholders ask for more features, projects often consume whatever time
and budget they receive. An overestimated project might achieve its objectives, but it might not deliver as attractive an ROI as it could have with a
more accurate estimate. As low estimates make ROI look better than it is,
high estimates depress project ROI, potentially below the minimum
required. Or a drawn-out schedule delivers a product too late, so the company decides to cancel the entire endeavor.

Another insidious problem with overestimating is that *other* worthy projects
get passed by. Most organizations use estimates to determine how many
projects they can run in a year based on the resources they have and the
project money that's available. A bloated schedule keeps resources tied up
and squeezes other projects off this year's project roster. In turn, the organization won't earn the profit that additional project could have provided.

The Problem with Padded Estimates

If you assume that project delivery dates and costs follow the typical bell
curve, you have a 50-50 chance of staying within the bounds of the budget
and schedule—not very comforting odds. And because tasks always seem to
take longer and cost more, bringing a project in on time and within budget
looks difficult indeed. Some people try to gain an advantage by padding
their estimates—adding extra time to their tasks so they can recover from
unexpected problems. True, padding increases individuals' chances of
delivering to their estimates, but if each level of management adds its own
padding, the resulting estimates look like sumo wrestlers by the time the
project sponsors see them. The games that begin with padding usually end
badly. One of the most common padding practices is when managers cut
every number they receive assuming they're padded. Team members

remember that their last estimates were cut so they thicken the padding the next time around. The final numbers end up the same, but the cycle of padding and cutting grows longer and trust drops lower.

Sensible Estimating Practices

The best way to get your estimates approved *and* see them become reality is by delivering realistic numbers and backing them up with data and analysis. The snag, of course, is how you get those realistic estimates in the first place. Estimating is both an art and a science, and mastering this skill takes time. This section introduces a few techniques that can help you reduce the inherent uncertainty of estimates and satisfy your stakeholders' desire for accuracy.

Get the Right People to Estimate

Good estimates start with experience. Someone who's never built a patio doesn't know the work involved or how long it takes. The people who estimate work have to understand the work that's being done. The best estimates come from the people who will do the work, because they take into account their capabilities or limitations. For example, one programmer needs a week to get up to speed on a brand-new assignment, whereas another needs only two days.

Best Practices

Padding that's public is a different story. Savvy stakeholders, executives, and project managers work together to reserve some money to act as a margin of safety for schedule and budget. Instead of every person or group having personal padding, the project shares a smaller pool and distributes the padding only to those who need it.

Project contingency funds are like the contingency funds a bank requires when you build a house, which is money reserved to resolve issues that might arise, such as price increases. Contingency time on a project works the same way. You set some time aside before the ultimate due date in case delays occur. Contingency funds and time are intended to handle known risks. You know they can happen. What you don't know is how bad they'll be if and when they do. Chapter 18, "Managing Risk," discusses contingency planning as a risk-management strategy.

Management reserve is a safety margin for unknown risks—potential problems that aren't in your risk-management plan (see Chapter 18). Management reserve time and money doesn't appear in a project plan, but management can dole it out at its discretion—without having to ask sponsors or customers for more.

Tip Commitment is another reason to obtain estimates from the people who do the work. Team members are more likely to try to meet the targets that they set themselves. However, it's impossible to include every team member in estimating on large projects. Choosing knowledgeable people for estimating is the next best option. As long as team members consider estimates realistic, they work to meet them. But they're likely to give up if they're given unrealistic estimates that someone else prepared.

Part Two:
Planning a
Project

On Time! On Track! On Target! Managing Your Projects Successfully with Microsoft Project

Improve Estimates As You Go

Estimates are almost always a trade-off of accuracy versus time and money. If you want to estimate how long it'll take to get to your aunt's house for Sunday dinner, a quick review of the mileage and road conditions is enough to get you there with 20 minutes to spare either way. But if you're estimating the time you need to make your flight for a much-needed vacation, you might consider the mileage, road conditions, the time of day, the line at the ticket counter, the line at security, the terminal your flight leaves from, and whether you have to stop for gas. You can't afford the increase in ticket price for the next flight, and you don't want to think about missing your cruise boat.

Get the Right Numbers

With several people providing estimates, you must make sure that you know what numbers you're getting. Suppose someone tells you that developing a brochure takes two weeks. Is that a total of 80 hours of work, or is it a two-week duration for a writer, copy editor, and graphic artist?

It doesn't matter whether you pick the estimated number of work hours (or days) or estimated duration and the number of resources for that time. However, if you have a preference, ask each estimator to provide you with the same kinds of estimates.

Organizations balance these trade-offs all the time. They don't need absolute accuracy for early go/no-go decisions. But they're willing to pay for that accuracy when a fixed-price bid is in the offing. Here are typical levels of estimate accuracy and when you're likely to use them:

1. *Go/no-go decisions* require the least amount of accuracy. For large projects, feasibility studies often determine if a project moves forward, whether the issue is cost, timing, or technology. Organizations spend some time and money up front so they don't waste lots more later on a dead-end project. Without feasibility studies, order-of-magnitude estimates are sufficient for early go/no-go decisions. For example, your client wants to build an office building that'll cost no more than $6 million and take no longer than a year. You can roughly estimate the usual cost and time per square foot for office construction to determine whether the time and budget is achievable.

2. *Project selection* requires more accurate estimates. To calculate potential finish dates and performance measures, you need to know something about the project scope and objectives, but not necessarily the entire project plan. For example, the scope is a 20,000 square foot office building, but you don't know if it will be a one-story or

multistory building. At this point, you can estimate the schedule within a few months and a few million dollars.

3. *More stringent project selection* requires even more accurate estimates, often produced after organizations fund projects through initial planning. For example, with a list of project objectives and scope on which all the stakeholders agree, you can develop a WBS and estimate the work required with reasonable certainty. After you know that the building has four stories, you can refine your estimate.

4. *Project milestones*, such as the completion of a phase, are good times to reevaluate estimates. When you have the final drawings for the building and construction bids in hand, you can estimate every construction task to tell your client that the building is going to take nine months and $5 million. When the steel framing is complete—a few weeks late—you can adjust your estimate if you can't make up that time on finish work.

Approaches for Estimating

You can choose from different methods of estimating depending on the type of project and your organization's experience. The right method is the one that is likely to produce the most accurate estimate for the project at hand. Learning to identify the best method is a matter of experience. This section describes a few of the more common estimating approaches used:

- *Top-down estimating* involves breaking up a project into pieces and gradually allocating time and cost to smaller and smaller components. Top-down estimates are accurate only if you start with reasonably accurate top-level estimates, so this method is best if your organization has performed similar projects in the past. For example, if your company has remodeled dozens of backyards in the past, you can use past projects to estimate that this remodel will take three months and about $30,000. From those high-level numbers, you can allocate time and dollars to the lower-level components, such as three weeks and $6,000 for building the deck.

- *Bottom-up estimating* starts at the bottom—the work packages for a project. You estimate the effort and cost for every work package and roll up the estimates at each level of the WBS until you have an estimate for the entire project. Project is perfect for generating bottom-up estimates, because summary tasks automatically calculate the cost, work, and duration of their subordinate tasks.

Part Two:
Planning a
Project

On Time! On Track! On Target! Managing Your Projects Successfully with Microsoft Project

■ *Parametric models* use factors to calculate the work and cost for a project, such as when contractors use square footage and the time or cost per square foot to estimate a construction job. Because construction is well documented, the industry has many estimating programs and databases of typical construction costs to help builders with their estimates.

If you don't have an industry-specific tool to help you estimate project costs, Microsoft Excel can calculate estimates based on parameters and formulas. For example, as shown in Figure 9-1, you can calculate the hours of effort by multiplying the square footage of a project by a factor.

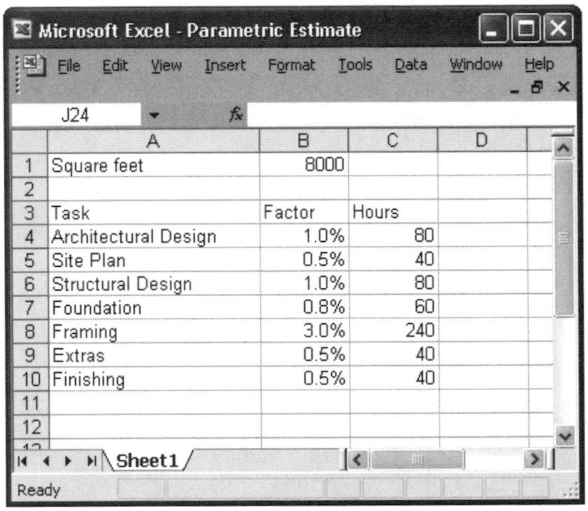

Figure 9-1 An Excel worksheet is ideal when you want to calculate estimates based on parameters.

Regardless of the method you choose to estimate a project, eventually, you want to add those estimates to a Project schedule. But walking around the office with a laptop running Project isn't the most effective way to gather estimates. Depending on how you receive estimates from others, you can write them on the WBS taped to your wall, type them into an estimating spreadsheet, or store them in a folder until you're ready to enter them into your Project schedule.

Statistical Estimating

Program Evaluation and Review Technique (PERT) is a method of estimating that looks at best, worst, and most likely results. For example, you expect a task for pouring foundations to take five days. However, if work goes incredibly well, the task might be completed in three days. On the other hand, if the weather doesn't cooperate or other problems arise, the task might take as long as eight days.

PERT comes to the rescue when there are too many unknowns to estimate tasks with certainty. You can create schedules based on three different durations for each task to show project stakeholders the shortest, longest, and most likely durations for a project.

The PERT Analysis toolbar in Project includes features to help you calculate PERT estimates and view the resulting schedules. To display the toolbar, on the Microsoft Project View menu, point to Toolbars and then select PERT Analysis. Here's what the features do:

- **Specify the worst duration, most likely duration, and best duration for each work package in a project** On the PERT Analysis toolbar, click PERT Entry Form to add Optimistic, Expected, and Pessimistic durations for each task, as shown in Figure 9-2 on the next page. The PERT Analysis toolbar also includes a button for the PERT Entry Sheet, which displays columns for Optimistic Duration, Expected Duration, and Pessimistic Duration in the Task Sheet pane.

The backyard remodel project with PERT durations, *Backyard Remodel Schedule PERT.mpp*, is available in the *Backyard Remodel Project* folder on the companion CD.

Complexity Takes Time

The time that tasks take increases exponentially with project size and complexity. One carpenter can hammer down decking in record time, but completed construction comes more slowly when hundreds of construction workers build a skyscraper.

Good communication is important when people work together. As you add people to a project, you have to factor in more time for communication and collaboration. Geographically distributed teams increase complexity and time. Despite e-mail, instant messaging, and collaboration Web sites, working with people in other places or time zones introduces delays. For instance, team members might have to wait for colleagues on the other side of the world to start their workday to resolve an issue. Even walking to meetings on a sprawling campus can eat up project time.

If you estimate a project from the bottom up by figuring the time needed for each work package, it's easy to forget about the additional time you need for communication and distributed collaboration. If your project is complex in some way, it's a good idea to increase your estimates to handle that complexity. Unfortunately, there's no handy guideline for choosing a complexity multiplier other than your experience or historical data. Because Project doesn't have a feature to incorporate complexity, increase your estimates for complexity *before* you enter any values in Project.

- **Weight PERT durations**   PERT calculations typically apply a weighting of 4 to the expected duration and a weighting of 1 to each of the

Part Two:
Planning a
Project

On Time! On Track! On Target! Managing Your Projects Successfully with Microsoft Project

optimistic and pessimistic durations. You can change these weightings. For example, if you want more weight on the bad news, change the weighting to 4 for the pessimistic duration and 1 for both optimistic and expected. To make these changes, on the PERT Analysis toolbar, click Set PERT Weights, which looks like a balance scale.

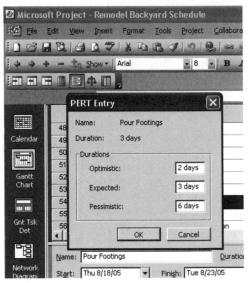

Figure 9-2 The PERT Entry dialog box includes fields for Pessimistic, Expected, and Optimistic durations.

■ **Calculate PERT durations** Click Calculate PERT to calculate the overall schedule durations based on the different PERT durations and weights you set.

Tip Project stores the three PERT durations you provide in the Duration1, Duration2, and Duration3 fields for each task.

■ **Display optimistic, expected, and pessimistic schedules** By clicking the Optimistic Gantt, Expected Gantt, and Pessimistic Gantt buttons, you can generate Gantt Charts based on the PERT durations and weightings you chose. For example, click Optimistic Gantt to produce the optimistic schedule, which finishes on September 2, 2005, shown in the top window in Figure 9-3. Click Pessimistic Gantt to produce the pessimistic schedule ending on October 27, 2005, shown in the bottom window in Figure 9-3.

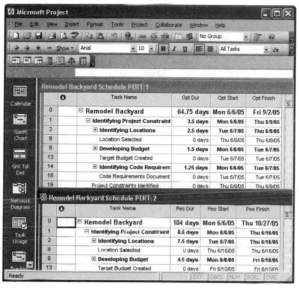

Figure 9-3   The schedule at the top of the screen is an optimistic schedule, whereas the one on the bottom is pessimistic.

Defining the Sequence of Work

Now that you know the work you must do and how long it should take, a project schedule also requires the order in which the work must be done. As tempting as it might be, college students can't take four years of courses in one semester and party the remaining seven semesters. Advanced statistics won't make much sense without probability theory as a foundation. Furthermore, there aren't enough hours in the day to attend all those classes and do all that homework.

The ideal schedule in Project is one that mirrors real life. Tasks are connected so that the schedule adjusts as you change task values. If one task experiences a delay, all the tasks that follow it are delayed as well. To achieve this ideal, every dependency that exists between tasks in real life must exist in the Project schedule as well. The next section describes the different options for linking related tasks in a schedule.

Types of Task Dependencies

Although tasks connected by dependencies are called successors and predecessors, a dependency is really about control not chronology. A dependency between two tasks specifies how one task controls the scheduling of the other, not which one comes first. The independent task (called

Part Two:
Planning a
Project

On Time! On Track! On Target! Managing Your Projects Successfully with Microsoft Project

the *predecessor*) determines the scheduling of the dependent task (the *successor*) and the predecessor can occur before, at the same time, or after its successor. You can choose from four types of dependencies:

- *Finish to start* is the most common type of dependency. It's also the easiest to understand, because control and timing follow the same order. When the predecessor task finishes, the successor task begins. For example, when a construction crew finishes setting up the forms for a concrete foundation, the crew starts pouring the concrete into the forms.

- *Start to start* dependencies mean that the start of one task triggers the start of the second. Start to start dependencies often come with a delay (called *lag*) between the tasks. For example, a road crew starts placing traffic cones to close a lane on the highway. Ten minutes after the crew begins, the line painting machine starts painting lines in the closed lane.

- *Finish to finish* represents one task that continues only as long as another task is in progress. For example, traffic flaggers stop directing traffic when construction work is complete.

- *Start to finish* is confusing, but isn't needed very often. With start to finish dependencies, the start of the predecessor controls the finish of the successor. The confusion arises because, in most cases, the predecessor occurs *after* the successor. For example, if you start evaluating requests for proposal (RFPs) on December 1, that date controls when vendors stop working on their RFPs. They deliver their documents in whatever state they're in and hope for the best.

Identifying the Correct Dependency Type

Most task dependencies are obvious, but you can identify the best type of dependency for less common situations by asking a series of simple questions. If you typically think about timing when choosing dependencies, use the following questions about control to identify the correct dependency type:

1. *What does this task need before it can start?* Identifying predecessors is usually easier than finding successors. Ask this question to find the tasks that act as predecessors for the task you're evaluating. With the predecessor and successor identified, you know which two tasks to link.

2. *Does the start or finish of the predecessor control the successor?* The answer to this question determines the first half of the task dependency type. For example, if the finish of the predecessor controls the successor, the dependency type must be either finish to finish or finish to start.

3. *Does the predecessor control the start or finish of the successor?* This question finalizes the type of dependency. For example, if the answer to question 2 is "finish" and the answer to this question is "start," the dependency type is finish to start.

Creating Task Dependencies

If you've ever calculated start dates, finish dates, and slack by hand, you already know the value of task dependencies in Project. When you create a dependency between two tasks, Project uses that relationship to recalculate the schedule whenever durations, start dates, or finish dates change. Building a schedule is simply adding all the dependencies between tasks, and they appear in the proper order. When you're done, the top-level project summary task shows the overall duration of the project (which is known as the critical path method or CPM).

Lag and Lead

In real life, tasks don't always follow each other immediately. Sometimes, there's a delay between tasks (called lag), and at other times, they overlap (called lead). In Project, you can further qualify the dependency between two tasks with a lag. For example, if you can't begin to paint until the primer has dried, the finish to start includes a four hour lag. To define an overlap between two tasks, you use a negative value for lag.

Adding lag time to task dependencies is perfect for showing waiting time (like concrete curing) or overlaps. In Project, you can define lag with either duration or a percentage of the duration of the predecessor task.

Because task dependencies are the foundation of scheduling in Project, it's no surprise that you can choose to create task dependencies in several ways. Here are the most common techniques and when they come in handy:

- **The Link icon**   The easiest way to create a finish-to-start dependency between two tasks is to select the predecessor task, then select the successor task, and finally, on the Standard toolbar, click the Link icon. Using the Link command is also helpful when you can't see both bars in the Gantt Chart at the same time.

- **Dragging between two tasks**   If you can see the bars for both tasks in the Gantt Chart (refer to the Dig Holes task in Figure 9-4 to see an example of a Gantt Chart bar), dragging from the predecessor to the successor gives you a visual cue that you're creating the dependency

Part Two:
Planning a
Project

On Time! On Track! On Target! Managing Your Projects Successfully with Microsoft Project

correctly. You see a link from the predecessor to a link of chain on the successor and a box pops up showing you the finish-to-start dependency you'll create when you release the mouse button.

Warning The drawback to both the Link command and dragging between tasks is that you can create only finish-to-start dependencies.

■ **Creating a dependency in a task form** If you want to create dependencies other than finish-to-start or you want to add lag to tasks, a form such as Task Entry or Task Details Form is the best solution. (On the View menu, choose More Views. In the More Views dialog box, double-click the name of the form.) As demonstrated in Figure 9-4, the start of the footing inspection lags five days after the footings have been poured.

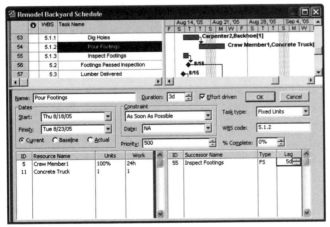

Figure 9-4 A task form includes fields for specifying the task dependency type and the lag between the two linked tasks.

Automated Dependencies

Project can adjust dependencies for you as you modify tasks—which can be a help or a hindrance. When you create a new project schedule in Project, the program automatically selects the Autolink Inserted Or Moved Tasks check box in the Options dialog box. With this option selected, when you insert a new task between two tasks, Project automatically removes the dependency between the two original tasks and creates finish-to-start dependencies to link the original predecessor to the new task and the new task to the successor.

While you are developing a schedule, these automated dependencies are a great timesaver. You can insert, remove, and rearrange tasks and let Project add or modify the dependencies for you. For example, if you add three tasks in a row to a project phase, Project automatically links all three to the existing predecessor and successor tasks as well as to each other.

After the schedule is set and the task dependencies are the way you want, clear this option's check box to prevent Project from making additional changes that you don't want. For example, you might want to reposition a task under a different summary task while maintaining all of its current task dependencies.

To turn off automated dependencies, do the following:

1.   On the Tools menu, choose Options.

2.   In the Options dialog box, click the Schedule tab.

3.   Under the heading Scheduling Options For <*project name*>, clear the Autolink Inserted Or Moved Tasks check box.

4.   Click OK to close the Options dialog box.

Making Schedules Easy to Maintain

When project execution begins, your project takes on a life of its own. The schedule that you carefully crafted during planning becomes obsolete almost immediately. To keep up with changes regardless of how many or how quickly they arrive, you need a flexible schedule in Project.

However, if you're new to Project, you might set specific start and finish dates to tasks or apply date constraints, such as the date when a task must finish; these constraints throw flexibility out the window. Even more frustrating, some scheduling shortcuts add date constraints that you don't realize you're creating. This section describes how date constraints can ruin your scheduling flexibility and how to use them properly along with other Project features to keep your schedule responsive to change.

The Right and Wrong Way to Use Date Constraints

Date constraints are not necessarily scheduling problems waiting to happen. When tasks occur on specific dates, such as training classes or conferences, date constraints are exactly what you need to keep those events tied to the correct dates on the calendar. For example, if your workers are attending a job safety class on September 22, you can create a task in the schedule and set a Must Start On date constraint to 9/22/2005.

Part Two:
Planning a
Project

On Time! On Track! On Target! Managing Your Projects Successfully with Microsoft Project

However, some project managers fall into a bad habit of setting dates instead of dependencies for tasks and that eliminates most of the benefits that a Project schedule provides. For example, if you set the start date for a task instead of linking it to its predecessor, you'll have to change that start date manually when the predecessor takes longer than planned.

Another pitfall is using the Finish No Later Than constraint in Project to represent a deadline. Its name makes it sound like it helps you meet your deadline. Unfortunately, not only does it not ensure an on-time delivery, but this date constraint leads to baffling behavior in Project. When a predecessor delays past the date constraint for its successor, Project must choose between keeping the date constraint for the successor and honoring the dependency between the two tasks. Date constraints are important, so Project honors the date constraint by default. As you can see in Figure 9-5, all this does is make it look like the Assemble and Install Stairs task meets its deadline—but it does so by overlapping the Assemble and Install Railing task that should precede it.

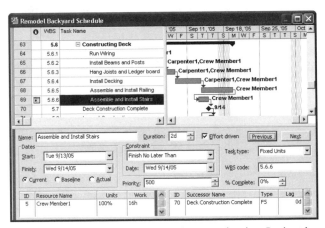

Figure 9-5   Missed date constraints can lead to Project ignoring important task dependencies.

Suppose you have a deadline with a costly late-delivery penalty and want Project to warn you when your schedule indicates you're going to miss the due date. A date constraint will tell you this—if you use it correctly. The trick is to tell Project to honor task dependencies instead of the date constraints, so your predecessors and successors run in the correct sequence. Project displays a Missed Constraint indicator if the schedule misses the date constraint you set, as shown in Figure 9-6.

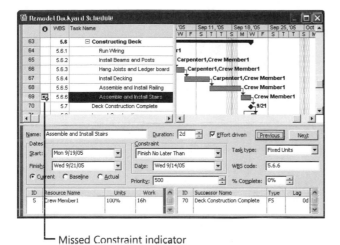

— Missed Constraint indicator

Figure 9-6   If you tell Project to honor task dependencies, it displays a Missed Constraint indicator to flag important dates that you miss.

To honor task dependencies rather than date constraints, do the following:

1. On the Tools menu, select Options.

2. In the Options dialog box, click the Schedule tab.

3. Clear the Tasks Will Always Honor Their Constraint Dates check box.

4. To honor task dependencies in the active project and all new projects, click Set As Default.

Deadlines

Deadlines are dates that you don't want to miss, but some deadlines are harder than others. For example, tax returns are due on April 15, but you can file for an extension with the Internal Revenue Service if your return isn't ready. However, if your company faces a $5 million penalty for delaying the opening of a new airport, you'll do everything you can to meet the deadline date. In Project, date constraints don't ensure that your schedule successfully meets required dates and can alter the behavior of Project in unsettling ways. For these reasons, the deadline feature is a better solution. It automatically tells Project to calculate the schedule based on the task dependencies you've set and highlights missed deadlines with an indicator similar to the Missed Constraints indicator.

Part Two:
Planning a
Project

On Time! On Track! On Target! Managing Your Projects Successfully with Microsoft Project

To add a deadline to a task, do the following:

1. Open the Task Information dialog box by double-clicking the task for which you want to add a deadline.

2. Click the Advanced tab.

3. In the Deadline text box, type the deadline date. You can also click the down arrow to display a calendar and then click the date.

4. Click OK.

When you add a deadline to a task, Project displays an arrow with a green outline at the task's deadline date in the Gantt Chart view, as demonstrated in the Assemble and Install Stairs task in Figure 9-7. If the Gantt bar for the task ends before the green arrow, it meets the deadline. But the task is late if its bar ends to the right of the green arrow. Project also displays a red diamond with an exclamation point inside it in the Indicators column.

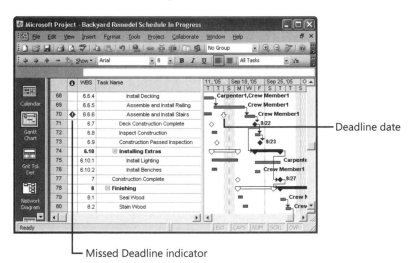

Figure 9-7   Project displays a green arrow to show a task deadline and displays a warning indicator if the task is scheduled to miss its deadline.

Adding Schedule Milestones

A WBS includes work packages and summary tasks, so you must also add milestones to your burgeoning Project schedule. Milestones highlight important project events whether they are hard deadlines or flexible dates. In the days of yore, a milestone was literally a stone that marked one mile from the last stone. For people working on projects, milestones don't measure distance, but mark progress, events, or achievements, such as the completion of a phase, a delivery of materials, or a payment for work performed.

In Project, the distinctive black-diamond shape for milestones provides easy-to-see cues for all kinds of events. You can use milestones to draw attention to significant events without worrying about delaying your project. In Project, milestones are tasks that have zero duration, so you can add as many milestones as you want without affecting finish dates one second.

Types of Milestones

The last task in almost every project schedule is a milestone, because it clearly shows the finish date—early, late, or right on time. However, milestones work equally well for many types of events. The following sections describe several uses for milestones.

Decisions

Moving forward on a project often depends on a decision. Many organizations commit to projects one phase at a time and decide to proceed to the next phase only if the results from the previous phase are acceptable. A milestone can act as the gatekeeper for these crucial decision points in a project, as Figure 9-8 illustrates.

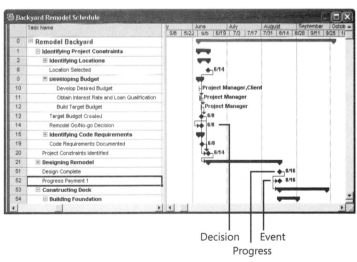

Figure 9-8 Milestones can represent decisions, events, or progress in a project.

- ■ **Decision** For many projects, particularly those with high risk and significant cost, estimates or feasibility studies might determine whether a project receives funding to continue. The estimating or feasibility

141

Part Two:
Planning a
Project

On Time! On Track! On Target! Managing Your Projects Successfully with Microsoft Project

study tasks link to a milestone, which represents the go/no-go decision. If the project is canceled, the milestone represents the end of the project. If it receives approval to continue, the successors to the milestone begin.

Some choices aren't as final as go/no-go decisions, but they affect a project so significantly that work can't continue until the choice is made. For example, construction on a house can't begin until the homeowner chooses the builder. A milestone for this type of decision makes it easy to delay the work that follows if the decision takes more time than you expect.

■ **Project start**   Starting a project with a milestone makes it easy to reschedule the entire project should the kickoff date change. For example, if the board of directors doesn't approve your project during its May meeting, you can move the entire schedule simply by changing the date for the starting milestone to the date of its August meeting.

Tip   An approval is a special case of a decision milestone. Often, additional work can't begin until previous work has been approved, such as when a county building inspector must approve the electrical wiring before the drywall crew starts finishing walls. Approvals can act like go/no-go decisions or as starting milestones for additional work.

Progress

The true progress for a project is hidden within its work packages, but you can view overall progress with milestones at key achievements throughout the life of a project. Just as a milestone is helpful at the beginning of a project, it's handy at the end of a project as well, particularly if the finish date is crucial to success. (See "Deadlines," page 139, to learn how to track deadlines in a project.)

Typically, you want to see progress long before you reach the end of a project. Keeping a project on schedule is much easier if you have checkpoints regularly spaced between the start and end dates. If you reach an interim milestone only to find that you're behind schedule, you can take corrective action while there's still time to recover. For example, if you're building a new superhighway, you could create milestones for every mile of road, so you aren't surprised by a multiyear schedule overrun.

Tip   Milestones are also handy for highlighting handoffs between teams. Although handoffs usually occur at existing project milestones, such as the end of a phase, a milestone indicating whenever a handoff occurs notifies the new owners of their responsibilities.

Events

You can use milestones to show brief events that occur during a project. For example, if you hold a team appreciation ice cream social once each quarter, you can add a milestone on that date. As long as the event is short in duration, you don't have to bother setting its duration or assigning resources to it. See "The Right and Wrong Way to Use Date Constraints" on page 137 to learn how to tie an event to a fixed date.

Deliveries

Many projects have external dependencies that are just as important as the work done by the project team. If you don't manage the work and simply expect deliveries on specific dates, milestones are the answer. For example, you don't manage the people at the building supply company who assemble the lumber order for the backyard remodel—but you want the lumber on site in time to begin construction. You can use milestones for any kind of external dependency: deliveries of raw materials, preassembled components, equipment, or the rockets for the next space shuttle launch.

Creating Milestones

Creating milestones is easier than creating work tasks. All you have to do to create a milestone is create a task and set its duration to zero (0). The task shape in the Gantt Chart changes from a bar to a black diamond. And because the duration is zero, you don't have to assign any resources to the milestone—unless you want the milestone to appear in repeats or views filtered by resource. (If you do want to assign resources to a milestone, see "Assigning Resources to Tasks," page 145, for instructions.)

Refining Task Names

When you built your WBS, you probably named work tasks and summary tasks so you could tell them apart (see "Good Task Names," page 91). When you add milestones to your schedule, the diamond shapes only help distinguish milestones when you view the Gantt Chart. Using different naming

Part Two:
Planning a
Project

On Time! On Track! On Target! Managing Your Projects Successfully with Microsoft Project

conventions for milestones, work tasks, and summary tasks makes it easy to tell tasks apart wherever you see them.

Naming Milestones and Deliverables

Unlike work tasks and summary tasks, names for milestones and deliverables don't include verbs. Deliverables are objects. Whether they're as ephemeral as a theme for your backyard design or as substantial as the lumber that's delivered, nouns are the perfect part of speech to use.

Milestones often relate to project deliverables. For example, design drawings are a deliverable, but the approval of those drawings might be a milestone that triggers a progress payment. To name milestones, begin with the deliverable name and add an adjective, such as Design Drawings Approved.

Unique Task Names

Good task names stand on their own. A common mistake that you're not likely to notice right away is duplicating the same brief task name within different phases of a project. In Project, tasks and their summary tasks don't appear together when you generate reports; group tasks with similar characteristics by applying the Group command, or hide summary tasks to inspect work packages. If you have duplicate names like "Phase complete," it's difficult to tell which task is which. To prevent mix-ups, add adjectives or qualifiers to task names to make them unique; for example, Pour Bldg 1 Foundation.

If your project plan uses similar task names in several phases, you don't have to type every unique task name in Project. You can create a set of tasks and copy them to each phase and then use the Replace command to replace the adjectives in each subsequent phase. To rename tasks from phase to phase, do the following:

1. In the Project Task Sheet, type the task names for the phase or summary task and include the adjective, such as Bldg 1, to associate the task names with the phase.

2. Select the summary task and its subordinate tasks, and copy the tasks to the Clipboard by pressing Ctrl+C.

3. Copy the tasks from the Clipboard to the next phase by selecting the row beneath the next summary task and pressing Ctrl+V.

   When you paste the tasks, they appear at the same level as the summary task. To make the tasks subordinate to the summary task, select the pasted tasks, and then, on the Formatting toolbar, click the Indent icon, which is an arrow pointing to the right.

4. To replace the qualifiers in the pasted tasks, open the Replace dialog box by pressing Ctrl+H.

Important Be sure that the Search box displays the word Down, indicating that Project will begin at the current task and search in all subsequent tasks in the Task Sheet.

---

5. In the Find What text box, type the qualifier for the first summary task (Bldg 1 in this example.)

6. In the Replace With text box, type the new qualifier for the pasted tasks, for instance Bldg 2.

7. Click Replace to replace the first occurrence of the qualifier.

8. Click Replace one more time for each task in the current phase.

Caution Do not click Replace All, which replaces the text in all tasks in the Project schedule.

Assigning Resources to Tasks

After you link tasks with dependencies, you're ready to flesh out the schedule by assigning resources to the tasks they are supposed to perform. Initial resource assignments are easy, although modifying assignments later on can be challenging until you learn the secrets (see the section "Adding Resources to Tasks to Shorten Duration" on page 283).

You can choose from several ways to assign resources. The method you choose depends partly on preference and partly on the details you want to specify for the assignment. The following sections describe three ways to assign resources.

Assigning Resources in the Task Sheet

If you want to add only one person to a task and assign that person with her maximum units (see "Creating Resources in Project," page 112), the Task Sheet is the easiest place to do so. All you have to do is choose the resource name in the task's Resource Names cell and press Enter. Project

Part Two:
Planning a
Project

On Time! On Track! On Target! Managing Your Projects Successfully with Microsoft Project

automatically assigns the resource to the task with the resource's maximum units from the Resource Sheet.

Here are the steps:

1. To display a table with the Resource Names column, on the View menu, point to Table, and on the submenu, choose Entry.

2. In the Task Sheet pane, click the Resource Names cell for the task to which you want to assign a resource.

3. In the list, choose the resource name.

4. Press Enter. Project assigns the resource to the task. If the resource's maximum units are 100%, all you see in the cell is the name of the resource. However, for any other value of units, Project displays the percentage in the cell after the resource name, as illustrated in Figure 9-9.

Tip   When you assign resources in the Task Sheet, you can copy resources from one task to another. For example, if several consecutive tasks use the same resources, position the pointer over the lower-right corner of the first task's Resource Names cell. When the pointer changes to a plus symbol, drag over the rows that use the same resources.

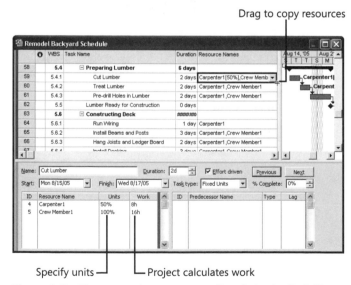

Drag to copy resources

Specify units — └ Project calculates work

Figure 9-9   You can assign resources directly in the Task Sheet or in the Task Form.

Assigning Resources in the Task Form

As soon as a resource assignment includes more than one resource or different units, a task form (Task Form, Task Details Form, or Task Entry) is easier to use than the Task Sheet. As you can see in the bottom pane of Figure 9-9, you can add several resources, each with its own units and work.

Here are the steps for adding resources and changing units:

1. If the Task Form isn't visible, point to the bottom pane in the Gantt Chart and then, on the View menu, select More Views. In the More Views dialog box, double-click Task Form.

    Tip   You can switch views between one pane and two. If only one pane is visible, double-click the rectangular box immediately below the vertical scroll bar to display the bottom pane in the view. To switch to a single pane, double-click the horizontal divider between the two panes.

2. In the Task Sheet, select the task to which you want to assign resources. The task information appears in the Task Form in the bottom pane.

3. In the Task Form, click the first blank Resource Name cell.

4. In the Resource Name list, choose the name of the resource you want to assign.

5. If you want to assign the resource at a specific unit percentage, click the Units cell in the same row and type the percentage, such as 50% for Carpenter1 in Figure 9-9.

    Tip   If you want to assign the amount of time that the resource spends on the task, click the Work cell and type the number of hours, days, or other periods. If you specify both the units and the work, Project recalculates the task duration automatically.

6. To add another resource, click the next blank Resource Name cell. Repeat steps 4 and 5 to assign the next resource.

7. After you assign all the resources, click OK. Project assigns the resources to the task. If you didn't specify values in the Work cells, Project calculates the work based on the units and the task duration.

Part Two:
Planning a
Project

On Time! On Track! On Target! Managing Your Projects Successfully with Microsoft Project

Using the Assign Resources Dialog Box

For a tool with all kinds of helpful features for assigning resources, on the Standard toolbar, click the Assign Resources icon (or on the Tools menu, choose Assign Resources). In the Assign Resources dialog box, shown in Figure 9-10, you can choose resources by clicking the cells to the left of their names. But you can do a lot more:

- Click the plus symbol to the left of Resource List Options to filter the list of resources you see. For example, you can locate resources who have enough time available to perform the task. When you click the plus symbol, it changes to a minus symbol, as shown in Figure 9-10.

- Click Replace to replace the selected resource with a different one, for instance, when your carpenter goes to the hospital after an accident.

- Click Graphs to see diagrams that show how much work the resource has or the time that the resource is available.

Tip   Unlike many of Project's other dialog boxes, which don't let you work in other parts of Project until you close them, the Assign Resources dialog box is especially useful because you can leave it open while you work in the Gantt Chart or other windows.

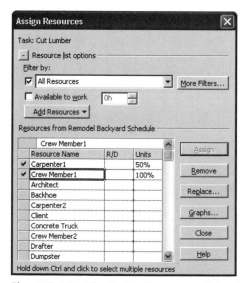

Figure 9-10   The Assign Resources dialog box is the most powerful tool for assigning resources.

Building Reality into a Schedule

The initial schedule you build based on estimated effort is an ideal rarely achieved in real life. Your initial work package estimates don't tell the whole story. You have to consider whether factors such as project complexity or remote project teams warrant increasing estimates before you enter tasks into Project. To make matters worse, team members attend training, take vacations, or have to focus on several assignments at once. In addition, people simply aren't 100 percent productive every working hour.

To deliver on time, you must take resource issues into account when you build a project schedule. For example, if the blasting crew is having a "blast" elsewhere and you don't trust the carpenter to remove some bedrock, you have to adjust the schedule for when the blasting crew is available. Understanding the factors that expand project schedules is only the first step to building a realistic schedule. Project offers features you can use to model these alternate realities and this section tells you how to apply each one.

Accounting for Productivity

One of the most dangerous project scheduling assumptions is that team members who work a 40-hour week actually spend 40 hours on their assigned project tasks. Attending staff meetings, filling out time sheets and insurance forms, and picking up snacks for the team uses up work time—sometimes reducing productive time by as much as 25 percent of each day.

Work environments can affect productivity, too. Project teams that are scattered on several floors of a high-rise building might spend time riding different elevator banks to meetings. Or a cube next to a loud and persistent sales rep could dramatically reduce someone's output.

If you schedule your project as if resources are always productive, your schedule is doomed to come in late. But good morale is another advantage to scheduling based on actual productivity. If you assign resources at 100%, most people have to work a 10-hour day to keep up. When you assign resources with the time they really have available, the team members know that you're doing the right thing and that, in itself, can boost productivity.

In Project, you can model productivity in a couple of ways. The easiest approach is to redefine the standard eight-hour workday to six hours, but that hides the problem with productivity. The more effective approach,

Part Two:
Planning a
Project

On Time! On Track! On Target! Managing Your Projects Successfully with Microsoft Project

which keeps the productivity level in view, is setting the units that resources work when assigned to a task. For example, to schedule team members for six hours of project work in each eight-hour workday, in a Task Form, set a resource's Units field to 75%. As you can see in Figure 9-11, reducing resource units from 100% to 75% increases a two-day duration to 2.67 days.

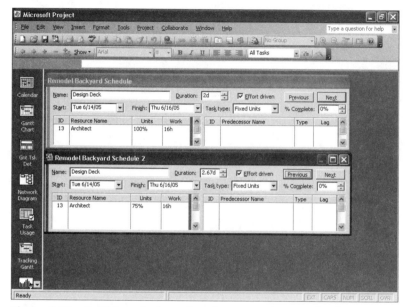

Figure 9-11   Setting units for task assignments changes the duration of tasks while showing the level of productive time.

Tip   If your company workday is nine hours, you can change the default setting for the hours in a day. On the Tools menu, choose Options. In the Options dialog box, click Calendar and type a new value in the Hours Per Day text box. You can also change the default hours per week or the number of working days in a month.

If you change the units you use for resource assignments, you might have to explain the apparent shrinkage of the workday to stakeholders or the functional managers who want to know why you aren't using their people full time.

Managing Part-Time Workers and Multitaskers

People who work part-time make tasks take longer, because they don't work eight-hour days to begin with. For example, working half-time doubles task duration. If someone works part-time, you must modify his maximum units in Project. For example, the maximum units for someone who works half-time is 50%.

Here are the steps for setting a resource's maximum units:

1. On the View menu, click Resource Sheet.

2. In the Resource Sheet window, in the Max. Units cell for the resource, type the percentage that the person usually works, such as 50% for half-time.

Note   Sometimes, part-time workers are more productive than full-time folks, because they don't attend as many meetings or perhaps don't earn time off. On the other hand, part-time workers have to spend time catching up on progress made while they were away.

People who work on several tasks at once spend only a portion of their time on each task. You might think assigning them to tasks is simply a matter of making sure that the units assigned add up to no more than their maximum units. But pulling people in too many directions comes with a hidden penalty. Each time they switch tasks, they have to reorient themselves and those small delays add up.

The best way to prevent this productivity drain is to limit the number of tasks that someone works on simultaneously to no more than three or four. To look for times when a resource is overcommitted, run the Who Does What When report. Generate this report by doing the following:

1. On the View menu, choose Reports.

2. In the Reports dialog box, click Assignments, and then click Select.

3. In the Assignment Reports dialog box, click Who Does What When and then click Select. When the report appears, look for weeks in which the resource has hours assigned to several tasks.

Part Two:
Planning a
Project

On Time! On Track! On Target! Managing Your Projects Successfully with Microsoft Project

Scheduling Around Nonworking Time

One of the serious drawbacks of team members is that they don't work five days a week every week of the year. Even if you reduce resource units to account for training, companywide meetings, and paperwork, you still have holidays, personal days, sick days, and vacations to consider. In Project, you use *calendars* to set the working days and nonworking days that the program uses to schedule work. Project doesn't schedule work to occur on days you define as nonworking time.

You can apply calendars with working and nonworking days to your entire organization, to specific resources, or to specific tasks:

- *The Standard calendar* that comes with Project applies to every project and task you create and every resource you assign. You can modify the Standard calendar to reflect your organization's holidays and time off that applies to everyone, such as the two-week closure at a manufacturing plant, shown in Figure 9-12.

    To modify the Standard calendar, on the Tools menu, choose Change Working Time. In the For list, select Standard (Project Calendar). (If a task-oriented view, such as the Gantt Chart, is visible, Project automatically selects the Standard calendar in the Change Working Time dialog box.) Modify the dates and click OK to close the dialog box.

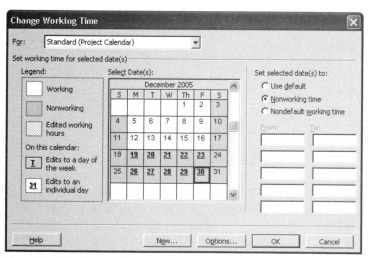

Figure 9-12   Project displays working days in white; nonworking days are gray and underlined; and nonstandard working days are white and underlined.

■ *Resource calendars* apply to specific resources that you use. If you schedule tasks around people's vacations, you can create a resource calendar for each person and change the vacation days to nonworking days.

To modify a resource calendar, on the Tools menu, choose Change Working Time. In the Change Working Time dialog box, in the For list, choose the resource whose calendar you want to change. Modify the dates and click OK to close the dialog box.

Tip Unless you want to spend your days updating resource calendars in Project, you're better off using reduced resource units in task assignments to account for sick days and personal days. Those days off come up with little notice and usually won't affect progress.

■ *Task calendars* are ideal for tasks that run during standard nonworking time. For example, if you run computer backups over the weekend, a calendar specifically created for the backup task won't affect resources or other tasks.

Setting a task calendar works differently from the Standard and resource calendars. Before you can apply a calendar to a task, you must create the calendar in the Change Working Time dialog box. Click New, name the calendar (for instance, Backups) and specify the working and nonworking time. For example, the Backups calendar might show every weekend as working time and every weekday as nonworking time. Click OK to close the dialog box.

To assign the calendar to a task, in the Gantt Chart, double-click the task to open the Task Information dialog box. Click the Advanced tab. In the Calendar list, choose the calendar for the task and click OK.

Adjusting Tasks for Resource Efficiency

The resources you obtain can affect the task durations you estimate. If you're lucky enough to get the fastest carpenter, the 80 hours of work you estimated might take only 60. If you have to make do with a less-experienced resource, the hours of work and task duration have to increase to reflect that the novice doesn't get as much done.

When you replace the assigned resource, adjust either the task duration or the value in the resource's Work cell to your new estimate. Add a note to the

Part Two:
Planning a
Project

On Time! On Track! On Target! Managing Your Projects Successfully with Microsoft Project

task explaining the reason for the change. (Select the task and click the Note icon on the Standard toolbar.)

Warning   Sometimes, physical constraints limit the scheduling you can do. For instance, if you have only three hammers, assigning more than three carpenters to the same task ends up with someone standing around. Add notes to your project tasks about these limitations, so you don't ignore them when you're trying to shorten project duration.

Shortening a Project Schedule

Most of the time, the schedule you build ends later than stakeholders had hoped. Before you start looking at paying people overtime or working the weekends, there are a couple of alternatives that can shorten schedules.

The Fast-Track to an Early Finish

You *fast-track* a project by scheduling tasks to run concurrently that were originally scheduled one after the other. Although they don't know it, the people you see driving to work while simultaneously drinking coffee, shaving, and reading the newspaper are fast-tracking their commute. And much like those harrowing trips, fast-tracking comes with its share of risks.

Projects usually have lots of tasks that you can overlap with few issues. For example, if you're painting a room, one person can finish painting the walls while a second person paints the trim around the windows. The problems arise when decisions made in overlapping tasks affect work that's already been completed. For example, a construction project pours the concrete foundations while the architects complete the final design. If a part of the design requires concrete in a different location, some rework is in order. The other problem with fast-tracking is that the overlaps between tasks leave less time to recover when something goes wrong. You might have no choice but to slip the schedule, reduce the quality, change the scope, or increase the budget.

Choosing Tasks to Fast-Track

The critical path is the sequence of tasks that determines the earliest finish date for a project. Any time you can shorten the critical path, you're bringing the finish date in earlier. To get the most from fast-tracking, check the longest tasks on the critical path for fast-tracking—they provide the largest potential decrease in duration with the fewest number of risks to manage and the least number of changes to the schedule.

Project makes it easy to find your attractive fast-track candidates. Applying a filter to show only the critical path and then sorting those tasks by duration quickly tells you what you need to know. To find fast-track candidates in Project, do the following:

1. Turn off the display of summary tasks. On the Tools menu, choose Options. Click the View tab and clear the Show Summary Tasks check box. Click OK.

2. To show only critical path tasks, on the Formatting toolbar, in the Filter list, choose Critical.

3. To sort the critical path tasks by duration, on the Project menu, point to Sort and then choose Sort By.

4. In the Sort dialog box, in the Sort By list, choose Duration.

5. Choose the Descending option to show the longest tasks at the top of the list.

6. Click Sort.

7. After you identify critical tasks with long durations, remove the Critical filter (choose the All Tasks filter) and re-sort your schedule by a field such as WBS or ID.

Partial Overlaps

Most of the time, you fast-track a project by starting the next task before its predecessor is complete. For instance, you might tell programmers to start coding before the design for all the Web pages is done. In Project, these partial overlaps are easy to add—all you have to do is apply a negative lag to the dependency between the two tasks.

You can edit a dependency by double-clicking the link line in the Gantt Chart view. If your schedule link lines look like spaghetti, an alternative is to double-click the name of the successor task in the Task Sheet. In the Task Information dialog box, click the Predecessors tab to see the predecessor tasks. To overlap the two tasks, in the Lag cell, type a negative number of hours, days, or other periods, as shown in Figure 9-13 on the next page. Click OK to save your changes.

Part Two:
Planning a
Project

On Time! On Track! On Target! Managing Your Projects Successfully with Microsoft Project

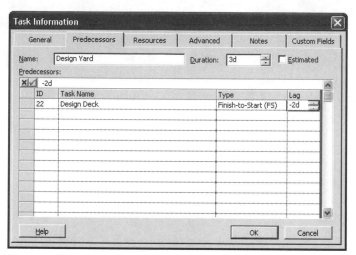

Figure 9-13   A negative value for lag between tasks results in an overlap.

Running Tasks in Parallel

Another way to fast-track a project is to schedule tasks concurrently—as long as they use different resources and the risks are acceptable. In Project, this approach requires adding and removing links rather than editing the dependencies that are already there. To run two tasks simultaneously, delete the dependency between them. In the Gantt Chart view, double-click the task dependency link line and, in the Task Dependency dialog box, click Delete.

The problem with this technique is that the successor task often disappears as soon as you delete its dependency. Without the predecessor, the successor doesn't know where it belongs, like mountain climbers without a sherpa. To prevent this disappearing act, link the successor to its new predecessor first and *then* delete the original dependency.

A Crash Course on Project Crashing

Adding more resources to a project to shorten its duration is called *crashing*, perhaps because of the traffic jams that occur when hordes of new team members try to pry their way into tasks that people are already working on. To nonproject managers, crashing seems like the most obvious thing to do— if Sam needs four weeks to develop a marketing plan, surely Sam and Rachel can produce it in only two.

If stakeholders offer more resources to shorten the project schedule, you're better off recommending other strategies, such as fast-tracking, first. Or you can spend some time optimizing your schedule in other ways like reducing lag times between tasks or eliminating nonessential items in the project scope (see Chapter 16, "Modifying the Project Schedule").

The Danger in Crashing Projects

You can't add more resources to a pregnancy to deliver a baby in five months instead of nine. In practice, adding resources stands as much chance of increasing duration as it does of shortening it. New resources aren't familiar with the tasks at hand and are less productive than current team members. And who guides the new members up the learning curve? Usually the experienced, most productive members of the project team do, and they should be working instead to finish tasks.

As well, the extra help that you receive is often less-than-qualified for the work. You might need HTML programmers and management gives you COBOL programmers instead. Even if the new resources have the right skills, they might have less experience than the people you already use. And, despite these risks, crashing typically costs more, as you'll see in the next section.

Time Versus Money

When you crash a project, you hope to trade off more money for less time. This strategy can make economic sense in the long run, for example, to bring products to market before they become low-margin commodities. Because stakeholders rarely want to spend more money than necessary, you'll probably be asked to show the trade-offs and recommend the best tasks to crash.

As you do with fast-tracking, you inspect the critical path for ways to shorten a schedule. Reducing duration on tasks that aren't on the critical path won't shorten the overall project duration one bit. But crashing a project isn't simply locating all the tasks on the critical path and assigning more resources to them. Some tasks cost more per week to crash than others. And the more you crash a project, the more expensive it becomes. Why spend $100,000 to shorten the schedule by 12 weeks, when 8 weeks and $50,000 will do?

By crashing the most cost-effective tasks first, you shorten the schedule to the duration you need for the lowest possible cost. *Crash tables* calculate the relative costs of shortening the critical path by crashing different tasks. For example, as the crash table in Figure 9-14 on the next page demonstrates,

Part Two:
Planning a
Project

On Time! On Track! On Target! Managing Your Projects Successfully with Microsoft Project

crashing one task might cost $1.5 million for each week you eliminate, whereas another task costs $10 million per week.

To analyze crash options, start with the longest tasks on the critical path. You'll need their duration and current cost. Of course, you have to determine how much you can decrease the task durations and how much that will cost. When you have that data, an Excel worksheet can help you calculate the crash cost per week for each task. Sorting the tasks by the crash cost per week quickly shows you the least costly tasks for crashing.

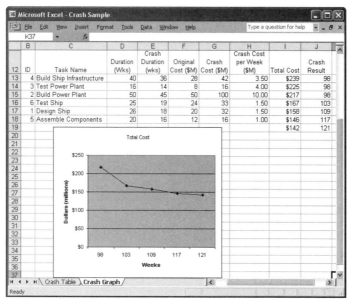

Figure 9-14 By sorting critical path tasks using the crash cost per week, you can identify the most cost-effective tasks to crash to obtain the schedule duration you need.

Tip For tasks with the same crash cost per week, crash the longer tasks first. You'll crash the fewest tasks to reach your goal.

In the worksheet in Figure 9-14, the Assemble Components task costs $1 million per week, and you can shorten the duration by four weeks for a total crash cost of $4 million. If you need to reduce the duration some more, you can crash either the Test Ship task or the Design Ship task. They both cost $1.5 million per week. However, the Design Ship task can crash seven weeks compared to the Test Ship's six weeks.

> **Warning** Crashing a task can change the critical path on the project, even adding a task to the critical path that wasn't there before. To accurately evaluate your crash decisions, you should review the critical path after every crash.

The chart in Figure 9-14 illustrates the benefit of crashing the least costly tasks first. As you can see, the initial reductions shorten the schedule significantly without much of an increase in overall cost. But, as you dig deeper for more reductions, each additional week comes at a higher and higher price.

In Summary

To build a project schedule, you need not only the tasks to perform and the resources assigned, but also how long you expect the tasks to take. The estimating method you choose depends on the type of project, your experience with similar projects, and other factors.

With work estimates in place, you can start to build your project schedule: first, by linking tasks to show the flow of work, and second, by assigning resources to tasks to determine their duration. Unfortunately, project schedules rarely finish soon enough to satisfy stakeholders. If you must reduce the project duration, you can use techniques such as fast-tracking or crashing.

Part Two:
Planning a
Project

On Time! On Track! On Target! Managing Your Projects Successfully with Microsoft Project

Chapter Ten

Working with a Budget

Why is there so much month left at the end of the money?

— *John Barrymore*

Projects, like most people, have to live within their means. When someone proposes a project, you can be sure that a few of the stakeholders will ask "How much will this cost?" or "How much money will this project make (or save) us?" In fact, by the time you receive your assignment to manage a project, its stakeholders probably have a number in mind, be it the price tag for the project, the return on investment, or the net present value.

As you'll see in this chapter and other chapters in the book, cost estimates, financial measures such as return on investment, and budgets are all inter-related. One of your tasks as a project manager might be to set—or reset—expectations and an estimate of project cost can help. An initial estimate helps win approval to get a project off the ground. More detailed estimates of the initial investment a project requires, what it will cost as time passes, and how much money it generates or saves, become part of a set of calcula-tions, known as *capital budgeting*, that can be used to answer questions such as "What return on investment will this project deliver?" or "If we commit resources to this project full-time for eight months, what other projects can we not take on?" If the capital budgeting analysis shows that the project can deliver financial measures that warrant moving forward with the project, estimated costs become the target that the project manager compares to actual costs as work is performed.

Cost estimates help stakeholders gain a better understanding of the scope of the project. They might start with an idea of what a project is likely to cost and that understanding might become the financial goal (the budget and target measures) for the project manager and project team. However, with thorough and realistic estimates as ammunition, you might convince stake-holders to reconvene to agree on changes to the scope to fit the budget they've set.

When it comes to managing a project, you need cost estimates that are developed in detail. Performance compared to budget is one of the key mea-sures of whether a project was successful. So, you need to set up a realistic budget from the start—a budget that reflects the project scope and goals defined by major stakeholders and decision makers. Corralling the costs for human and material resources as well as the costs of project tasks helps flesh out your project plan. Moreover, these costs serve as the foundation of a baseline budget that you monitor and control throughout the life of the project.

This chapter begins with an introduction to capital budgeting. A few project managers are lucky enough to not be held to financial performance measures. However, by understanding the budgeting process that your

Part Two:
Planning a
Project

On Time! On Track! On Target! Managing Your Projects Successfully with Microsoft Project

organization uses, you are better equipped to manage stakeholders' expectations and use resources effectively to make your projects a success.

The section "Estimating Work on Estimated Scope" on page 125 describes how to estimate the *work* for project tasks, which, in turn, helps define the *duration* of those tasks. This chapter describes how to add cost rates to human and material resources in your Microsoft Project schedule to coax Project to calculate costs. But you still need to get those costs over to whatever tool you use for capital budgeting. The last section in this chapter describes how to export task costs from Project. To learn about managing a project budget after a project is under way, see Chapter 17, "Balancing the Budget and Other Project Variables."

Understanding Capital Budgets

Money isn't everything, but it ranks right up there with oxygen.

— *Rita Davenport*

Most organizations and executives use capital budgeting to make financial decisions—including which projects to undertake. Similar to the analysis that investors use to evaluate investment opportunities, capital budgeting calculates financial measures such as a project's internal rate of return (see "Internal Rate of Return," page 20) and the period of time that will elapse before the project benefits offset its initial investment (see "Payback Period," page 17).

Calculating potential financial results helps identify the projects that meet an organization's financial goals and those that are likely to fall short. Capital budgeting can help an organization decide which projects seem the wisest to pursue and which ones should be removed from the docket. Because organizations usually don't have the financial or human resources to take on every project, they turn to capital budgeting to find the projects that provide the greatest cost-benefit trade-offs.

Important   If terms like *internal rate of return*, *payback period*, and *net present value* are not yet part of your vocabulary, the section "Prioritizing Projects" on page 16 describes and provides examples of these financial measures.

Putting Capital Budgeting into Practice

Not every project you manage goes through a capital budgeting process. And you might not be responsible for performing the capital budgeting analysis. But understanding these concepts puts you in a better position to influence and defend decisions about which projects are approved and which ones are rejected or postponed. Executives generally end up choosing the projects that make the most of the money available. With capital budgeting in your toolbox, you'll be able to obtain the support of decision makers—or know that a project isn't worth the effort.

Capital budgeting is more than just a financial modeling tool. The forecasted financial returns for a project might *look* favorable, but you must evaluate those measures in the context of potential risks and other factors such as resource constraints. Capital budgeting can help pin down the benefits and risks associated with a project, with the ultimate aim being to accurately quantify benefits, costs, and risks for the project in both the short term and the long run.

Using a Capital Budgeting Tool

Most organizations use some sort of capital budgeting tool to evaluate investments and projects. A template helps keep analysis consistent from project to project so stakeholders can compare results with confidence. If your organization doesn't have a tool for capital budgeting or you want to experiment with one to learn how capital budgeting works, you can download a capital budgeting Microsoft Excel template, shown in Figure 10-1, from Microsoft Office Online (*http://office.microsoft.com/en-us/templates/ TC011589891033.aspx*). After you enter your data, the spreadsheet calculates the rate of return on an investment, the net present value of the investment, and the payback period (in years).

In the template, you identify benefits that the project delivers and quantify the costs and financial benefits for three years after the project is complete. For example, benefits might include cost savings due to increased productivity, additional revenue from increasing customer satisfaction and earning more repeat business, or, in the manufacturing world, savings from streamlining production and reducing errors and waste.

Part Two:
Planning a
Project

On Time! On Track! On Target! Managing Your Projects Successfully with Microsoft Project

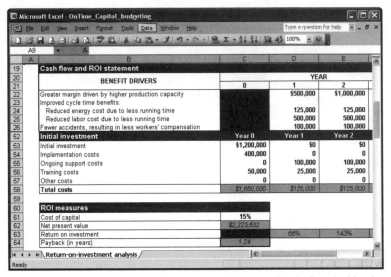

Figure 10-1 An Excel worksheet can perform any kind of capital budgeting calculation you need.

The worksheet calculates overall project costs based on the values you provide for the initial investment (year 0) and the costs you expect to incur in the three years that follow (Year 1, Year 2, and Year 3). The example shown in Figure 10-1 includes costs for implementation, training, and support, but you can change these categories to reflect the costs for your project. For example, you could add costs for the new computers you must purchase or the salary for the high-paid systems architect you've hired.

The other value you provide is the cost of capital. In most cases, cost of capital represents the rate of return your organization pays for the money it

Quantifying Qualitative Benefits

How do you quantify benefits such as fewer errors? Suppose that a project to improve manufacturing processes is planned to reduce errors made in assembly by about 20 percent each month. From quality assurance reports, you know that approximately 1000 errors occur on the assembly line each month and that correcting each error takes about half an hour. You also know that the burdened hourly rate (see "What Goes into Labor Rates?," page 167) for workers on this assembly line is $60. Using these numbers, you can quantify the benefit as follows:

Errors eliminated per month	20% of 1000 = 200
Time saved per month	200 errors * .5 hour = 100 hours
Cost savings per month	$60 * 100 hours = $6000

invests in the project. For example, if the company borrows money at 6 percent to fund the project, the cost of capital is 6 percent. The project has to provide a return on investment of at least 6 percent to come out ahead.

Alternatively, you might use *opportunity cost* as the cost of capital. For example, if your company keeps its project bankroll earning interest in short-term notes paying 4 percent, taking money out of those notes to fund a project means the 4 percent return is history. The project has to provide more than 4 percent return for the company to come out ahead. But opportunity cost is usually tougher than low-risk returns. Most organizations measure opportunity cost as the highest return provided by alternative investments. In this case, the opportunity cost is the highest rate of return for other projects competing for part of the project bankroll.

Caution Of course, you can't ignore capital budgeting measures after your project starts. Higher than expected costs reduce net present value and internal rate of return, on which the project was originally approved. If your project falls behind, its financial benefits also lag, either because the project takes longer (which almost always costs more) or, more drastically, because the scope of the project is reduced to get the project back on track.

Calculating Costs in a Project Schedule

If your outgo exceeds your income, then your upkeep will be your downfall.

— *Bill Earle*

Most project costs come from the resources that a project requires. The people assigned to perform tasks and the equipment and material resources needed to get the work done all have costs associated with them. By assigning cost data to resources in the Resource Sheet view in Microsoft Project, you can derive a good deal of labor and material costs you need for capital budgeting. The type of cost information you provide for project resources depends on the types of resources (see Chapter 8, "Project Resources") and how you pay for them. Here are the different types of costs that Project supports and how you use them:

■ *Standard rate* (Std. Rate in the Project Resource Sheet view) and *overtime rate* (Ovt. Rate) usually represent how much a resource costs for a unit of time. Whether you use employees or contractors, they have a

Part Two:
Planning a
Project

On Time! On Track! On Target! Managing Your Projects Successfully with Microsoft Project

labor rate, whether it's $50 per hour or $60,000 per year. In the back-yard remodeling project, work resources such as carpenters and crew members have hourly rates. Equipment sometimes has a daily rate. For example, if you rent a backhoe, you might pay $500 per day.

When you add rates to resources and then assign them to tasks, Project multiplies the number of hours (or other units) by the rate to calculate the cost of the hours you use the resources on those tasks. The more hours the resources spend, the higher your labor or equipment costs will be.

If you pay more to use resources past the end of a standard workday, the overtime rate kicks in. For instance, if the standard workday is 8 hours, you might pay a carpenter $40 per hour. The $40 goes into the Std. Rate field for the carpenter. If you ask the carpenter to work 10 hours one day, his rate for the last 2 hours might jump to $60 per hour. By entering $60 in the Ovt. Rate field, Project multiplies the first 8 hours by the standard rate and the last 2 hours by the overtime rate.

Tip   The Std. Rate field works just as well calculating costs for units other than time. For example, suppose your crew members go through drill bits like water and you want to include the cost of those bits in your estimates. You can create a resource for a drill bit and enter the cost for each one in the Std. Rate field. Then, when you assign the crew members to a drilling task, you can add the drill bit resource to the task as well. In the Units field for the task assignment, enter the number of drill bits you expect the crew members to man-gle. Project multiplies the cost per drill bit by the number of units to calculate the total cost of drill bits.

■ *Cost/use* is another field for the costs of material resources (and some work resources). This type of cost is perfect when you pay a fee each time a resource is used. For example, in the backyard remodeling project, the dumpster and the concrete truck each have a per-use fee; every time the hauling company empties the dumpster, you pay $450. As you'd expect, the total cost for this per-use resource depends on how often you fill the dumpster.

In Project, cost fields aren't mutually exclusive, which is good, because some resources have a time-based rate and a cost/use rate. For example, the dumpster costs $450 each time you fill it, but the hauling company also charges $50 for each week it sits on your construction site.

■ *Fixed costs* are associated with tasks rather than resources. For example, if you're concerned about the productivity of the crew working on remodeling your backyard, you might ask the builder to quote a fixed price for the job. Then, instead of calculating costs based on the number of hours that the carpenters and other construction workers work, you can assign the fixed price to the task's Fixed Cost field. Unlike the costs derived from hourly rates, fixed costs stay the same even when the task takes longer than expected or the amount of work exceeds initial estimates.

Specifying Rates for Work Resources in Project

You use the Resource Sheet view in Project to add any kind of rate other than a fixed price. The following steps explain how:

1. With your Project file open, on the View menu, choose Resource Sheet.

2. In the Resource Sheet table, select the Resource Name cell for the resource to which you want to add rates. To add a new resource, select the Resource Name cell in the first blank row and type a name.

3. In the Std. Rate field, type the rate for the resource. You can enter the rate and the time period, such as $50.00/hr, as demonstrated by the Carpenter1 resource in Figure 10-2, or $1000.00/day.

4. In the Ovt. Rate field, type the rate when you use the resource beyond the standard workday. Some companies don't pay overtime at all. Some pay the same hourly rate for overtime hours; the luckiest employees receive a premium hourly rate for extra work hours.

What Goes into Labor Rates?

Labor rates for employees within your organization are not as clear-cut as how much they're paid. First of all, hourly rates can vary for employees in the same role, and you probably don't want to track the different rates for each person on your project team. More important, payroll information is usually confidential and not readily available to you as a project manager.

The labor rates you'll use most often are *burdened labor rates,* which you can obtain from the human resources department or possibly the accounting team. A burdened rate represents the average amount that it costs an organization to employ someone—salary or wages, benefits, and a portion of overhead costs. For example, carpenters might earn $20 an hour. But by the time you include the cost of benefits and some extra money to cover overhead expenses, the burdened hourly rate for a carpenter might be $35. Average burdened hourly rates often take into account job classifications and the level within that job class. For example, an apprentice carpenter might have a burdened hourly rate of $35, whereas a master carpenter who's faster than a novice with a nail gun might carry a burdened hourly rate of $75.

Part Two:
Planning a
Project

On Time! On Track! On Target! Managing Your Projects Successfully with Microsoft Project

5. If a resource has a fee for each use, in the Cost/Use cell, type that
    value, as illustrated by the Dumpster in Figure 10-2.

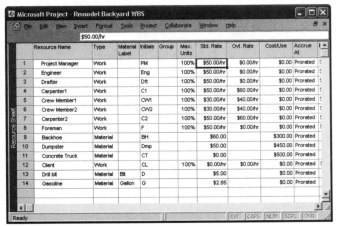

Figure 10-2   A resource can include rates for standard hours, overtime hours,
and cost per use.

You can also create up to five *different* rates for a resource, which is helpful
when a resource costs a different amount for a different type of work or to
reflect increases in wages or salary that will take effect at some point in a
project's schedule. For example, the carpenters cost $50 per hour in 2005,
but as soon as the 2006 construction season begins, their hourly rate goes
up to $55.

To add multiple rates to a resource, in the Resource Sheet, do the following:

1. Double-click the resource with the multiple rates.

2. On the Costs tab of the Resource Information dialog box, click the A
    (Default) tab and then type values in the Standard Rate and Overtime
    Rate cells.

3. In the next row of the table, type a new rate or a percentage change
    from the previous rate. To have this rate begin as of a specific date, in
    the Effective Date cell, type the date that the rate change goes into
    effect.

4. You can use the B, C, and other labeled tabs to define additional sets
    of pay rates for the resource.

5. Click OK to close the dialog box.

Entering Rates and Quantities for Material Resources

Project can calculate costs associated with material resources such as lumber, drill bits, and gasoline. In addition to specifying the rate for the material, you can also specify the units the material comes in. For example, drill bits come by the bit, whereas gasoline is priced by the gallon. When you assign a material resource to a task, Project calculates its cost using the material resource rate and the quantity of material used to complete the task. Here are the steps for specifying costs for materials:

1. With your Project file open, on the View menu, choose Resource Sheet.

2. In the Resource Sheet table, select the Resource Name cell for the material resource to which you want to add rates. To add a new resource, select the Resource Name cell in the first blank row and type a name.

3. Select the resource's Type cell and from the list box, select Material.

4. In the Material Label cell, type the unit of measure. This unit of measure might be board feet for lumber, cubic yards for concrete, or gallons for gasoline, as shown in Figure 10-2.

5. In the Std. Rate field, type the price per unit of material, such as $5.00 for each drill bit or $2.85 for each gallon of gas.

6. If the material resource has a cost per use, in the Cost/Use cell, type the charge for each use.

Best Practices

Budgets include direct costs for labor, equipment, and materials that they use. These expenses depend on the work required or the volume of use. But you also need to account for expenses such as overhead (rent, utilities, insurance, and the like), travel, employees working in staff roles, and capital equipment that isn't used specifically on projects. Because each project has to help pay for these indirect costs, you need to add them to your project estimates. Indirect costs remain fairly static, so the simplest way to include them is by using burdened labor rates, as explained in the sidebar "What Goes into Labor Rates?" on page 167.

If you use burdened labor rates, be sure you know the costs they cover. If they cover only labor expenses and employee benefits, you'll still have to add indirect costs to the capital budget. If burdened labor rates also include allocations for overhead, you're free and clear. Adding overhead costs separately would count overhead costs twice.

Another method for factoring in indirect costs is adding a multiplier to the total project budget. For example, you might add 10 percent to the project budget for indirect costs, much like some catalog merchants charge for shipping based on the cost of an item instead of its weight.

Part Two:
Planning a
Project

On Time! On Track! On Target! Managing Your Projects Successfully with Microsoft Project

Setting a Fixed Cost for a Task

Fixed costs work differently than resource and material costs. Regardless of the amount of material or the hours of work, the price stays the same. Here are the steps for setting a fixed cost for a task:

1. On the View menu, choose Gantt Chart.

2. On the View menu, point to Table: <*name of current table*>, and then choose Cost. The menu option you see changes depending on the table that is visible. For instance, if the Entry table is visible, the menu option is Table: Entry.

3. In the Fixed Cost field for a task, type the fixed cost amount, such as 5000 for a $5000 subcontractor's fee.

Important If a fixed cost represents the only cost for a task, remove the resources assigned to the task. Otherwise, Project adds the costs of those resources to the fixed cost when it calculates the total cost for the task.

Exporting Costs from a Project Schedule

You can do a lot with cost information in a Project schedule: calculate the costs for summary tasks from the work packages within them, track variances between budgeted amounts and actual values, and see how the actual cost of a task compares to its percentage of completion. But some of the financial analysis and reporting that you want to do is often easier in a software application other than Project—Excel, for example. Export maps make it easy to export your costs from Project for in-depth scrutiny.

In Microsoft Project, an *export (or import) map* controls the type of data you export (or import), the order in which the data transfers, and the field names at the destination. You can export data to Microsoft Access as well as to Excel or to file formats such as HTML or XML. Project comes with built-in maps for exporting information, and the one you want for your budgeting activities is Cost Data By Task.

The following example illustrates how to export cost data, using the Project file for the backyard remodeling project located on the companion CD. Because organizations use different spreadsheets and tools for capital budgeting, you'll probably have to modify the options and other settings to work with your organization's budgeting tools.

> The schedule for the backyard remodeling project, *Backyard Remodel
> Schedule.mpp*, is available in the *Backyard Remodel Project* folder on the
> companion CD.

You don't want to export costs for summary tasks, because you run the risk
of counting costs twice—once for work package items and again within the
subtotal for the summary tasks. By filtering out summary tasks before you
export cost information, you prevent this double counting. Unfortunately,
Project doesn't include a filter that limits tasks only to work packages, so
the example starts by creating the filter you need.

Creating a Filter to Show Only Work Packages

Here are the steps for creating a filter that hides summary tasks:

1. On the companion CD, in the *Backyard Remodel Project* folder, open
   the file *Backyard Remodel Schedule.mpp*.

2. On the Project menu, point to Filtered For: All Tasks, and then choose
   More Filters. (The menu entry you see depends on the filter that is
   currently in place. For instance, if the filter is for all tasks, the menu
   entry is Filtered For: All Tasks.)

3. In the More Filters dialog box, click New.

4. In the Filter Definition dialog box, type a name for the filter (such as
   Work_Packages).

5. In the Filter area, in the first Field Name cell, select Summary from the
   list box.

6. In the Test cell, select Equals, and in the Value(s) cell, type **no**. The
   dialog box should appear as follows:

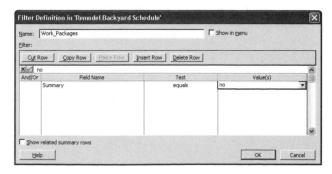

Part Two:
Planning a
Project

On Time! On Track! On Target! Managing Your Projects Successfully with Microsoft Project

7. In the Filter Definition dialog box, click OK, and then, in the More Filters dialog box, click Close.

Exporting Costs from a Project Schedule

Here are the steps for exporting task costs to an Excel workbook:

1. In Project, on the File menu, click Save As.

2. In the Save As dialog box, from the Save As Type list box, select Microsoft Excel Workbook (*.XLS), and then click Save. You'll see the Welcome page of the Export Wizard. Click Next.

3. On the Export Wizard - Data page, keep the Selected Data option selected and click Next.

4. On the Export Wizard - Map page, verify that the New Map option is selected and click Next.

5. On the Export Wizard - Map Options page, select the Tasks check box to export costs associated with tasks. Verify that the Export Includes Headers check box is selected so that column headings appear in the spreadsheet you create.

6. Click Next. You'll see the Export Wizard - Task Mapping page.

    The Task Mapping page (and a similar page for resources) is the crux of the export map. On this page, you can choose a filter for tasks (such as the Work_Packages filter created earlier). You can also specify the fields in Project that contain the data you want to export.

7. From the Export Filter list box, select Work_Packages.

8. To quickly select cost fields to export, in the row of buttons below the field table, click Base On Table. In the Select Base Table For Field Mapping dialog box, select Cost, and then click OK. The Task Mapping page should look like the following graphic.

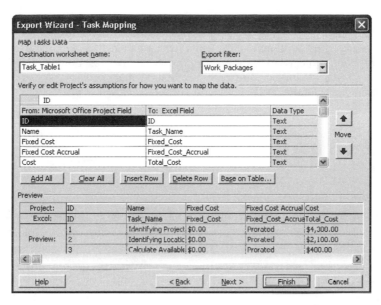

9. Because the Cost table includes some cost fields you don't need, in the From: Microsoft Office Project Field list, select Fixed Cost and then click Delete Row. Repeat this action to delete the rows for Fixed Cost Accrual, Baseline Cost, Cost Variance, Actual Cost, and Remaining Cost. The deleted fields don't contain values other than $0.00 because the project doesn't have actual costs yet.

10. Click Next, and then click Finish. Here's the resulting Excel worksheet:

Part Two:
Planning a
Project

On Time! On Track! On Target! Managing Your Projects Successfully with Microsoft Project

Tip Getting the export map right could take a couple of tries, experimenting with its options and the fields you want to include. When the Excel workbook contains what you want, run the wizard one last time, and on the End Of Map Definition page, click Save Map so that you can use the map again in the future.

In Summary

Chances are your organization uses some form of capital budgeting to decide which projects to undertake. Although you might receive a budget along with a project management assignment, understanding capital budgeting and financial measures can help you keep your projects on track to meet stakeholders' expectations. As you develop your project plan, you can enlist Project to help calculate estimated costs. And, you can export those costs to another program, such as Excel or your company's budgeting tool, for further analysis.

Part Three

Carrying Out a Project

In this part

Chapter Eleven   **Executing the Project Plan** 176

Chapter Twelve   **Evaluating Project Performance** 184

Chapter Thirteen **Managing Project Resources** 208

Chapter Fourteen **Communicating Information** 220

Part Three:
Carrying Out a
Project

On Time! On Track! On Target! Managing Your Projects Successfully with Microsoft Project

Chapter Eleven

Executing the Project Plan

Pray that success will not come any faster than you are able to endure it.

— *Elbert Hubbard*

After all the activity and excitement of the project planning phase, project execution sounds simple. Carry out the plan. But before the first hard copies of project planning documents settle in the printer tray, something will happen that requires changes to your plan. So, project execution is more of a blur of everything you do between the end of project planning and reaching the project goal.

This chapter acts like a kickoff for the most visible of your duties as a project manager. It begins with a reminder of the items that you should complete before you execute the project, such as an approved project plan, a filing system for your project documents, and a baseline of the plan to which you'll compare progress. It also summarizes the tasks you perform while executing the plan and controlling progress. However, the rest of the chapters in Part Three, "Carrying Out a Project," and Part Four, "Controlling a Project," fill in the details.

A Quick Checklist

To start managing the project that you've so carefully planned, you need a few key components. Most of the time, you complete these items during the planning phase and you're all set to start. However, just as you pat your pockets for your house keys before you lock the front door, it's a good idea to ensure that you have everything you need to launch project execution.

Approvals and Commitments

During planning, you worked hard to get people to agree on the plans and commit to the project. As you reached agreements and obtained commitments that resources were available to your project, you asked the project sponsor, customers, and other stakeholders to formally sign documents to approve the plan.

If you're glancing around nervously and shaking your head no, don't panic. Many projects have to start before the project plan is complete and approved. It's risky, but it's a common occurrence in the world of project management. You have to execute and control the project according to the plan as it is, while continuing to push to complete the plan and obtain approval on it.

Part Three:
Carrying Out a
Project

On Time! On Track! On Target! Managing Your Projects Successfully with Microsoft Project

The following checklist includes the items that are (ideally) complete with signatures that represent stakeholder support:

- The project sponsor has signed and distributed the project charter to everyone involved with the project (see "The Project Charter: Publicizing a Project," page 25).

- The project sponsor and all stakeholders have signed the project plan, including completion criteria, indicating their approval and support for it.

- The functional managers for the resources you need have notified you of the resources they are providing to the project.

- Any contracts that are required, for instance with subcontractors or vendors, have been signed by both parties.

- Any additional steps or procedures that your organization has for obtaining funding or budget approval are complete and project funding is officially available.

The Project Notebook

The project plan is a collection of text documents, spreadsheets, project schedules, diagrams, memos, and more. Moreover, after you begin managing project execution, you'll be awash in more paperwork: status reports, change requests, e-mails with questions from team members, and so on. If you haven't already, now's the time to create a repository for the project notebook, whether it's a set of ring binders with tabbed separators, hanging folders in a filing cabinet, or electronic folders on a computer. (See Chapter 21, "Archiving Historical Information," to learn about different ways to store project information electronically. Figure 21-1 on page 344 shows a sample index for a project notebook.)

The best approach to a filing system depends on the type and size of the project, your dedication to keeping information organized, and the technology your organization has available. Setting up the ring binders or computer folders beforehand ensures that you have a home for every piece of information you generate or receive. However, if time is already tight, set up the following binders or folders as a minimum:

- *A project plan binder* contains all the documents that compose a project plan: the text document for the overall plan, the project schedule, the budget, text documents for component plans, and so on.

Tip If you make major changes to the entire plan or to parts of it, don't place the revisions in chronological order. Keep the most recent versions in the front of a physical binder and store the older versions in the back. If you store files on a computer, use one folder for the current version of a document and a second folder as an archive of previous versions.

- *A communication binder* covers so much of a project that it is sure to expand as the project progresses (see Chapter 14, "Communicating Information"). You can include tabs (or subfolders) for status reports, variance reports, all forms of correspondence, and meeting minutes. Or you can set up separate binders for each one.

- *A change management binder* stores the documentation for change requests and their status (see Chapter 15, "Managing Project Changes"). Depending on how you manage changes, this binder can include the original change requests, estimates, approvals, rejections and the reasons for them, and a regularly updated status of all changes requested so far.

- *A risk management binder* contains risk plans, reports, and status for risks that have occurred or are still only potential problems (see Chapter 18, "Managing Risk").

Project Baselines

You're anxious to start managing your project and comparing progress to the plan. But before you can do that tracking, you need to save the numbers from the plan so you can compare your actual results to them. The numbers you've planned for are called baselines and Microsoft Project can save them for any values you track in the program.

Baseline Schedule

Project includes baselines for both the schedule and costs, but it doesn't set them automatically. When you receive approval for the project schedule, you can set a baseline in Project to save baseline values for start and finish dates, duration, work, and cost. To save your initial baseline in Project, do the following:

1. With the schedule open in Project, on the Tools menu, point to Tracking, and then select Save Baseline.

Part Three:
Carrying Out a
Project

On Time! On Track! On Target! Managing Your Projects Successfully with Microsoft Project

2. In the Save Baseline dialog box, make sure that the Save Baseline option is selected.

3. In the list underneath the Save Baseline option, choose Baseline, which indicates the baseline that Project uses to calculate variances. (See "Modifying Baselines" on page 284 for information on saving additional baselines.)

Best Practices

Because Project calculates variances based on the values in the Baseline fields, consider reserving Baseline for the values from your most recent baseline. After you save your original plan values to Baseline, immediately save the same values to Baseline1, to keep a permanent copy of this baseline. (On the Tools menu, point to Tracking, and then select Save Baseline. In the Save Baseline list, choose Baseline1 and click OK.) By doing so, you store your original baseline values in Baseline1 and your most recent baseline (which at this point is the same as the original) in Baseline.

When you save a revised baseline, for instance to incorporate a major change to the project, save it to the next empty baseline—Baseline2, Baseline3, and so on. At the same time, save a copy of those values in Baseline, so your variances are based on the most recent baseline values.

4. Under the For heading, verify that Entire Project is selected.

5. Click OK. Project stores the values in fields for the baseline.

If you save a baseline for the entire project, you can be sure that Project dutifully copies your estimated values to its baseline fields. However, if a few small changes come in or you want to check that you've saved the correct baseline values, the Baseline table in Project includes every field for the primary baseline: Baseline Duration, Baseline Start, Baseline Finish, Baseline Work, and Baseline Cost, as shown in Figure 11-1. Here are the steps for applying the Baseline table to a view, such as the Gantt Chart:

1. With the Gantt Chart view visible, on the View menu, point to Table, and then choose More Tables.

2. In the More Tables dialog box, select Baseline, and then click Apply.

You can see baseline dates for tasks in the Task Details Form, also shown in Figure 11-1. Initially, the Task Details Form opens with the Current option selected, which shows your current estimates for task start and finish dates. However, when you select the Baseline option, the dates in the Start and Finish boxes change to your baseline dates.

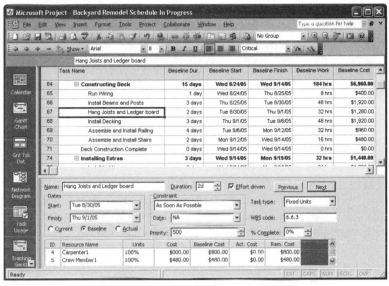

Figure 11-1 The Baseline table shows the fields for the primary baseline in Project.

Baseline Budget

Your schedule in Project includes baseline costs, but you might need an additional budget baseline if your organization uses another tool for budgeting (see Chapter 10, "Working with a Budget"). If you use a capital budgeting spreadsheet or another stand-alone tool, your baseline might be as simple as making a backup copy of the file. Baselining an overall budget is even easier if your accounting system provides budget versus actual reports, as most do. However, accounting systems usually don't track project costs to the level of detail you want as a project manager, so the baseline costs in Project are still worthwhile.

A Day in the Life of a Project Manager

When you begin to execute your project plan, you divide your time between tasks that keep the project moving forward and those that steer it in the right direction. As it turns out, managing a project isn't a linear process. It's a cycle that starts with the initial planning of the project, but it repeats the following basic tasks until the project is done:

- **Communicate** As the project manager, you coordinate the work the team members are supposed to do. As work continues, you must also

Part Three:
Carrying Out a
Project

On Time! On Track! On Target! Managing Your Projects Successfully with Microsoft Project

inform people of progress and changes, whether due to change requests or to correct course.

■ **Evaluate**   You regularly evaluate how the project is doing. Is it on time? Is it within budget? Are the objectives being met?

■ **Revise**   If the project isn't on track, you work with the stakeholders and the project team to find out why and then revise the plan to get the project back in line—which means communicating the changes to the team.

In Summary

Project execution takes up the largest part of a project schedule, but the goal for this process is simple: carry out the project plan to achieve the project objectives. As project manager, you make sure that people are working on what they should be; you see whether they're making progress as they should; and if they aren't, you come up with changes to the plan to recover. Doing that is a balancing act of skills and tasks. You must lead resources, communicate with everyone involved, evaluate project performance, solve problems, and revise the project plan while you simultaneously manage risks that might occur and respond to change requests.

Part Three:
Carrying Out a
Project

On Time! On Track! On Target! Managing Your Projects Successfully with Microsoft Project

Chapter Twelve

Evaluating Project Performance

*An unsophisticated forecaster uses statistics as a drunken man
uses lamp-posts—for support rather than illumination.*

— Andrew Lang

The more time you have to correct the course of a project, the more likely you are to succeed in getting things back on track. As a project manager, you can prevent unpleasant jolts of adrenaline by regularly reviewing your projects for early signs of trouble. Knowing where a project is relative to the planned schedule and budget helps answer questions such as "Are the hours allocated to tasks realistic?" and "Are team members working as productively as we estimated?" which, in turn, can help you decide how to rein in your project. And with a bit more analysis, you can answer the questions the stakeholders ask, such as "Will the project meet our objectives?" and "What's the return on investment?"

This chapter describes how you go about analyzing project performance. The first task, of course, is to collect the information you need to compare actual progress to the plan. Then, you can track work completed and other task status to begin to measure schedule and cost performance—reviewing actual values versus baseline values, for example. Microsoft Project provides several tools for tracking progress and spotting early warning signs: views, tables, filters, and reports. You'll learn which ones to use and when. You'll also learn about a technique known as *earned value analysis*, which indicates whether your project is on time and within budget by comparing the relationships among actual costs, budgeted costs, scheduled work, and completed work.

Gathering Data

The progress of cost and schedule for a project is an extension of the resources that it requires. To determine where a project stands, you mainly need to know how much time resources are spending on their tasks and when. If you have costs that you track outside your project schedule, you need to know how much of those your project has incurred as well. As difficult as it can be to gather numbers for time and cost, you also need to know other, less easily quantifiable measures of project progress—how closely the work conforms to the project requirements, quality, and whether the project is making the customer happy. This section describes the information you need to gauge progress and provides some guidelines for how to obtain it.

The Data You Need

The data you need to evaluate progress depends on what's important to you and project stakeholders. Because "Are we on time?" and "Are we within budget?" are the most frequently asked questions, you know you

Part Three:
Carrying Out a
Project

On Time! On Track! On Target! Managing Your Projects Successfully with Microsoft Project

need information about the work that's been done and the labor costs to do it. But there's more to progress than time and money. This section introduces some of the data you might want to collect to evaluate project performance.

Progress on Work Packages

When all the work packages are complete, the project is done, so tracking progress on work packages is a great place to start. Work packages that are completely finished are comparatively easy to measure. Each work package should have completion criteria (see "Detailing Work Packages," page 101), so a work package is complete when it's met those criteria. You also need to know how much time team members spent, when they did the work, and any additional costs beyond labor that the work incurred.

But because you gather data while work packages are in progress, you also want to know what it's going to take to finish the work that's in progress. You also need to know the accomplishments that team members have achieved. Besides providing bullet points to include in your status report, what work resources have finished can help you determine whether their forecasts for completion are realistic.

Tip   If you ask people to report the percentage that their tasks are complete, don't bother asking for precise values. Percentages such as 0, 25, 50, and 100 are easier for them to estimate and for you to update in your schedule.

Here are some examples of the data you might collect for different situations:

- For salaried employees, the easiest way to determine progress is by finding out when they started, when they expect to finish, and what percentage of their days they spend on your tasks. This approach is ideal when resources work full-time on tasks or their allocation to a task stays steady from day to day. With these three pieces of information you can calculate the cost and duration so far as well as the estimated cost and duration when the task is complete.

  If you prefer more detail, you can collect work hours instead of daily allocation. You still need to know when they started, and you also need to know how many hours they think it will take to finish.

- For hourly employees, hours worked and estimated hours to finish become more important, particularly if a task requires a lawyer who charges $500 an hour. You still need to know when they started and when they expect to finish.

- If a vendor is delivering work on a fixed-price bid, all you really need to know is when the vendor expects to achieve major milestones in addition to when the vendor will finish, because the actual hours and cost don't affect your project at all.

Quality

Quality measures can alter the picture of the progress you've made. For example, if you find defects faster than you can fix them, you might not be as far along on completed software as what your team members are telling you.

For product-related projects, keep your eye on defect statistics, such as the number of open defects, closed defects, and new defects found or reopened. In addition, watch trends in quality measures. For instance, the number of open defects usually increases during the early part of testing, when the most defects exist and testers find the most obvious ones. Eventually, the number of open defects hits a peak and begins to decline.

Tip   The cost to fix a defect is an important measure, but it can be misleading. For example, if you plan a project to prevent defects, the cost per defect is higher but the total cost of fixing defects is lower. Moreover, if the cost per defect increases with time, team members might be fixing the easiest defects first, which means that the rest of the defect-fixing iceberg could still be waiting.

One way to maintain quality throughout your project is to schedule reviews. For example, reviewing the project plan is essential for your project to solve the right problem in the right way. Reviewing requirements is another way to keep your project on track. Work performed to deliver the wrong or unnecessary requirements wastes time and money—and decreases morale when team members find out the work they did was for naught.

Tip   As you hand over deliverables to customers, you can survey them to see whether they like what they've gotten so far. The feedback you receive can also help you adjust future work to more closely align to what they want.

Part Three:
Carrying Out a
Project

On Time! On Track! On Target! Managing Your Projects Successfully with Microsoft Project

Problems That Could Lie Ahead

Another key category for determining true progress is what can and could go wrong. You need to know what issues team members have and what risks have arisen (see Chapter 18, "Managing Risk"). For example, for the backyard remodel project, tasks in the planning phases could be ahead of schedule, but then you find out that the hippopotamus that took up residence in the homeowners' backyard mud hole is a bigger problem than anyone imagined. Until you know how many permits you have to obtain and how long it's going to take to relocate the creature, your project progress could be stuck.

As well, when risks occur, you have to snap your risk management plan into action. Depending on the risk, your response might include dipping into the project's contingency funds and time. Or you implement your other responses, such as submitting an insurance claim for the tree that the bulldozer knocked down. And for some risks, you'll have to rework the schedule.

> **Note** You might measure progress in other ways, depending on the project and what stakeholders care about. For example, measuring productivity can help you gauge how much work is left and can help you improve estimates in the future.

Obtaining Time and Status

Obtaining time and status is essential to tracking progress. Some people are happy to oblige, but others might be reluctant to report time in the way you require. Perhaps they don't see the value of recording the hours they've spent on a task. Or they could be so busy that a few minutes to track time are minutes they don't get to sleep. To make matters worse, you might need to understand the ins and outs of your organization's time-tracking system to see whether it helps or hinders collecting the information you need.

Work resources that bill and are paid by the hour should have plenty of incentive to report the time they spend on tasks. But salaried employees are paid the same amount whether they spend two days or two weeks completing a task. People offer lots of reasons for failing to accurately report the time they spend on project tasks. For one thing, work resources might divvy up their days among several tasks. Remembering to account for 30 minutes preparing a report for one task, an hour-long meeting to plan work for three other tasks, and half a day to finish still another task is tedious at best. And performed in hindsight, keeping track of relatively short periods of time on several tasks can involve more guess-work than accuracy

---

Tip   Many organizations use compensation systems, such as pay-for-performance and reviews, to ensure that salaried employees perform the work for which they're responsible. Rewarding people for doing what you want is a big motivator. If your organization doesn't include project results as employee compensation goals, talk to management about adding these new measures.

Another factor in how time is reported is a single-minded drive for quality. Perhaps a few key resources, once they get going on a task, conclude that doing the job right will take more than the week allocated in the budget. They spend 50 hours completing the work but report the original 40. The lower number of work hours helps the budget, but it doesn't provide a true picture of the project's costs. Moreover, it might not help the schedule either if the resources should have been paying attention to other tasks.

The first step to getting the time-reporting accuracy you want is to explain the benefits of recording actual labor hours to team members. Accurate time reporting can help:

- Improve estimates in the future

- Persuade the customer and stakeholders of the time required to produce quality work

- Negotiate additional money and time for change requests

- Identify potential problems with a project schedule and budget early enough to take corrective actions

When the Accounting System Is an Adversary

The accounting or time-tracking application that you and your team members must use can present problems for tracking project work hours. The systems and programs that many organizations use track time by role, by customer, or by entire project. They aren't designed to track time for discrete tasks within a project, which, unfortunately, is exactly the information you need. As a result, you might need to ask team members to track their task time separately so that you can incorporate it into the project schedule and budget.

Suppose the accounting department asks you to record hours that you've spent on one task to a different task. For example, the actual hours exceed the estimated hours (or the number of hours specified in the contract). The accounting department might want to record the hours against different tasks rather than amend the contract or track variances. If you follow this advice, you won't know whether your estimates are over the budget, under budget, or right on track. You might not have any choice but to do what the accounting department says. However, if you track detailed task time outside of the accounting system, you have a record of actual hours. The challenge in this situation is to keep track of both the actual project hours and the numbers that accounting uses so you can explain any discrepancies between your project performance calculations and accounting's calculations.

Part Three:
Carrying Out a
Project

On Time! On Track! On Target! Managing Your Projects Successfully with Microsoft Project

Asking people to track their time to a meaningful increment of time might be the most successful approach. You probably don't need to know how each minute of the workday is spent. You might get better results and more participation by asking team members to estimate their time to the nearest hour (or day for long tasks).

Tracking Schedule Progress

Progress on the schedule is your first measure of progress, because the longer a project takes, the more it usually costs. However, to get an accurate picture of schedule progress, you have to track what's been accomplished, not just how much time has passed or how many hours have been billed. Completed work packages are your most dependable guides to real progress, which is why you want to break work into relatively small chunks (see "When to Stop Building a WBS," page 93). This section introduces some techniques for reviewing schedule progress in Project as well as how to use some of its built-in reports to do the same.

> **Important** If the scope of your project has changed, tracking progress against your original schedule doesn't give a clear picture of progress. See Chapter 15, "Managing Project Changes," and "Modifying Baselines" on page 284 to learn how to update your schedule to reflect the current scope.

As long as you enter the information that Project needs to calculate remaining duration and finish dates for tasks, you can view progress in a couple of ways. The quickest way to see an overall picture of project completion and cost is in the Project Information dialog box. On the Project menu, select Project Information and, in the Project Information dialog box, click Statistics to see high-level status for duration, work, and cost, as well as the project start and finish dates. As you can see in Figure 12-1, the Project Statistics dialog box shows baseline values, Project's current estimate at completion, actual amounts so far, and remaining amounts.

> You can view a schedule with actual values added in *Backyard Remodel Schedule In Progress.mpp* in the *Backyard Remodel Project* folder on the companion CD.

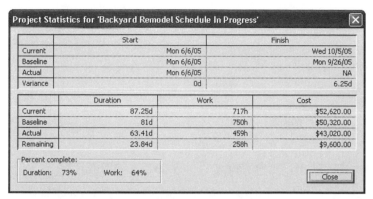

Figure 12-1   At the bottom of the Project Statistics dialog box, if the percentage of work that's complete is less than the percentage of duration that's passed, your project is falling behind.

Reviewing Schedule Progress

As you might expect, you can view progress for your schedule in several ways in Project. But by far the easiest way to see where tasks in the schedule stand is with the Tracking Gantt view. This view shows two sets of taskbars,

How Project Calculates Values and Variance

Project keeps track of several sets of start dates, finish dates, durations, work, and cost, which it uses to calculate performance. You provide baseline and actual values and Project uses those to estimate values at completion and how much remains. By understanding the difference between these values, you can track and interpret your progress more easily.

Scheduled values are always the most up-to-date values for your schedule regardless of whether you are still planning or work has begun. As you build and fine-tune your schedule, the values that you see in fields in the Task Form are your current planned values. (The Task Details Form lets you choose the values you see by including three options for Current, Baseline, and Actual.) After you begin tracking actual values, scheduled values become Project's estimates of the values at completion. Project combines actual dates, effort, and costs for completed work with the estimated dates and costs for the work that remains.

Baseline information represents the estimates that you put together and to which stakeholders have agreed. When you save a baseline (see "Project Baselines," page 179), you copy the current scheduled values to baseline fields.

Actual values, of course, are the values that come true: the dates that tasks actually started and finished, the work hours that team members actually spent, and the resulting actual durations and costs. Project subtracts scheduled values from baseline values to determine variance.

Remaining values are merely scheduled values minus actual values—how much duration, work, or cost remains.

Part Three:
Carrying Out a
Project

On Time! On Track! On Target! Managing Your Projects Successfully with Microsoft Project

as demonstrated in Figure 12-2: one using baseline start and finish dates and the other using scheduled start and finish dates. Because the Tracking Gantt displays tasks on the critical path in red, you can see tasks on the critical path that are pushing past the baseline finish date and focus on pulling them back in (see "A Crash Course on Project Crashing," page 156). Project includes the Tracking Gantt view on the View menu and in the View Bar. To switch to the Tracking Gantt view, on the View menu, choose Tracking Gantt.

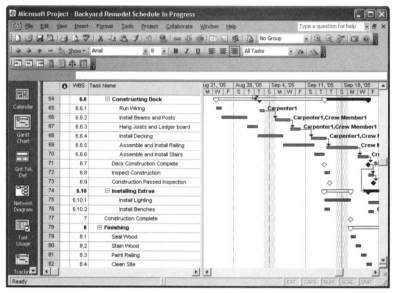

Figure 12-2   When the scheduled taskbars occur later than the baseline taskbars, you know that your tasks are running later than you planned.

> **Tip**   If you save more than one baseline, for instance, to show the baseline at the end of each phase (see "Modifying Baselines," page 284), the Multiple Baselines Gantt view displays the bars for Baseline, Baseline1, and Baseline2. If tasks start to fall further behind from baseline to baseline, it's time to identify and resolve the problem before it gets worse.

In Project, views, tables, and filters work together to help you spot potential problems. Views, such as the Tracking Gantt, format information so progress is easy to see. The fields in tables you apply to the Task Sheet come in handy for identifying estimated finish dates, finding tasks with slack time, or seeing whether the schedule variance is getting worse or better. And filters restrict the tasks that appear to ones that might require attention.

Note Project recalculates scheduled values as you update tasks with actual values, so the dates, durations, costs, and variances you see are always up to date.

Tables with Schedule-Related Fields

To apply a table to the current view, on the View menu, point to Table: *<current table name>*, and then click the name of the table you want. Here are tables in Project that include different fields for evaluating schedule performance:

- **Summary** The Summary table shows the scheduled values for the most common progress measures: Duration, Start, Finish, percentage complete (% Complete), Cost, and Work. If a stakeholder asks when the project will finish or how much it will cost, this table has the answers.

- **Variance** This table includes both scheduled and baseline start and finish dates and also shows the time variance between those dates.

Tip One way to spot schedule trends is to display the Variance table and then sort tasks by finish date. If the values in the Finish variance field continue to increase, your project is falling further and further behind schedule.

- **Schedule** The Schedule table includes the Free Slack and Total Slack fields, which are helpful when you're looking for tasks whose resources you can reassign to shorten tasks on the critical path.

Tip A checklist for progress analysis can remind you of the views you want to see and the filters you want to apply, particularly if you create customized views and filters. One way to keep your checklist nearby is to store it as a note attached to the top-level summary task in your project file. Select the summary task and then, on the Standard toolbar, click the TaskNotes icon. In the Summary Task Information dialog box, type the checklist points you want to perform.

Part Three:
Carrying Out a
Project

On Time! On Track! On Target! Managing Your Projects Successfully with Microsoft Project

Filters for Checking Schedule Progress

Most of the time, the majority of tasks run without incident. You want to keep your eye on the ones that are falling behind or are at risk of doing so. Project includes several built-in filters for finding these at-risk tasks. To apply a filter, on the Formatting toolbar, choose the filter you want to apply in the Filter list. Here are a few filters for checking the schedule:

■ **Slipping Tasks**   Use this filter to check for tasks whose finish dates have slipped. This filter shows tasks that are already in progress and whose scheduled finish dates are later than the baseline finish.

■ **Slipped/Late Progress**   This filter looks for potential schedule slippage in two ways. The filter looks for tasks that haven't started or are in progress whose scheduled finish is later than the baseline finish and those whose work performed is less than the work scheduled.

■ **Should Start By**   You can look for delayed tasks with this filter, which shows tasks that should have started, but haven't. For this filter, you type the start date you want.

■ **Should Start/Finish By**   This filter looks for delays in both start and finish dates. It filters for tasks that should have started or finished by the date you specify, but haven't.

■ **Work Overbudget**   The Work Overbudget filter shows tasks whose estimated work is greater than the baseline work, which often leads to delays.

■ **Slipping Assignments**   This is a resource filter that you can apply to views such as Resource Usage to show resources that might need help. The filter shows tasks in progress whose scheduled finish date is later than the baseline finish.

Note   Instead of filtering the list of tasks in a Gantt Chart view, you can use the Slipping Tasks report to show the same information in a tabular format. The report lets you review baseline costs and any variances between baseline and total costs. Tasks are sorted by total cost so you can start examining the most expensive ones first. To generate the report, on the View menu, select Reports. In the Reports dialog box, double-click Current Activities. Double-click Slipping Tasks.

Reviewing Cost and Cost Variance

After you've set up a budget for a project, you track costs so you can compare them to the original estimate (the baseline). The simplest measure of cost performance is whether actual costs are more or less than budgeted costs, whether you look at a few tasks or the project as a whole. As you keep an eye on the status of tasks as resources work on them, the actual cost and cost variance are easy ways to spot problems.

This section describes some straightforward procedures you can follow to review costs in Project as well as how to use its built-in budget and cost reports.

Viewing Cost and Cost Variance

A baseline budget reflects the costs approved by a project's stakeholders. In a perfect world, the actual costs line up precisely with the baseline. But in reality, some tasks cost more than you estimated and some cost less. As long as you enter the information that Project needs to calculate estimated and actual costs, you can view costs in a couple of ways.

Applying the Cost table to the Task Sheet displays columns for all kinds of costs as well as the variance between the baseline and actual costs, as described in the next section. Project recalculates the scheduled cost as you enter fixed costs, work, or task completion percentages, so the costs and variances you see are always

Evaluating Financial Measures

Project cost performance isn't limited to how much you spend. Sometimes, it depends on how much more money your organization makes or how much it saves. You should check all the financial assumptions included in the project's capital budget. (For more information about capital budgeting, see Chapter 10, "Working with a Budget.") For example, has the project met the revenue projections used to establish its return on investment? If you assumed that the project would reduce the cost of processing orders by 15 percent, has the project saved that amount of money? If the capital budget assumed that the cost to support and train users for the first three months after project completion would be $75,000, what were the support and training costs?

Project calculates cost based on resource rates (see "Specifying Rates for Work Resources in Project," page 167) and the amount of work performed or the percentage of the task's duration that's complete. You set up resource rates in Project when you build your project team in the Microsoft Project Resource Sheet (see Chapter 8, "Project Resources"). When you assign resources and the amount of work they do to tasks (see "Assigning Resources to Tasks," page 145), Project can calculate the projected task cost. Now that work has begun on those tasks, you and the project team must track the amount of work done and the percentage that's complete so that Project can also calculate the actual task cost and the variance from your estimate.

Part Three:
Carrying Out a
Project

On Time! On Track! On Target! Managing Your Projects Successfully with Microsoft Project

up to date. Here are the steps to view costs and variances for tasks in Project:

1. On the View menu, select More Views.

2. In the More Views dialog box, select Task Sheet, and then click Apply.

3. On the View menu, point to Table: *<current table name>*, and then select Cost. (The Table command will change to indicate the name of the current table.) Project applies the Cost table in the Task Sheet view.

Tip   You can also apply a table to a view by right-clicking the blank cell immediately above the first ID cell and then choosing the name of the table you want to apply, such as Cost.

Figure 12-3 shows the backyard remodel project with the Cost table applied. Here are the fields that the Cost table includes by default:

■ **Fixed Cost**   If a task includes a fixed cost, such as a $2,000 fixed bid for the concrete on a construction project, enter the value of the fixed cost in this field.

■ **Fixed Cost Accrual**   This field tells Project when to apply a fixed cost to the schedule. Prorated means that the cost is distributed over the duration of the task. Start and End represent the cost occurring at the start or the finish of the task, respectively.

■ **Total Cost**   This field is the scheduled cost and includes the labor costs and fixed costs for the task.

■ **Baseline**   This field represents the baseline cost for both labor costs and fixed costs.

■ **Variance**   Project calculates variance by subtracting the baseline cost from the total cost. If the variance is positive, the project is over budget.

■ **Actual Baseline**   This field represents the actual cost for both labor costs and fixed costs.

■ **Remaining**   Project calculates the remaining value by subtracting the actual cost from the total cost.

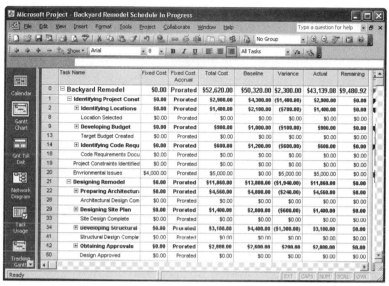

Figure 12-3   The Cost table provides a quick view of the status of costs and variances.

Important   If your variances are all zero, you aren't necessarily right on track. You can view cost variances only if you've entered pay rates for resources (or fixed costs for tasks) and saved a baseline.

Finding Costs That Are Over Budget

One of the first steps to controlling a budget is regularly checking the tasks and resources that have exceeded their budgeted amounts. Project includes both views and reports for examining costs that are over budget. Here are the steps to view cost overruns by applying a filter to the Task Sheet. You'll learn more about viewing cost reports in "Project Cost Reports" on the next page.

1.   On the View menu, select Task Usage to display a view that includes values not only for tasks but for each resource assigned to each task. By using this view, you can evaluate task overruns and which resources are over and under budget.

2.   On the View menu, point to Table: *<current table name>*, and then select Cost.

Part Three:
Carrying Out a
Project

On Time! On Track! On Target! Managing Your Projects Successfully with Microsoft Project

3. To view only over budget tasks, on the Formatting toolbar, in the Filter list, choose Cost Overbudget.

With large projects, you probably don't want to spend time on tasks that are only slightly over budget. In addition to the Overbudget Tasks report, described in the next section, you can show the tasks with the largest cost overruns in the Task Sheet. First, hide summary tasks (on the Tools menu, select Options, and on the View tab, clear the Show Summary Tasks check box). On the Project menu, point to Sort, and select Sort By. In the Sort dialog box, in the Sort By box, choose Cost Variance. Select the Descending option and then click Sort.

Note To view cost overruns by resource, follow the same steps, except in step 1, choose Resource Usage.

Project Cost Reports

Reports in Project don't offer many formatting options, so you might not use them that often. To generate a cost report, on the View menu, select Reports. In the Reports dialog box, double-click Costs to display Project's built-in cost reports:

- *The Cash Flow report* shows when the project will incur costs based on the project schedule. This report totals all costs associated with a task (assigned work resources, materials, equipment, fees, and fixed costs) and the costs show up depending on whether they accrue at the beginning, end, or throughout the duration of tasks.

- *The Budget report* shows the fixed costs, total costs, baseline costs, variance costs, actual costs, and remaining costs for budgeted tasks. The report lets you review baseline costs and any variances between baseline and total costs tasks are sorted by total cost so you can start examining the most expensive ones first.

- *The Overbudget Tasks report* shows you all tasks for which actual or scheduled costs exceed the baseline costs. (You must save a baseline in order to generate this report.) Tasks are sorted with the highest variance first.

- *The Overbudget Resources report* shows resources for whom actual costs exceed the baseline costs. Like the Overbudget Tasks report, this report sorts the resource with the highest variance first.

■ *The Earned Value report* shows the standard measures used in earned value analysis, including budgeted cost of work scheduled, budgeted cost of work performed, actual cost of work performed, cost variance, and others.

Tip   If Project reports don't provide the information you need—or don't provide the information in the way that stakeholders want to view it—you can export Project cost information to Microsoft Excel (see "Exporting Costs from a Project Schedule," page 170, for detailed steps); to a format that is compatible with a database application, such as Microsoft Access; or to a reporting engine such as Crystal Reports. If your organization has more demanding reporting requirements, you can export cost information to a Microsoft SQL Server database and then work with a database designer to create the reports that fit your needs. And if your organization uses Microsoft Project Enterprise Project Management tools, you can use Online Analytical Processing tools (informally known as the OLAP cube) to drag and drop fields to build reports that present project data in almost any way you can imagine.

Earned Value Analysis: Schedule and Cost Performance

The comparison of how much you've spent to what you've planned to spend can be deceiving. For example, suppose a project is through half of its scheduled duration and you've spent roughly half the budget as well. If half the work is done as well, you're right on track. But if the budget and schedule are half spent and the team has finished only 30 percent of the work, the picture isn't as bright. You have 50 percent of the budget and duration left but you still must complete 70 percent of the work. *Earned value analysis* takes into account not only actual and budgeted costs, but how much actual and estimated work is complete to give you a better idea of where your project stands. For example, if you've spent more than was budgeted for the current status of the project, you could be ahead of schedule rather than over budget. Because you performed more work than you planned in the time that's passed, the higher costs are to be expected.

Note   Earned value analysis gets its name because you identify the *value* that the project has *earned* so far (the money that's been spent to perform the work that's complete). The U.S. Department of Defense and other government agencies require an earned value analysis for their projects, but businesses use it to evaluate projects as well.

Part Three:
Carrying Out a
Project

On Time! On Track! On Target! Managing Your Projects Successfully with Microsoft Project

Earned value analysis calculates how much of a budget should have been spent given the amount of work that's been performed to a specific date. Earned value uses the following concepts to measure status:

- Project tasks earn value as work on the task is completed.

- The earned value compared to actual and planned costs shows cost performance and forecasts future costs.

- Work completed is measured in dollars so that cost performance and schedule performance are money-based measures.

Earned Value Status Measures

The measures that initiate earned value analysis are budgeted cost of work scheduled (BCWS), actual cost of work performed (ACWP), and budgeted cost of work performed (BCWP). Here is what each one of these measures represents:

- *Budgeted cost of work scheduled (BCWS)* is sometimes referred to as planned value or PV, because it is the baseline cost up to the status date for tasks as they were originally scheduled in the project plan. It is how much of the budget you planned to spend by the date on which you measure BCWS. For example, if the cost of tasks that you planned to complete by September 15, 2005 is $10,000, BCWS on that date is $10,000.

- *Actual cost of work performed (ACWP)* is also known simply as actual costs and represents the actual costs for the work performed up to the status date, whether you've completed more or fewer tasks than you had planned so far. ACWS is whatever you've spent up to September 15, 2005.

- *Budgeted cost of work performed (BCWP)* is also called earned value or EV, because it measures the value of the worked performed, thus earned, up to the status date. This measure calculates how much of the cost should have been spent given the work that's actually been done and has nothing to do with when the work is performed. For example, if the budgeted cost for all the task work completed so far is $8,000, BCWP is $8,000. Although you calculate BCWP for each task individually, you analyze earned value at the project level.

Analyzing an Earned Value Graph

An earned value graph is the best way to view earned value because you don't even have to see any numbers to know whether your project is on schedule and within budget. You'll typically see BCWS, ACWP, and BCWP compared as shown in Figure 12-4. By plotting each measure over time, you quickly see how your project is doing compared to your planned schedule and budget. The y-axis in the earned value graph represents cost, whereas the x-axis shows time.

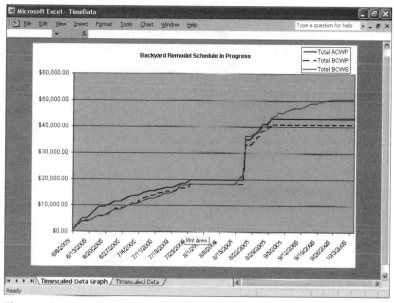

Figure 12-4 An earned value graph visually depicts the relationships among BCWP, BCWS, and ACWP, so you can easily identify trends.

Here's how you read an earned value graph to determine both the schedule and budget status for a project:

- The BCWS line represents the amount of money you planned to spend over the course of the project, so it's no surprise that it continues to rise throughout the project's duration. As the shaded BCWS line in Figure 12-4 illustrates, the budgeted cost increases until it reaches the $50,000 planned budget.

Note In this example, the flat section in the middle of the graph is due to a several-week wait to obtain the construction permit from the county. And the big spike in price represents the cost of the materials delivered just before construction.

Part Three:
Carrying Out a
Project

On Time! On Track! On Target! Managing Your Projects Successfully with Microsoft Project

- The BCWP line represents the cost you estimated for the work that has been performed and is shown as a heavy dashed line in Figure 12-4. When construction begins (after the spike in price), the BCWP line is below the BCWS line. Mathematically, this means that the cost of the work you've done is less than the cost of the scheduled work. In project status terms, this translates into the project is behind schedule.

- The ACWP line represents what you actually spent and is the solid line in Figure 12-4. When construction begins, the ACWP line is above the BCWP line, which means that you spent more to complete the work than you had budgeted—in short, your project is over budget.

Tip   Here's a summary of what you *want* to see in an earned value chart. The project is ahead of schedule when the BCWP line is above the BCWS line. The project is under budget when the ACWP line is below the BCWP line.

You can create an earned value graph by exporting data from Project to Excel, which is described in detail in "Creating an Earned Value Graph in Project" on page 206.

Earned Value Performance

Earned value analysis also calculates variances and indexes to help you determine whether you have enough money left in the budget to complete the project or whether the project is on track to finish on time. The following are other earned value measures you can calculate and what they tell you:

- *Cost variance (CV)* is the budgeted cost of work performed (BCWP) for a task minus the actual cost of work performed (ACWP). If the variance is positive, the actual cost is under the budgeted amount; if the variance is negative, the task is over budget.

Important   Don't confuse the CV and Variance fields in Project. For example, in the Cost table, Variance is the actual cost minus the baseline cost, so a positive variance in Project means that the task is over budget. However, the CV field is BCWP minus ACWP, so a positive CV means that the task is under budget.

- *Schedule variance (SV)* is the budgeted cost of work performed (BCWP) minus the budgeted cost of work scheduled (BCWS). SV shows the difference in cost between the work that has been performed and the work that was originally scheduled. A positive schedule variance means that the project is ahead of schedule.

- *The cost performance index (CPI)* is an indicator of whether a project will go over budget. CPI is the ratio of budgeted costs of work performed to actual costs of work performed (BCWP / ACWP), and the CPI for the entire project is the sum of BCWP for all tasks divided by the sum of ACWP for all tasks. A CPI greater than one indicates the project is under budget, because budgeted costs are greater than actual costs. A CPI less than one means the project is over budget. For example, a CPI of 0.7 means that the budgeted cost is 70 percent of the actual costs.

- *The schedule performance index (SPI)* is an indicator of whether a project will be on time and can help you estimate the project completion date. SPI is the ratio of the budgeted cost of work performed (BCWP) to the budgeted cost of work scheduled (BCWS). An SPI greater than one indicates that the project is ahead of schedule, because the work performed exceeds the work scheduled. An SPI less than one indicates that the project is behind schedule.

- *Budget at completion (BAC)* is simply the budget approved for the entire project.

- *Estimate at completion (EAC)* is an estimate of the total cost of a task or project based on progress as of the status date. EAC is calculated using the formula EAC = ACWP + ((BAC − BCWP) / CPI).

- *Variance at completion (VAC)* is the difference between the budget at completion (BAC) and the estimate

Best Practices

Earned value analysis might sound a little daunting, and when you throw in acronyms like BCWS, BCWP, and the like, you might think that the calculations must take more time than you have available. The good news is that Project can calculate earned value measures for you. To obtain Project's assistance, you must assign costs to tasks, set a baseline, keep track of actual costs in Project, and set up tasks that don't run from the project start to project finish. (Project uses completed tasks to calculate earned value.)

Although you certainly want to find out why a CPI is less than one, don't panic. For example, the CPI might have improved from last month's report, which means that the project is coming back closer to the original budget.

Finally, even if your analysis reveals a positive schedule variance, take a look at the tasks that must be completed to reach major milestones. If secondary tasks are all on track, but a few major tasks are behind, that positive schedule variance could disappear.

Part Three:
Carrying Out a
Project

On Time! On Track! On Target! Managing Your Projects Successfully with Microsoft Project

at completion (EAC). In Project, the Total Cost field represents EAC and the Baseline Cost field is BAC.

- *Estimate to complete (ETC)* is the amount of money needed to finish the project. To calculate ETC, subtract ACWP from EAC.

- *To complete performance index (TCPI)* is the ratio of the work remaining to the budget remaining (as of a status date). The formula for TCPI is (BAC − BCWP) / (BAC − ACWP). A TCPI value greater than one indicates performance is on track. A value less than one indicates that performance must improve to meet your goals.

The % Complete and Physical % Complete Fields

Earned value calculations are based on the budgeted cost of work performed (BCWP), so the results you obtain depend on whether you use the % Complete or Physical % Complete field to indicate completion. The % Complete field shows the percentage of a task's *duration* that has been completed. Depending on how you track progress, you can enter a value in the % Complete field or have Project calculate it. For example, if you estimated the work on a task to be 16 hours and you enter 8 hours of actual work, Project calculates the % Complete as 50 percent.

The value in the Physical % Complete field is always a value you enter. Physical % Complete is often a more accurate depiction of the amount of actual work performed or work remaining.

Here's an example of how % Complete and Physical % Complete differ. You estimate that pouring 100 concrete pads will take 10 days. Because it rained, you've poured 30 concrete pads at the 5-day mark. % Complete is 50 percent, because 5 of the 10 days have passed. Physical % Complete is 30 percent because you've poured 30 of the 100 concrete pads. Because it's difficult to speed up most tasks, the Physical % Complete is usually a better measure of completion.

Earned Value in Microsoft Project

Project can calculate values for BCWS, BCWP, ACWS, and the other earned value measures, but you have a few tasks to complete first. You must check that options related to earned value are set the way you want. You must save a baseline (at least one). If you save more than one baseline, you must know which baseline you want to use for earned value comparisons. And you must choose between using the % Complete field or the Physical % Complete field as the basis of the calculations, which is described in the sidebar, "The % Complete and Physical % Complete Fields." After you've completed these steps, you can view earned value analysis in several ways.

Setting Options for Earned Value

Here are the steps for setting up options for earned value calculations:

1. On the Tools menu, select Options, and then, in the Options dialog box, click the Calculation tab.

2. Click Earned Value, which is tucked away about halfway down the dialog box.

3. In the Default Task Earned Value Method list, choose % Complete or Physical % Complete for calculating budgeted cost of work performed (BCWP).

> **Important** Changing the value of this option affects only the tasks that are added to your Project file *after* the option is changed. To change this setting for a task that already exists, double-click the task to open the Task Information dialog box, and then click the Advanced tab. Choose the field you want in the Earned Value Method list.

---

4. In the Baseline For Earned Value Calculations list, select the baseline you want Project to use when it calculates earned value totals.

5. Click Close.

6. In the Options dialog box, click OK.

Viewing Earned Value in a Table

In a Project schedule, you can see earned value in the Earned Value table and in the Earned Value Cost Indicators table. (On the View menu, point to Table: *<current table name>*, and then select More Tables. In the More Tables dialog box, double-click either the Earned Value or Earned Value Cost Indicators table.)

- The Earned Value table shows the fundamental earned value measures, including BCWS, BCWP, ACWP, SV, CV, EAC, BAC, and VAC. You can use this table to spot variances and the different values at completion.

- The Earned Value Cost Indicators table includes some of the same columns as the Earned Value table, but also includes indexes, such as CPI and TCPI. Check the values of CPI and TCPI to see whether the project is on budget and schedule. If CPI is less than one, the task or project is over budget. The value of TCPI indicates how much you need to increase project performance on remaining work to stay within the budget.

Part Three:
Carrying Out a
Project

On Time! On Track! On Target! Managing Your Projects Successfully with Microsoft Project

---

Note   The Earned Value report is a standard cost report in Project. The report includes the fields from the Earned Value table. However, in most cases, it's more effective to view earned value in the Task Sheet, so you can dig deeper when you find a problematic task.

Creating an Earned Value Graph in Project

Project provides a command to export data, so you don't have to perform the typical steps to export data. Here are the steps to creating an earned value graph like the one shown in Figure 12-4:

1.   On the View menu, point to Toolbars, and then choose Analysis, if it isn't already displayed.

2.   On the Analysis toolbar, click Analyze Timescaled Data In Excel. The Analyze Timescaled Data Wizard starts.

3.   To export the entire project, keep the Entire Project option selected and click Next.

4.   In Step 2 of the wizard, Ctrl-click ACWP, BCWP, and BCWS, and then click Add to add the fields to the Fields To Export list.

5.   In the Fields To Export list, select Work and click Remove. Click Next.

6.   In Step 3, the wizard automatically fills in the project start and finish dates. If you want to see the graph for the entire project duration, leave these values as they are. To graph up to a status date, in the To box, type the status date, such as 9/15/2005.

7.   In the Units list, choose Days, Weeks, or Months, depending on the length of the project. Click Next.

Tip   For example, for the two-month backyard remodel project, choosing Days or Weeks is fine, but choosing Months won't provide enough data points for a meaningful earned value graph. For long projects, choose Weeks or Months, because daily changes provide too much data.

---

8. In Step 4 of the wizard, keep the "Yes, Please" option selected, and click Next.

9. In Step 5 of the wizard, simply click Export Data to open the resulting workbook in Excel.

In Summary

Regular checkups are the best way to keep a project healthy. If you spot signs of trouble early, you have time to make changes. To review progress, you need information. Team members must provide accurate data about what they've accomplished, the time they've worked, and how much time remains. Project includes tools for looking at your schedule and costs in detail. But to see the big picture of project performance, you need the indicators that earned value analysis provides, comparing baseline costs to how much of the budget has been spent and how much should have been spent for the completed work.

Part Three:
Carrying Out a
Project

On Time! On Track! On Target! Managing Your Projects Successfully with Microsoft Project

Chapter Thirteen

Managing Project Resources

Pull the string, and it will follow wherever you wish. Push it, and it will go nowhere at all.

— *Dwight Eisenhower*

Managing a project team is a tough job. The people who work on your project usually report to other managers who have more control over their salaries and chances for promotion. Although you work with team members for relatively short periods of time, to optimize their performance, you must work with them as if you've known them for years. Furthermore, you must lead the group to turn it into a team in more than just name.

Managing people is a skill that's enhanced over time, but never truly mastered, so this chapter introduces a few approaches to managing people on a project. What's important is that there's no one way to manage team members. Your goal should be to continually increase your repertoire of people skills.

Part of managing people is evaluating their performance. In this chapter, you'll learn how to review resource progress in Microsoft Project. More important, you'll also learn about performance factors that no software program can help with.

Motivating Project Resources

A leader is best when people barely know he exists, not so good when people obey and acclaim him, worse when they despise him. But of a good leader who talks little when his work is done, his aim fulfilled, they will say: We did it ourselves.

— Lao-tzu

Demanding, dictating, wresting, or wringing work out of people might deliver results initially. Over the long term, your project performance will deteriorate along with your relationships with your team members. Leading people is a big part of a project manager's job. Ideally, you'll entice them to do their best without making them cringe every time they see you. Building good relationships is especially important in today's business world, as team members try to juggle multiple projects in addition to day-to-day responsibilities. Team members are more responsive to project managers who get to know them and respect their expertise and time.

The challenge, of course, is determining how to get the best out of each person on the team, because each one is different. Some people want nothing more than to develop an elegant solution to a problem. To them, the achievement is its own reward. Others might want interesting work, recognition, advancement, or personal and professional growth. Still others might crave more tangible results: more money, more vacation, fewer hours

Part Three:
Carrying Out a
Project

On Time! On Track! On Target! Managing Your Projects Successfully with Microsoft Project

at the office, less stress, or never ever having to speak in public.

Sitting in your office, collecting status from team members and assembling it into project status reports will not tell you what's really going on in your project. You need to get out and talk to people. Much of your job is about communicating *effectively* and that can change depending on who you're talking to. Here are some guidelines for developing strong working relationships with most, if not all, people who work, albeit temporarily, as part of your project team.

- **Clearly delineate and communicate roles and responsibilities**   If you've ever dodged left and right as you and someone else try to get out of each other's way, you know that deciding what you're going to do and communicating it clearly can solve a lot of problems. The same approach is equally effective for working with project team members. Work flows more smoothly and relationships are stronger when team members know what *they* are supposed to do, as well as what *you*, the project manager, do. For example, change requests can turn scope creep into a scheduling scramble if team members speak directly to the customer and make changes without telling you. But if team members know that they are supposed to report change requests to the person in charge of the change management process (see Chapter 15, "Managing Project Changes"), you can manage change requests and work with the customer to handle them properly. At the same time, team members need to know that they are still part of the change management process, because they must estimate the effect of requested changes and estimate the time it will take to complete them.

  Similar to building a responsibility matrix with stakeholders (see "The Responsibility Matrix" on page 105), discussing roles and responsibilities with team members helps identify points on which you disagree. There's no guarantee that you can resolve those disagreements, but knowing that they're there helps you work around them.

  Tip   Many team members have no idea what a project manager does or, worse, remember only what the last project manager did—good or bad. By explaining your role to team members and how you plan to help them accomplish their work, you begin to build trust and respect.

- **Assign specific and attainable goals**   Whether you assign a single work package to people or assign a major section of a project to a team leader to manage, specific goals give them a target on which to focus. Telling a group to develop an eye-catching advertisement won't help if the group doesn't know the product being advertised or the audience you're trying to reach. Assigning specific goals isn't difficult, because they're much like project plans in miniature; they have their own objectives, completion criteria, due dates, and budgets.

Important   Don't be afraid to set challenging (yet attainable) goals for your people. Objectives that are *too* easy to accomplish can make team members think you doubt their capabilities. Eventually, thoughts like those become self-fulfilling prophecies, as demoralized team members do less or deliver lower-quality work. On the other hand, if you find out what your team members like to do and give them tasks that fit their work preferences, you barely have to direct them at all.

- **Provide the tools people need to do their jobs**   Trying to perform surgery with a butter knife wouldn't be pleasant for a doctor *or* a patient. Part of your job is to ensure that team members have what they need to do their work, whether that's the proper equipment, enough time, or a sufficient budget.

- **Treat team members as valued and important individuals**   There are a few people who are driven from within and don't need motivation from others, but most people want to know that they are of value to the project. Of course, you can tell people directly that they're important, but simply treating them with respect is a more sincere and powerful approach. For example, saying "thank you" is simple, quick, and incredibly effective.

Warning   In contrast, treating people as if they are incompetent or untrustworthy is a fast track to poor project relationships. And bureaucratic procedures with unending forms, reports, checkpoints, evaluations, and rules tend to convey that message. One challenge to project management is balancing your need for information with team members' needs to do their work and feel as if they are in control of their assignments.

- **Remove obstacles**   Suppose your project is falling behind schedule, tasks are taking too long, or quality is an issue. You might wonder if

Part Three:
Carrying Out a
Project

On Time! On Track! On Target! Managing Your Projects Successfully with Microsoft Project

team members are shirking their responsibilities, but chances are good that obstacles are getting in the way. The best way to uncover obstacles is to ask team members what's standing in their way. Then, go to work removing those hurdles so that team members can focus on their jobs.

- **Provide frequent feedback**   Your team members are people. Nonetheless, some techniques that work for training children are equally effective for helping team members succeed. Give people positive reinforcement as soon as they do something good. And if they do something wrong, quickly explain the problem and how they can perform better in the future. By providing feedback to people quickly, they can use it immediately to improve or continue their performance.

- **Be honest**   Face it. From time to time, getting project work done isn't fun—or optional. If you need results from team members, tell them the truth. At the same time, you can use the opportunity to also remind them that you have faith in their abilities. People respond more favorably when they know *why* you're asking for them to push. For example, "Getting this project done in one more month is clearly a challenge, but I know that we can do it. Our customer benefits from reduced inventory and faster payments. I will do everything I can to provide what you need to meet this goal. Just ask."

- **Have fun**   Project work can become very serious, so finding ways to have fun while meeting project goals is a great morale booster. Small gestures can mean a lot, such as hanging a miner's helmet on the wall of the tester who found the most interesting defect the past week. Casual competitions are another approach. Because

Best Practices

Obstacles aren't necessarily easy to eliminate. You might have to find a way to obtain equipment that the accounting department cut from the budget, protect team members from a salesperson who wants to know every five minutes when the product will ship, or streamline administrative procedures that are consuming a few hours of each workday.

You can't remove every barrier that stops team members' progress. The important point is that your team members know that you're there to help if they run into trouble.

One common problem is that people are asked to work on several projects at the same time without any guidance on project priority from management. Don't let your team members flounder over which task to do first or struggle to complete all project tasks at once. As project manager, investigate the priorities of different projects and urge management to formally communicate those priorities.

Paying attention to and acting on team members' requests doesn't only remove the obstacles in their way. You also gain team members' gratitude and support, which comes in handy when you do have to ask for favors.

project teams enjoy turning the tables on managers, prizes that involve managers making fun of themselves are extremely popular. For example, if someone finds that the project manager made an error, a fun and harmless way to relieve stress is to have the entire project team bombard the project manager with marshmallows for 30 seconds as "punishment."

- ■ **Enable excellence** Everything might be going well, but why not strive to do even better? Besides asking about obstacles in people's way, ask team members what you can do to help them excel.

Tip As you get to know team members, make a point of finding out what they enjoy doing. If you can assign them the type of work they like, they'll work harder and enjoy it more. For example, ask people who love to fix things to troubleshoot problems.

Developing a Team

Teams don't start out as well-oiled machines. Nor do they become effective by accident. Teams of people mature just as individuals gain wisdom and better judgment over the years. And, yes, teams go through awkward adolescent stages on their way to high performance. You can choose from several models of team behavior, such as Bruce Tuckman's "Forming, Storming, Norming, and Performing," but the models all describe similar stages. Typically, teams mature over time; they increase their abilities as relationships develop between team members; and leaders of teams must adjust their leadership style as their teams move through each stage.

Teams that deliver the highest performance tend to be small groups of people, so you shouldn't expect an entire project team to become a close-knit group. Nonetheless, as a project manager, you can help your team become more effective by understanding each stage of team behavior and changing how you interact with the team as it matures. For example, giving inexperienced team members detailed task instructions is a good idea, but the reaction when you give an expert the same directions will be totally and unpleasantly different. Here is an introduction to the stages using Bruce Tuckman's nomenclature and the most effective leadership style for each:

- ■ **Forming** During the forming stage, teams aren't yet teams, so they rely on the leader for direction. The team members haven't sorted out their roles and responsibilities with each other and often don't agree on their goals as a team. As the leader, you must define the goals

Part Three:
Carrying Out a
Project

On Time! On Track! On Target! Managing Your Projects Successfully with Microsoft Project

clearly, direct the team members, and answer their questions about what they are supposed to do and how they fit into the big picture of the project. What's more, forming teams resist authority, so you can expect them to challenge your leadership and the guidelines you've provided.

■ **Storming** Many situations have to get worse before they can get better and team performance is one of them. As team members establish their relationships with other team members, you can expect some power struggles over who does what. As the leader, your authority is a target for challenges from members. Factions often form within the group, which makes decisions difficult to reach. However, the struggles and disagreements mean discussion and that communication helps the group clarify its purpose. However, if the team begins storming over issues not related to the project at hand, you, as project manager, must help them focus on more productive discussions. The tension and emotions are distracting, so the leader must coach the team to focus on its purpose and objectives. Furthermore, the leader must help the team reach decisions—and compromises, if necessary.

■ **Norming** When the storm quiets down, you'll find that the team is finally a team. The team members understand the purpose of the group and their roles and responsibilities in achieving the team objectives. The team makes major decisions while leaving smaller decisions to individuals or subgroups. The team continues to grow by refining how the group works together and by having fun together. At this point, you, as the leader, can back off and delegate some of the leadership to the team. Your role becomes facilitation—someone who takes action only if the

Best Practices

Many teams reach the norming phase, but the leap to a performing team is a big one. Depending on your generation, you might think of the Harlem Globetrotters, the Blue Angels, Cirque du Soleil troupes, or other groups that perform at a level of perfection that's hard to believe. Leaders don't take an active role within these performance teams, but they can engender their development.

To achieve high performance, teams need two ingredients that only management can provide:

■ **A direction or challenge** Teams reach a high level of performance in part by shaping their purpose, which is a direct response to a challenge or opportunity that the team receives from the project manager, project sponsor, or customer.

■ **Specific performance goals** Similar to individuals, teams thrive when they receive specific goals that are challenging, but attainable. Challenging goals are what pushes a team to increase its performance. Otherwise, any team at the norming level will do.

team requests it or gently guides the team if it veers off on an inappropriate tangent.

- ■ **Performing** A team at this level has a clear vision of what it is doing and why, so it has little need for a leader. In fact, the team leads itself, so you simply delegate tasks or subprojects to the team and let it work out how best to meet your criteria. Although disagreements don't disappear, the team can resolve them effectively and even modify the team processes or relationships to improve team performance.

Evaluating People's Performance

Evaluating people's performance is more challenging than evaluating the performance of a project, because human performance is not always easy to quantify. For example, do people work well with others on the team? Do they build a level of synergy with other team members that enhances the performance of the entire team? Or, do they disrupt the team by complaining or not delivering what they're supposed to? This section describes what you can do to evaluate the qualitative performance of people on projects and how to handle problems if they arise. It also provides a few techniques for reviewing people's performance using Project.

Watching for People's Performance

Management by walking around is the best way to see how people are performing on your project. Team members don't necessarily announce that they have problems with other people and, when the project is going well, they often simply keep their heads down and pump out work. You can tell a lot just by talking to team members. With a few insightful and open-ended questions (see "Initiate Discussion with Open-Ended Questions," page 321), you can learn about what's going well and what could be better. And reading between the lines in those responses, you might also learn about people who are doing well or not so well. Symptoms vary with the people on the project. Problems can lead to more bickering than usual, but an unusual silence can be the indicator as well.

Status meetings and lessons learned sessions (see "Collecting Lessons Learned," page 318) provide additional opportunities for learning about performance. The mood of the group, people joking with each other, strained discussion, and other interaction can tell you how work is going.

Part Three:
Carrying Out a
Project

On Time! On Track! On Target! Managing Your Projects Successfully with Microsoft Project

> **Important** Identifying and resolving issues is much easier when you focus on improvement, not who's to blame. See "Getting Better, Not Blamed" on page 323 for some techniques that can help keep a positive focus.

What to Do with Problem People

Despite all your efforts to build an effective project team, some people problems are bound to arise. Team members might not deliver what they're supposed to, might not get along with other members of the team, and could exhibit any of an almost infinite variety of performance-deteriorating behaviors. As you learned in "Motivating Project Resources" on page 209, attending to the problem quickly is crucial. In many cases, people don't understand what you expect of them or don't realize the effect their actions have on others. You can often resolve these issues with a clear, yet tactful, discussion.

The first step is determining whether people have the capability to perform satisfactorily. Are they qualified for their assignments? If not, you have to decide whether your project can handle the additional time, additional cost, or reduced quality that the resources can deliver. (Of course, you must review your work packages and communication with functional managers to ensure that you were clear about assignments and skills you needed.) If your project can't afford the burden of someone who doesn't have the qualifications you need, you must work with the functional manager to transfer the person to a more suitable assignment and get someone else for your project. If transferring the person isn't possible, you must work with stakeholders to reset their expectations for cost, quality, or schedule. Another option is to assess the impact of dismissing team members and *not* replacing them. Although this option puts a burden on other team members and you, it may be easi?er than working with team members who aren't qualified for their assignments.

If people's qualifications are acceptable, the next step is determining whether they want to perform. If someone *doesn't* want to meet your expectations—of productivity, quality, team spirit, attitude, or whatever else—it isn't fair to the rest of the team to keep that person on board. Poor performance and negative attitudes can be disruptive to both the team and your project. When people don't want to perform, you must work with the functional manager, project sponsor, and perhaps the human resources department to decide what to do and how to proceed.

> **Warning**   Solving people problems can require documentation. If you
> plan to ask the project sponsor for help, be prepared to provide a brief
> summary of the problem, what you've tried, and what you recommend. If
> the problem is more severe and could lead to dismissal, the human
> resources department can tell you and the functional manager the steps
> you must perform.

Reviewing People's Performance Compared to the Plan

In addition to task filters, Project includes several built-in resource filters for finding assignments that aren't sticking to your plan. However, these filters can't pinpoint schedule problems due to resource assignments. For example, a resource filter can show assignments that are scheduled to finish later than you planned, but it can't tell if the delay is due to the resource's productivity, the resource not being available to work on the task as much as you estimated, or that the task itself started late.

A better way to look for resources who might need help is to use the Overbudget Resources report. This report shows resources whose actual costs on their assignments exceed the baseline costs and sorts the report with the highest variances first, as shown in Figure 13-1. Because you see overbudget costs by resource, you know that the person is spending more time than you budgeted. But you'll still have to talk to the person to unearth the real problem.

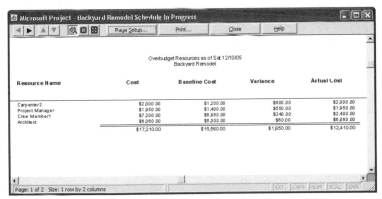

Figure 13-1   The Overbudget Resources report shows assignments that cost more than you planned, whether the problem is an optimistic task estimate or the productivity of the assigned resources.

Part Three:
Carrying Out a
Project

On Time! On Track! On Target! Managing Your Projects Successfully with Microsoft Project

Here are the steps for generating the Overbudget Resources report:

1. On the View menu, select Reports.

2. In the Reports dialog box, double-click Costs.

3. In the Cost Reports dialog box, select Overbudget Resources, and then click Select.

Tip   If you want to modify the Overbudget Resources report before you generate it, select Overbudget Resources and then click Edit. For example, you can choose a time frame in the Period list to show variances for days, weeks, months, the entire project, or several other time frames. To display different fields in the report, choose the table you want to apply in the Table list.

To apply resource filters, you must first display a resource-oriented view, such as Resource Usage. (On the View menu, choose Resource Usage.) Then, on the Formatting toolbar, choose the filter you want to apply in the Filter list. Here are some of the resource filters that help you evaluate progress by resource:

■ **Slipping Assignments**   This resource filter shows assignments in progress whose scheduled finish date is later than the baseline finish. Slipping assignments could indicate that the resource isn't making progress as quickly as you had planned. However, this filter doesn't check whether the task started on time, so the late finish might be due to a late start date, not the assigned resource's productivity or availability.

■ **Resources/Assignments With Overtime**   This filter shows assignments that include overtime hours, which might be due to resources trying to catch up on work. However, if you ask people to work overtime to meet deadlines, you'll see those assignments as well.

■ **Cost Overbudget**   Tasks that are taking longer than planned or requiring more work hours than you estimated often lead to costs higher than the baseline cost. This filter shows any assignments in which scheduled cost is greater than baseline cost (and a baseline cost exists). Although the problem might lie with your estimate, you can review these assignments to see whether the assigned resources need help.

In Summary

Managing the team members for a project is challenging for several reasons. People report to other managers, so you must share management responsibilities with someone else. In addition, you work with people for short periods of time. Finally, each person is different, so you must tune your techniques depending on who you're working with. You can use Project to gauge how people perform on delivering their assignments according to your plan. And you might use other tools to measure productivity. But evaluating people has more to do with understanding them and motivating them than it does with numbers.

Part Three:
Carrying Out a
Project

On Time! On Track! On Target! Managing Your Projects Successfully with Microsoft Project

Chapter Fourteen

Communicating Information

The greatest problem in communication is the illusion that it has been accomplished.

— *George Bernard Shaw*

As a project manager, you use tools such as a WBS, Gantt chart, and earned-value graph, but project management is mainly about communicating with people. Project communication is about ensuring that customers, stakeholders, and team members know what they need to do their jobs, whether you're trying to get stakeholders to agree on project objectives, telling team members about their assignments, or working with a group to resolve an issue that's delaying the project. But keeping everyone informed about project status is an important part of project communication, too.

You can spend years learning to communicate effectively. Ideally, what a project needs is effective communication between every person involved. An impossible goal? Yes, but you, as the project manager, can do a lot to improve communication on your projects. This chapter discusses methods for communicating information to people on the project. You'll learn about who needs information, what they usually need to know, when they need to know it, and the best way to get it to them—which sums up the purpose and contents of a project communication plan, a project planning document that describes the tools and techniques you will use to communicate on your project. But you'll also learn how to communicate effectively, whether you're talking to people, running meetings, authoring reports, or sending e-mail.

Knowledge Is Power

Many people think that the person with the knowledge is the one who has the power. For projects, power comes from everyone being in the know. Here are a few ways that good communication contributes to project success:

- **Focus on the goal**   After stakeholders define the problem that a project is supposed to solve and what constitutes success, they must communicate these items to the entire project team to gain their support and help them understand what they are supposed to do.

- **Better decisions**   Everyone on a project—from the sponsor to individual team members—needs information to make good decisions. With project information readily available, people can make the right choices, take advantage of opportunities, and fend off problems.

- **Increased productivity**   Team members can get more done if they have the information they need or know how to find it easily. By communicating effectively, you can ensure that team members are doing the right work the right way. To the contrary, when communication is

Part Three:
Carrying Out a
Project

On Time! On Track! On Target! Managing Your Projects Successfully with Microsoft Project

lacking or unclear, time spent delivering the wrong results or duplicating effort hurts the project schedule, budget, and team morale.

- **Fewer errors**   Team members make fewer mistakes, and if problems do arise, team members can identify and fix them quickly.

- **Better project management**   As a project manager, you have a selfish reason for sharing information—your job is easier. When people don't know what's going on, they usually ask questions—often with a great deal of impatience and at the worst possible moment. The other reaction to not knowing is not acting; people sometimes ignore tasks if they aren't sure what they should do and don't want to ask. By distributing the information that people need to know *before* they need to know it, you can spend more time proactively managing your projects.

- **Continuous improvement**   Communication doesn't stop at the end of a project. By documenting information about completed projects, you can provide guidelines for project teams to follow on future projects (see Chapter 19, "Learning Lessons").

- **Enhancing collaboration**   Sharing information helps build teamwork and increases people's satisfaction with their work.

The Communication Plan

For small projects, communication can be quite simple. Communication for the project of heading home after the holidays might be no more than "Call us when you get there." But good communication grows complex as the scope of the project increases, more people are involved, and teams are scattered around the world. For example, a conference call that includes people in Europe, Asia, and North America is going to keep someone up late and get someone else up early, and you don't want to make those decisions at the last minute. By planning your approach for communication in advance, you can provide the right information to the right people, at the right time, in the right format, and with the right emphasis. Your road map is the project *communication plan,* illustrated by the first page of a sample communication plan in Figure 14-1. This section describes the components of a communication plan, how you choose the communication methods appropriate for your project, and how to create a communication plan.

---

1. Communication Plan

This communication plan describes the approach for communicating and collaborating on the Fabrication Design System project. The plan identifies the audiences for the project, the information to communicate, and the communication methods to use. This plan can help facilitate effective and coordinated communication between all project audiences.

Project Audiences

Because of the short schedule and limited budget for the Fabrication Design System, the communication plan includes communication to four main audiences:

- The *Project team* includes the stakeholders and all people assigned to work on the project.
- *Fabrikam, Inc., stakeholders* are the management stakeholders employed by Fabrikam, Inc.
- *Internal Fabrikam, Inc.,* represents all Fabrikam, Inc., employees.
- *Vendors* are the project contacts from the vendors who are working on the project.

Project Information

For this project, we have created six categories of information to simplify project communication:

- *Approval* information represents documents, change requests, budget requests, or project deliverables that require stakeholder approval.
- *Stakeholder project status* includes high-level summaries of completed milestones, major accomplishments, current schedule and budget performance, and any issues or risks that have occurred.
- *Detailed project status* includes completed and in progress work packages, team accomplishments, issues that need resolution, and lessons learned.
- *Project reference* represents all project documents and document-based deliverables.
- *Collaboration* information includes change requests, issues, risks, and lessons learned.
- *Publicity* represents high-level overviews and status.

Communication Methods

Because of the small Fabrication Design System team, we will use only four methods of communication:

- *E-mail* is the preferred method for sending information that people are supposed to act on, whether they are to approve documents or begin work on an assignment.
- *Voice mail* is a secondary method for requesting action.
- *Meetings* will be kept to a minimum.
- The *SharePoint Web site* contains project reference information.

Figure 14-1   A communication plan can be as simple or as sophisticated as your project requires to deliver information to the people who need it.

A sample communication plan, *OnTime_Communication_Plan.doc*, is available in the *Sample Documents* folder on the companion CD.

Who Needs to Know?

The first step to creating a communication plan is identifying who needs to know something about the project. Stakeholders are obvious audiences for project communications, but other groups often need—or want—project

Part Three:
Carrying Out a
Project

On Time! On Track! On Target! Managing Your Projects Successfully with Microsoft Project

information. Here are some typical audiences, both stakeholders and ancillary groups, you might include in a communication plan:

■ *The project team* is the core of communication. Team members work on the project every day. They need to know what's going on with the project, but they also contribute a lot of the information that you communicate to others.

■ *Management stakeholders* aren't dedicated to the project, but they make key decisions about it. Management stakeholders share similar needs for project communication and can include customers, the project sponsor, a steering committee or leadership team, members of the change management board, functional managers, and so on.

> **Important**   *The customer* is part of the management stakeholder group, but often wants different information delivered in different ways.

■ *The project sponsor* is also part of the management stakeholder group, but is usually involved more intimately with the project. For example, you might send the project sponsor the same information that you provide to other management stakeholder groups, but also meet face to face for in-depth discussions.

■ *Supporting groups* might be involved in your project from time to time and need to know specific information. For example, sales and marketing might want to know what the product features are and when it'll be ready to sell. The legal department gets involved only to work on contracts or to review documents for legal issues. Other supporting groups include operations, manufacturing, IT, and other departments.

■ *External audiences* can be very involved in your project. For example, vendors, suppliers, partners, and the project managers who work for them can belong to your core team. However, you typically don't tell external audiences as much as you do internal team members. For example, if you're trying to resolve issues, you'd include external audiences in those discussions only if they are directly affected. Investors and regulatory agencies (such as the IRS or a public utility commission) might represent additional external audiences. For these audiences, the format and schedule of communication is often already specified, such as the financial statements that the SEC requires.

Warning It's better to send information to too many people than too few. Leaving out stakeholders can hurt your chances of success, particularly if the stakeholder you forget is a key decision maker for the project. As you build your communication plan, ask stakeholders and other groups you've identified as audiences if there's anyone else who needs to know something about your project.

What Do You Communicate to Audiences?

Sad but true, people hear only what they want to hear. Your customer might care deeply about the return on investment of the project, but using return on investment to inspire team members to complete a work package more quickly probably won't deliver the results you're hoping for. For each audience that you've identified, the next step is to determine what they *need* to know, what they *want* to know, and what information *you* want to tell them. For example, the customer, project sponsor, and management stakeholders need status reports, but they also want information about the project strategy and issues and risks that might affect the business objectives for the project. Functional managers need status information in order to plan their people's time.

Usually, you want to distribute some information that audiences don't think to ask for. For example, you communicate the benefits of your project, the mission statement, and its objectives to everyone involved, even though team members might *want* to know only what their task assignments are. For another example, if a project is going to change how processes in your organization are going to work, you can begin to tout the benefits of the changes.

Best Practices

As you develop your communication plan, keep these two guidelines in mind:

- *The audience gets what it wants.* Just as a Gantt chart might make perfect sense to you and not one whit to the customer, the methods of communication you choose must actually get the message through to your audience. And if that means you have to prepare a Microsoft PowerPoint presentation for the steering committee, a Microsoft Excel worksheet for the accounting department, a Microsoft Word document for project teams, and a Microsoft Windows SharePoint Services site for the developers, so be it. After all, your job as project manager is to make the project a success, and communicating information successfully is a big part of that.

- *Too much communication is as bad as not enough.* Telling people more than they need or want to know can give audiences the wrong impression, similar to strangers who want to show you their surgical scars. Some people might think you can't handle your job, but more likely and more dangerous, they'll simply start ignoring information that you send.

Part Three:
Carrying Out a
Project

On Time! On Track! On Target! Managing Your Projects Successfully with Microsoft Project

You can categorize project information in different ways. For example, you might categorize information based on what different groups need to know: planning, day-to-day detailed status, high-level status, and general information. You might also categorize information by whether it's required, desired, or merely for reference. This section describes information you typically communicate in projects and then categorizes it by the groups that use it.

Tip   Keep track of each type of information that you provide to each audience, because the distribution method and timetable you choose may vary based on the information. For example, you might distribute project status every week while the stakeholders want a thorough financial update once a month.

Types of Project Information

The information that you communicate varies depending on whether you're planning, executing, or closing the project. Here are types of project information that you distribute by phase in a project:

- **Project planning**   The components of the project plan (see "The Components of a Project Plan," page 50) help people involved with the project understand the purpose of the project and their roles in completing it successfully. From the project mission statement to the schedule and the communication plan, each component describes how you plan to run the project. Some audiences review planning documents in detail and approve them, whereas other groups use them simply as direction for the work they perform.

- **Project execution and control**   Once the plan is approved and you begin to execute that plan, people need to know the rules. You have to provide people with procedures, such as reporting time and expenses, requesting time off, escalating issues, and so on. For most of the project duration, people need to know the status of the project and what's planned for the near future.

  The status you provide varies by the needs of the audience. For example, the elegant programming shortcut that is helpful and fascinating to the development team would put management stakeholders to sleep. On the other hand, the financial measures that the management stakeholders can't live without would be equally boring to most technical folks.

- **Project closure**   You wrap up projects with reports that summarize the performance of the project (see "Project Closeout Reports," page 331).

- **Project publicity**   Regardless of the phase a project is in, you want to build enthusiasm and commitment for it. Publicizing a project early on (see "Kickoff Meetings," page 245) might include announcements in the company newsletter, contests to name the project, or road shows that describe the purpose and benefits of the project. During project execution, you might use a project newsletter to publicize accomplishments, host celebrations upon completion of significant milestones, or distribute pens or coffee cups emblazoned with the project logo. And nothing beats meeting stakeholders and team members one-on-one to build commitment.

Management Stakeholders

Management stakeholders, including the customer, project sponsor, and other high-level stakeholders, typically care about the overall business goals of a project. Early on, they evaluate the project plan to ensure that it meets their needs. During project execution, they frequently review performance, such as how much progress has been made, how much money has been spent, and the quality of the results that have been achieved. Most of the time, they don't want to know the details, although they will for significant issues, such as someone absconding with project funds.

Part Three:
Carrying Out a
Project

On Time! On Track! On Target! Managing Your Projects Successfully with Microsoft Project

Note As internal customers, company executives often require more detailed project information than external customers. They must evaluate project performance compared to the entire portfolio of the company's projects and business objectives.

Here is some of the information that management stakeholders want to receive:

- **The project plan** During planning, management stakeholders must ensure that the proposed plan satisfies their needs. Later, if requirements or criteria change, these stakeholders revisit the project plan while negotiating change orders, contract revisions, or modifications to the project goals.

- **Project status** Executive summaries of project status focus on high-level performance and accomplishments (see "Project Status Reports," page 249). Management stakeholders want to know about major milestones that have been completed, summaries of costs and schedule performance (the project is one month behind schedule and $20,000 over budget), and major issues and risks that could prevent the project from achieving its goals. If you are measuring other aspects of project performance, such as lines of code written or statistics about defects found and fixed, they want to know whether the metrics are good or bad and about the trends in performance.

- **Financial information** These stakeholders understand and care about the financial measures for projects, so they want to know the current financial results, including performance compared to the budget and other metrics, such as return on investment.

- **Change requests** Some management stakeholders need to know about change requests. For example, the customer, project sponsor, and members of the change management board must evaluate change requests to see whether they should be approved or rejected (see Chapter 15, "Managing Project Changes").

Tip Executives plan for the long term, so they also want to know what is in store for the project in the future. Is the project going to deliver on time and under budget? Will it deliver the financial results they want? Will it achieve its objectives? Or are changes necessary?

Functional Managers

Functional managers usually provide the people who perform the project work, so they need to see project plans to understand the skills required, to know when their people are needed, and to be aware of any constraints, such as cost or availability. Once people are working on assignments, functional managers want to know how much longer those people are needed or might ask if they can substitute someone else.

Here is typical information you might communicate to functional managers:

- **The project plan**   During planning, functional managers must understand the big picture of the project, but they focus on work packages, the skills needed, and when assignments are scheduled to occur.

- **Project status**   Functional managers need to know when their people will be done with their assignments, so they can line up more work for them in the future.

Team Members

Initially, team members must understand the work they are supposed to perform as well as how that work fits into the big picture of the project. This information helps them make good decisions in their day-to-day work. As work progresses on the project, team members need to know detailed status about completed work and the work that's scheduled for them in the near future. Here are some types of information that team members need:

- **Assignments**   Team members want to know what work they are supposed to do and when.

- **Status**   They also need to know the status of their work and related tasks. With status updates, team members can collaborate with their colleagues and help devise solutions to problems.

- **Issues**   Team members need to know about issues that might affect them, proposed solutions, and how closed issues were resolved.

- **Lessons learned**   Team members can work more effectively if they can take advantage of tips, shortcuts, or practices to avoid.

- **Decisions**   Team members must know about any decisions that affect the direction or objectives of the project, so they can conform to the new guidelines.

Part Three:
Carrying Out a
Project

On Time! On Track! On Target! Managing Your Projects Successfully with Microsoft Project

What Communication Method Should You Use?

The last step to developing a communication plan is to determine the best methods for getting each type of information to your audiences. You must decide how often audiences need information, the best method for delivering information, and the best format in which to deliver it. For example, everyone involved in the project needs a project status report, which you distribute via e-mail to the entire team but review in a meeting with stakeholders. Your organization's executive team meets once a month and wants an executive summary of project status with emphasis on the budget and financial measures. The project sponsor prefers to meet in person to review status, issues, and risks. And team members have asked you to distribute the detailed status reports of team accomplishments every week.

Communication methods come in many guises and each one has its advantages and disadvantages. For example, face-to-face communication is best for delicate discussions or to brainstorm solutions. Conference calls and e-mail come in handy for teams that are distributed geographically. Documents in paper or electronic format are ideal for communicating large amounts of information that require study.

Here are some considerations for communication methods:

- *Status reports* can contain different types of information depending on the audience. Moreover, whether you produce paper or electronic status reports depends on the audience as well. Sending status reports to people makes it easy for them to read the information, and they can choose to scan the reports for pertinent topics—or ignore them if time is at a premium.

Important   When you distribute documents electronically, you have to consider the software formats that your audiences can read. For example, if some team members have older versions of Word, you might choose to distribute reports in Adobe Acrobat format. Don't forget that most people in your audiences won't have Microsoft Project, so you should save Gantt Charts and other Project views as pictures or Adobe Acrobat files.

- *Meetings* can vary from one-time kickoff meetings to daily meetings of small groups of team members, weekly or monthly executive updates, or occasional all-hands meetings (see "Meetings That Work," page 240). Although you can't guarantee that people will pay attention in a meeting, getting people in the same room is ideal for discussions, brainstorming, and decision making.

You have options for how you deliver information in face-to-face meetings. For example, an executive update meeting might start with a presentation of project status followed by an energetic discussion. Other meetings, such as lessons learned sessions, can be completely dedicated to group discussion.

- *Conference calls* are an option for meetings when people are distributed geographically; however, they are not ideal if you are working through issues or dealing with a team that is "storming" (see "Developing a Team," page 213). In situations in which tension is high, a video-conference or Microsoft Office LiveMeeting provides more effective interaction.

- *Sending documents* to people is preferable if you want the recipients to take action. For example, if you want stakeholders to review and approve your project plan, you should send the plan to them for review. However, the best way to obtain approval and signatures is to hold a meeting.

- *Storing documents* is a reasonable solution for information that only some people need only some of the time. For example, you can store any document-based deliverables, such as the current project plan, requirements, specifications, change requests, and other project

Resolution Is What's Important

If you want someone to do something, sending an e-mail or leaving a voice message is *not* the same as getting something done. If you have an issue that's delaying your project, you can't afford to wait until the person you contacted decides to act. The most effective way to obtain a response to a request is to tell people up front what you want them to do and when. For example, an e-mail that scrolls for pages before you get to the point will be deleted long before the recipient knows what you're asking for. Put requests in the first paragraph of an e-mail, memo, or other written communication. State requests in the first sentence of voice messages. You can follow up with the whys and hows after that.

After you've sent requests for action, you must follow up if you don't receive a response when you expect. If a return e-mail doesn't arrive, follow up with another e-mail or a telephone call. (E-mail gets caught in spam filters all the time, so don't begin your follow-up with an accusation.) If a voice message goes unanswered, find the person or someone else who can help.

Some folks don't respond no matter what you do. One way to coax responses from people who do that is to tell them what you plan to do if you don't hear from them by a specific time or day. If your contingency plan is something you know they don't want, you're almost guaranteed to receive a response when you need it. For example, "Hi, Dale. I really need the graphic for the brochure by tomorrow morning at 9 A.M. If I don't have it by then, I'm going to use the photograph of the meerkat. Thanks for your help." If someone still doesn't respond, diplomatically escalate your request. If you do ask for help, it's a good idea to tell the managers you ask what you would like them to do. Otherwise, they might apply more pressure than you intended. Of course, you must be willing to go with the meerkat if you still don't get a response.

Part Three:
Carrying Out a
Project

On Time! On Track! On Target! Managing Your Projects Successfully with Microsoft Project

information in a shared folder, on a Web page, or in a shared work-space (see "Ways to Build a Project Archive," page 345). People who need the information can retrieve it when they need it.

■ *Newsletters and e-mail distribution lists* work well for announcements and other information you want to disseminate to broad audiences. You can distribute information to many people without much effort, but the readers can skip the message if it doesn't apply to them.

When you choose communication options, opt for the ones that get infor-mation to audiences with the least amount of effort. For example, don't send hard copies of status reports if everyone on the project checks e-mail every day. An e-mail distribution list is much easier than printing and dis-tributing dozens of hard-copy memos. However, for some information, such as reports that government agencies require, you have to use their format and transmission methods.

Tip Although the ideal approach is to provide every audience with exactly what they want, some communication methods can be extraordi-narily time-consuming. If communication demands threaten to consume every workday, try suggesting to stakeholders alternatives that require less time.

Building a Communication Plan

The communication plan begins with sections that list the audiences for the project, the information you plan to communicate, how you will compile the information, and the communication methods you plan to use. But the heart of the communication plan is a matrix that shows how you plan to communicate information to each project audience, as illustrated in Figure 14-2.

Tip Although the communication plan is often a part of the project plan, it's a good idea to publish the communication plan as a stand-alone docu-ment. That makes it easy to keep a copy handy for quick reference.

The Communication Matrix

The communication matrix shows how we plan to communicate information to the project audiences. The matrix also includes the frequency of communication for different types of information and the method of communication.

Given the small size of the team on this project, communication is relatively simple. Team members will copy all e-mail to the entire team. The project manager will document telephone calls and meetings and post notes to a shared workspace. The project manager will maintain a folder in Microsoft Office Outlook for all e-mail correspondence. In addition to the project deliverables, Contoso, Ltd., will distribute biweekly status reports to the project team. The status reports will cover the previous two weeks and include tasks completed, tasks in progress with percent completed, upcoming tasks, copies of the current issues list, assignment list, defect list, and report of earned value against the project baseline.

Audience	Information	Method	Frequency
Project team	Detailed project status	E-mail	Weekly
Project team	Collaboration	E-mail	As required
Project team	Collaboration	Meeting	Every other week
Fabrikam, Inc. stakeholders	Approval	E-mail/voice mail	As required
Fabrikam, Inc. stakeholders	Stakeholder project status	Meeting	Monthly
Vendors	Detailed project status	E-mail	Weekly
Vendors	Collaboration	E-mail	As required
Internal Fabrikam, Inc.	Publicity	E-mail	Weekly
Internal Fabrikam, Inc.	Publicity	Meeting	Quarterly

2

Figure 14-2 A matrix like the one included on page 2 of the sample communication plan is helpful for showing the information you communicate to audiences and the methods you plan to use.

Creating Communication Reminders

After you complete your communication plan and begin executing the project, days and weeks can pass before you realize it. As project manager, you can set up your communication tasks as milestones in Project so you see reminders about communication along with the rest of the tasks you review regularly. If you prefer more obvious reminders, you can create tasks with reminders in Microsoft Outlook so you don't forget to send important information to project audiences or schedule meetings.

Part Three:
Carrying Out a
Project

On Time! On Track! On Target! Managing Your Projects Successfully with Microsoft Project

In Outlook, you can set up recurring tasks for e-mail, reports, and regularly scheduled meetings. In fact, you can send meeting requests to attendees to schedule meetings and keep track of who has accepted and who can't attend.

Here are the steps for creating a communication reminder:

1. In Outlook, on the File menu, point to New, and then choose Task.

2. In the Untitled – Task dialog box, in the Subject text box, type the name of the communication task, such as "Prepare stakeholder status report."

3. On the toolbar, click Recurrence.

4. In the Task Recurrence dialog box, choose the option for the time period. For example, to set up a status report that you send every other week, select Weekly.

5. In the Recur Every . . . Week(s) On text box, type the number of periods between each occurrence. For example, for every other week, type **2**.

6. Select the check box for the day of the week on which you perform the task.

7. In the Range Of Recurrence section, you can keep the No End Date option selected to receive reminders until you decide to delete the task. If you're certain that the project will end when you expect, you can choose either the End After . . . Occurrences option when you know the number of occurrences or the End By option when you know the last date for the task to occur.

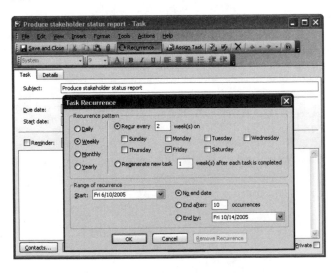

8. Click OK to close the Task Recurrence dialog box. Click Save And Close to save the recurring task.

Guidelines for Good Communication

Most conversations are simply monologues delivered in the presence of a witness.

— Margaret Miller

You listen to team members explain something and you answer the question that they ask only to have them blurt out in disgust, "You just don't understand!" Years ago, you learned to pronounce words and found out what they meant. You learned how to string them together into sentences, written and spoken. And you learned how to recognize the words that other people say or write. So, why don't you understand? For that matter, why does everyone have so many problems with miscommunication? The answer is that most people aren't taught to communicate effectively.

What Is Communication?

Communication is actually a *two-way* process with information successfully passing from one person to another. Effective communication entails several achievements, each one more useful—and more difficult—than the last. If you're having a problem with communication, review these steps to see where the breakdown might be.

- *Transmitting information* is the first and easiest step. Speaking to someone, sending a letter or an e-mail, and folding your arms over your chest while scowling all represent transmitting information. But, similar to the television broadcasts we've transmitted into space, there's no guarantee that someone hears your speech or reads your message. Recipients can block out what you say or delete your e-mail messages without reading them.

- *Receiving information* is the next step after transmitting but it still doesn't guarantee communication. Someone can play a voice mail or open an e-mail, which is, in principle, receiving information. After all, a read receipt in Outlook can confirm that someone received and opened your e-mail message. But the person still might delete the e-mail without reading the words.

Part Three:
Carrying Out a
Project

On Time! On Track! On Target! Managing Your Projects Successfully with Microsoft Project

- *Understanding the message* is the first step that represents communication and it can be a big challenge, as illustrated here in Abbott and Costello's famous give-and-take about baseball players:

Costello:	*Well then who's on first?*
Abbott:	*Yes.*
Costello:	*I mean the fellow's name.*
Abbott:	*Who.*
Costello:	*The guy on first.*
Abbott:	*Who.*
Costello:	*The first baseman.*
Abbott:	*Who.*
Costello:	*The guy playing...*
Abbott:	*Who is on first!*
Costello:	*I'm asking YOU who's on first.*
Abbott:	*That's the man's name.*
Costello:	*That's who's name?*
Abbott:	*Yes.*
Costello:	*Well go ahead and tell me.*
Abbott:	*That's it.*
Costello:	*That's who?*
Abbott:	*Yes.*

  In a *successful* communication, someone transmits a message and someone else receives the message *and understands* its contents. Understanding what someone else is trying to convey can involve a lot more than grasping the meaning of their words. You might have to learn something new, interpret the hidden meanings in messages, or ask questions to clarify points that aren't clear to you.

- *Obtaining agreement* is the next step toward effective communication. If you ask the project steering committee for more money and its members say no, they've understood your message, but they don't agree with it. In order to turn communication into decisions and results, you must obtain agreement from the other party. Similar to understanding, obtaining agreement can be a complicated undertaking. Negotiation, compromise, collaboration, and many other approaches all strive to reach some kind of agreement so that work can continue.

- *Acting on communication* is nirvana. In project management, you communicate to move your project to completion. Every communication is about getting something to happen. For example, suppose the project steering committee tells you that you can have more money, but it never gives the accounting department the approval to disburse the money. You obtained agreement but still didn't get the money you needed.

How to Get Messages Through

Diplomacy is the art of letting someone have your way.

— *Daniele Vare*

If you are trying to make a point or convince someone else to do something, the responsibility for communicating well is yours alone. Of course, communication is easier if the other person cooperates. But the hard truth is no one else cares as much about what you want than you. Here are some guidelines for getting your messages through to your audience:

■ **Talk in the audience's terms**
Stephen Covey describes this approach as "Seek first to understand." If you want to convince others to see as you do or to do what you want, you must first understand what's important to them and what they are concerned about. Only then will you have any chance of showing them why your request is important to them. For example, if you want functional managers to provide or keep people on your project, first understand the pressures that they face. If they're measured by the group's billable income, you might focus on how your project needs their people full time for several months. On the other hand, if you know that

the biggest challenge is a heavy workload, you can show the functional managers how you've planned the project to prevent overtime and last-minute deliveries.

Don't Assume Anything

Making assumptions is one of the most common communication problems. For example, you ask someone to prepare a report and, in your mind, you know that you want to see a summary of the labor costs broken down by employees and subcontractors and that you need it before a stakeholder meeting on Monday. In fact, you know what you want so clearly, you forget to tell the person these important details. If you stomp into his office on Friday demanding the report, you're likely to meet a blank stare or the question, "Well, when do you need it?" If you respond with a huffy "In two hours," you're still in trouble. If he didn't know when you needed the report, it's likely he doesn't know what should be in the report either.

The best approach for getting what you want is to clearly state what you expect and be proactive about confirming that the person understands your request. For instance, "Joe, what questions do you have about the report content?" or "Joe, tell me how you plan to present the information for the report." However, if a miscommunication occurs, it's more productive to start a conversation by clarifying the request instead of yelling or accusing the person of dropping the ball. "Have you completed the report I asked you to prepare? I need it today so we have time to revise it, if necessary, before the stakeholder meeting."

Part Three:
Carrying Out a
Project

On Time! On Track! On Target! Managing Your Projects Successfully with Microsoft Project

■ **Be accurate**   Check the accuracy of the information you are present-ing and avoid speculation or gossip at all cost. If you don't know an answer, don't bluff. Admit that you don't know, promise to find the answer, and then do as you promised. Credibility is much easier to keep than to gain back.

■ **Be persuasive**   Although accuracy is important, dry facts and pages of data will lose your audience faster than a fire alarm in the building. Try telling stories (relevant to the topic, of course) or using interesting analogies.

■ **Be brief**   No one enjoys a presentation that seems to go on forever. Take the time to prepare your message, so you can present it clearly and succinctly. Follow the lead of newspaper reporters and assume that no one will read past the first paragraph.

■ **Accentuate the positive**   Publicize project successes frequently and make sure that the customer, key stakeholders, managers, and project team hear about them. Back up project success stories with perfor-mance data.

On the other hand, if people make mistakes, work with them individ-ually to help them improve. Blaming others or targeting the person instead of the behavior ruins any chance of effective communication. If others on the team begin to blame others, jump in and redirect their conversation to the issue at hand (see "Accentuating the Positive," page 322). If *you* make a mistake, admit it, explain how you will pre-vent it in the future, and then do just that.

Tip   In "Motivating Project Resources" on page 209, you can learn more about how to communicate effectively with team members, including being clear about roles and responsibilities, and treating people with respect.

You might be forgiven for poor or inappropriate communications, but your message will never be forgotten. Before you communicate, consult the fol-lowing checklist to see whether you need to say anything at all, and if you do, whether the message you're sending will produce a positive result:

■ Is my message necessary?

■ Is my message true?

■ Is my message considerate?

■ Is my message better than no message at all?

Learning to Listen

Because communication is a two-way process, listening to the messages you receive is as important as sending your own. Unfortunately, hearing and listening are two very different things. Your ears might sense the sound waves from your team members talking, but without your brain listening to the message, you'll have no idea how to respond to their questions. Here are some suggestions for improving your listening skills:

■ **Give your full attention to the speaker** As a project manager, you've learned to work on multiple tasks at once. However, when you're meeting with someone or talking to them on the phone, you must switch gears and give them your undivided attention. Try to meet in a quiet place and turn off your cell phone or pager. (Taking calls in the middle of meetings doesn't demonstrate importance—only rudeness.)

Tip If someone interrupts a meeting with you, say something like "Well, I assume the meeting is over, so I'm going to get back to work." The person will either confirm your statement or refocus his attention on you.

■ **Listen for what is communicated without being spoken** Only a small percentage of meaning is in the words that are spoken. In fact, facial expressions convey the majority of a message, and the *way* words are said contributes almost all the rest. For this reason, you must focus even more on telephone calls even though the temptation is to work on other tasks at the same time, because the other person can't see you.

■ **Keep an open mind** If you enter a conversation with preconceived notions and predetermined responses, there's little point in the discussion, because you've already made up your mind. Concentrate on what other people have to say and make your decisions only after you've listened to their points.

Being Responsible

Some people feel as if they are controlled by events. Others make a point of choosing their responses. People who say "He doesn't understand," or "You didn't tell me to do that," push responsibility for their action (or inaction) onto someone else. People who accept responsibility for their actions say instead "I'm not making myself clear," or "I forgot to ask about that."

As a project manager, choosing your responses is an important part of dealing with the challenges you face every day. Eventually, it might even make you a little more comfortable in uncomfortable situations. If you tend to blame others for your choices, you must learn to accept responsibility for your actions. The easiest way to recast your comments is to start your sentences with "I" and complete them with what you can do to improve the situation.

Part Three:
Carrying Out a
Project

On Time! On Track! On Target! Managing Your Projects Successfully with Microsoft Project

■ **Repeat or paraphrase what you have heard**   The best way to acknowledge that you've listened is by repeating what the other person has said. If you put it into your own words, you can demonstrate that you listened and that you understand. In the worst case, you give the other person a chance to correct any misunderstanding you might have.

Tip   Body language says a lot. If you meet with people face-to-face, make eye contact and avoid distracting habits, such as yawning and fidgeting.

Meetings That Work

Many team members dread meetings, and for good reason. Regularly scheduled meetings that occur without a specific purpose or framework can be boring wastes of time. Pointless meetings drive people to distraction and eventually they look for any excuse to miss the meetings you schedule. What's more, meetings are extraordinarily expensive in time and cost. A status meeting for a team of 12 that lasts two hours costs your project three person-days and $1,200, assuming a $50 an hour labor rate. That's time that someone could spend completing a work package or money that could provide people with the equipment they need. However, if you take advantage of the interaction at meetings, you can resolve problems, make decisions, and share information more effectively than in any other method of communication. In short, if you're going to hold a meeting, make it count. This section provides some guidelines for getting the most out of your meetings and describes different types of project meetings you might schedule.

From Education to Communication

Communicating project information is a challenge when the rest of the organization is not familiar with project management practices. And if you're new to project management as well, communication practically comes to a halt. You probably know the drill. You're happily mixing chemicals in the lab and mostly not blowing things up when your boss tells you you're going to manage a project to expand the lab. Little do you know that without project management training or knowing how to communicate with project teams, you can watch something really explode—your project and the folks on the team.

You have to understand the benefits of the project management practices you use before you can convince team members, customers, functional managers, and anyone else involved in a project to follow your example. Of course, your first tentative explanations and answering the questions that arise can increase your understanding, too. As your knowledge of project management grows, so should the success of your projects. And that success provides even more fuel for convincing people in your organization to use project management.

Guidelines for Good Meetings

Productive meetings don't just happen. They require foresight, facilitation, and follow-up. The sections that follow describe the steps for running productive meetings.

Setting Up Meetings

If I am to speak ten minutes, I need a week for preparation; if fifteen minutes, three days; if half an hour, two days; if an hour, I am ready now.

— Woodrow Wilson

One reason for unproductive meetings is lack of preparation. If you don't know what you're trying to accomplish with a meeting and the attendees don't come prepared to discuss the topic, you can easily waste precious time with "What do you think?" and "Well, I don't know. What do you think?" Preparing for a meeting can be short, although prep time increases with the importance of the outcome. For example, a brief agenda might be sufficient for a team meeting to resolve a small issue that's come up, but you're likely to spend considerable time preparing concise yet persuasive handouts and presentations for a go/no-go meeting with stakeholders for a multimillion dollar project. Regardless of the detail involved in meeting setup, the steps are simple:

1. *Determine the purpose of the meeting.* What do you want to accomplish with the meeting? What results do you expect at the end of the meeting? For example, are you trying to obtain status information, a decision from stakeholders, or resolution to an issue?

2. *Identify the right attendees.* Meetings run longer than you plan if too many people attend. To the contrary, any time spent in a meeting with the *wrong* people is usually wasted. Based on the reason for the meeting, decide who must attend. (And if others show up when the meeting starts, politely shoo them away.)

3. *Develop the agenda.* Prepare an agenda that identifies the topics to discuss and the order in which you plan to discuss them. Estimate the time you'll need for each topic and add those estimates to the agenda. When you run the meeting, you can refer to the estimated times to cut short unproductive discussion. Or can you decide to defer a few topics to another meeting if the discussion is worthwhile. An agenda can also provide the first introduction of the ground rules you set for meetings, such as "Arrive on time" or "Keep it constructive."

Part Three:
Carrying Out a
Project

On Time! On Track! On Target! Managing Your Projects Successfully with Microsoft Project

A template for a lessons learned meeting agenda, *Lessons Learned Agenda.dot*, is available in the *Templates* folder on the companion CD.

4. *Schedule the meeting.* Choose a date and time that works for the attendees you need. Reserve the meeting location for the date and time you've selected. Then, send a meeting invitation with enough advance notice that the attendees can prepare for the meeting. For example, if you want to obtain approval for your project plan, stakeholders need enough time to fit a thorough review of the plan into their schedules.

5. *Prepare and distribute meeting materials.* At least a few days before the meeting, distribute any materials that attendees must review for the meeting. Prepare any other materials, such as PowerPoint presentations, that you plan to use during the meeting.

Running Meetings Well

Although preparation is a good start for a good meeting, a group of people will quickly go astray if you don't keep them focused on the meeting objective. And maintaining focus in a meeting requires a subtle yet valuable skill called facilitation. As project manager, you will often facilitate meetings. However, if you have many other duties in a meeting, such as presenting status or discussing issues with stakeholders, you might choose to assign someone else to facilitate the meeting.

The meeting facilitator ensures that the time spent in the meeting is effective. Here are some of the skills and techniques that facilitators use to keep meetings under control:

■ *Kick off the meeting* by identifying the purpose of the meeting, introducing the attendees, explaining the ground rules, and initiating the discussion. By taking the lead at the beginning of the meeting, people will be more likely to defer to you when you direct the discussion or move the meeting on to another topic. Selecting a position of authority in the room helps you to control the meeting without overt actions. For example, the head of the table, the middle of a long table, or in the front of the room are all positions of authority.

> **Tip** People might be familiar with the rules by which you run meetings. However, reviewing the rules at the beginning of the meeting Is always a good idea, just like paying attention to flight attendants explaining safety procedures—you never know when the rules will come in handy.

- *Direct the meeting* to maintain focus on the agenda topics. If the discussion begins to digress, quickly jump in to get it back on track. If the conversation is totally off the topic, say something like "We're supposed to be discussing the identified project risks. Let's get back to that." However, if the discussion is of value, you can interrupt and tell people that you've added the topic to the end of the agenda. Or, if the new topic is very valuable, you might ask the attendees if they want to modify the agenda to continue the discussion and eliminate another topic.

  Keep your eye on the agenda during the meeting. By following the agenda, you can ensure that you cover the important points, keep discussions on track, or make good decisions about changing the agenda to incorporate new topics.

> **Important** If it becomes clear that only a few people are involved in a discussion, you can keep the meeting on schedule and earn the never-ending gratitude of the other attendees by asking the people talking to finish their discussion after the meeting. For example, if two people disagree about the best way to resolve an issue, ask them to pick up their discussion after the meeting and notify you and the rest of the attendees of their decision.

- *Help people communicate* by promoting discussion, asking open-ended questions, making notes on a flip chart or white board, and suggesting methods for setting priorities. Guide the group through making decisions. For example, "Sara, you suggested that we fast-track the project. Does everyone else agree?" If the group members get stuck on a point or conflicts arise, step in to identify the problem and help them resolve their issues.

  You can also help people communicate by paraphrasing what they say. For instance, if someone is struggling to explain a point, jump in and describe the point in a different way. For example, "Meg, I think you're asking if the engineering team can deliver a prototype before the end of the year. Is that correct?"

Part Three:
Carrying Out a
Project

On Time! On Track! On Target! Managing Your Projects Successfully with Microsoft Project

Warning Silence is not the same as agreement. If a decision is required, be sure to get people's verbal agreement.

■ *Meeting notes* are an essential part of successful meetings. Have you ever attended a meeting in which dozens of action items were identified, but nary a one written down? The chances of those action items ever seeing action are slim. It's a tough job to facilitate a meeting, present information, and take notes at the same time, particularly if the meeting includes several people enthusiastic about their ideas.

As the facilitator, you use a white board to collect action items and commitments along with who's responsible for them. But a better solution, if it's feasible, is to appoint a scribe to take thorough notes. Someone who is familiar with the project and fast on a keyboard can take notes about discussions, disagreements, action items, and decisions.

Best Practices

To limit the length of meetings, start and end them on time. People tend to follow the unspoken lead of people in charge, so set an example and show up on time for the meetings you schedule. If people who aren't crucial to the discussion haven't shown up, you can start without them. But don't stop to review when they do appear, or you'll teach everyone that they can be late without penalty. A more lasting approach is to publicly call laggards to the meeting—a call from a speakerphone with all the attendees who are present chiming in is a powerful incentive to show up on time for the next meeting.

If crucial attendees aren't present, try to round them up quickly—say within 10 minutes. Longer than that, you're better off rescheduling the meeting.

During the meeting, stick to the agenda. Or, if something important comes up, make a conscious decision to change the agenda. Another way to keep meetings short once everyone is present is by standing up. If possible, stack the chairs or move them to the corner of the room. If that isn't possible, purposefully remain standing with your chair pushed under the table.

Meeting Follow-Up

After the meeting is over, edit the notes from the meeting and quickly distribute them to the attendees and any other people who need to know (as identified in the communication plan described in "Building a Communication Plan" on page 232). This gives people a chance to catch any mistakes in the notes or ask questions about the content.

Be sure to emphasize the action items and the people responsible for performing them. Follow up on action items to ensure that they're completed.

Kickoff Meetings

At the beginning of a project (and at the beginning of phases in large projects), a kickoff meeting is a great way to launch the project or next phase of work. By getting stakeholders and team members together, you can build commitment to the project, help team members get to know one another, and have a little fun before the hard work kicks in.

Take advantage of the energy that a new beginning provides. When the project plan is approved and you're ready to begin the execution phase of the project, hold a kickoff meeting to tell people about the project, introduce all the players, and get them excited about the project. Here are a few of the activities you can schedule for a kickoff meeting:

- The project sponsor reviews the purpose of the project and why it's important to the customer and key stakeholders (see "The Project Mission Statement," page 64). In addition, kickoff meetings are a great time for project sponsors to introduce and announce their support for the project managers they assign.

- The customer amplifies the importance of the project or provides a different perspective of its benefits.

- Depending on the size of the project team, the project sponsor can introduce team members or groups, including any vendors or subcontractors working on the project.

- Coordinate team-building activities to help people get to know each other and develop camaraderie. For example, give everyone at the meeting "project bingo" cards with the names of stakeholders on them. Give small prizes to the first several people who get signatures from the stakeholders whose names appear in a column or row on the card.

Tip If you are going to give people pens, coffee mugs, or other products, hand them out at the kickoff meeting to build team spirit *before* the project starts.

Project Status Meetings

Most team members don't need a meeting to understand the tasks that are complete, delayed, or overdue to start. The benefit of project status meetings is gathering team members to discuss and resolve issues, coordinate

Part Three:
Carrying Out a
Project

On Time! On Track! On Target! Managing Your Projects Successfully with Microsoft Project

work, make decisions, and build relationships. You might have to hold one project status meeting for customers and other key stakeholders that reviews the project in less detail but with more of a business focus. You then schedule additional, more detailed project status meetings for teams within the project. Here are topics and activities you can include in project status meetings:

- *Communicate progress on work packages.* In particular, review tasks that should have started or completed, but haven't. If you distribute a report of tasks that are slipping or should have started or finished (see "Filters for Checking Schedule Progress," page 194), team members can come to the meeting prepared to discuss the delays and potential changes to the project plan.

- *Inform the team about decisions and changes* from the customer, project sponsor, or other groups involved in the project. And if stakeholders have offered positive feedback, be sure to announce that at the meeting.

- *Share lessons learned* to help team members be more productive (see Chapter 19 to learn about collecting lessons learned).

- *Brainstorm issues and solutions* if they are small enough to tackle in a status meeting. Take advantage of the face-to-face discussion to collect suggestions or find out why some solutions might not work. As you identify next steps, add them to the issues tracking log and also document them as action items for the meeting (see "Running Meetings Well," page 242).

Issues are problems or obstacles that must be resolved for work to continue or complete successfully. If your organization uses the Microsoft Enterprise Project Management Solution (EPM), you can use its collaboration features to track issues. However, you can also easily maintain an issues tracking log with Excel. The basic information to store about issues includes ID, status (open or closed), a description of the issue, the status and last action taken, the next action, the person assigned to the issue, the date the issue was identified, and the target or actual completion date. For an issue tracking template, open *Issue Tracking Log.xls* in the *Templates* folder on the companion CD.

Management Meetings

Meetings with management don't occur that often, but they are valuable opportunities to obtain support for your project or changes you want to make. One common mistake that some project managers make is giving executives too much information about items they don't care about. As a project manager, your job is to manage the day-to-day activities of your project, so you spend much of your time with project details. Meetings with executives require a different perspective because they want to see the big picture of progress and consider only major issues and risks.

Warning   Unlike team members, who simply try to avoid meetings they find pointless, executives are quick to tell you that you're missing the mark or wasting their time. And you won't get more than a couple chances to get your executive-level presentations right. If your first management meeting meets with disapproval, go back to your communication plan (see "The Communication Plan," page 222) and revise it based on the executives' feedback. You can also ask your project sponsor for some assistance putting the right emphasis on high-level project information.

Here are a few rules for satisfying the needs and tight schedules of executives:

- Be clear and concise at all times. Take time to prepare your materials and practice your delivery.

- Highlight project successes.

- Describe issues and risks and provide options for resolving them.

- Summarize project status including the schedule and cost, as illustrated in Figure 14-3 on the next page.

- Present requests or recommendations persuasively. Back up your presentation with compelling facts and statistics.

Part Three:
Carrying Out a
Project

On Time! On Track! On Target! Managing Your Projects Successfully with Microsoft Project

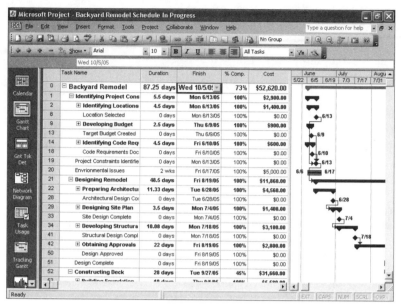

Figure 14-3   Rolling up summary tasks in Project is an easy way to show management schedule and cost status.

Here are the steps for formatting the Gantt Chart view in Figure 14-3:

1. On the View menu, choose Gantt Chart.

2. On the Formatting toolbar, select an outline level, such as Outline Level 2, from the Show list, to display the top two levels of summary tasks in your project schedule.

3. If necessary, you can compress the timescale to shorten the taskbars in the Gantt Chart view. Right-click the dates above the Gantt Chart and choose Timescale on the shortcut menu.

4. In the Timescale dialog box, click the Middle Tier tab and then, in the Units list, choose Months (or Quarters for multiyear projects). Click the Bottom Tier tab and then, in the Units list, choose Weeks or Months. Click OK.

5. To display the table with the fields that the executives are interested in, on the View menu, point to Table: <*table name*>, and then choose the table you want, for instance, Summary or Cost.

Project Status Reports

Project status reports keep people informed about the progress that's being made on your project and what's happened in the recent past. These reports are important and can be chock full of information, but brevity is a virtue. The key to reporting project status is to be concise while still delivering information that people need or want to hear. Here are some guidelines for producing effective project status reports:

- **Use a standard format**   The people in your audience can find the information they need more quickly if you deliver project status in the same format each time, as demonstrated by the project status report template in Figure 14-4 on the next page. Develop a template for your project status report and include notes about how to fill it in.

- **Begin with a project status summary**   Key stakeholders appreciate a summary of status, so they can decide whether they must review the entire report in detail. Include major accomplishments, issues, risks, and plans for the next period.

- **Review the budget and project schedule**   Summarize the budgeted and actual costs and the planned and actual dates for the status period, and explain significant variances (more than 10 percent).

Important   As project manager, be sure to define the meaning of significant variance during project planning. A two percent variance on the backyard remodel project might be insignificant. The same two percent variance would have been catastrophic for a Y2K remediation project that was scheduled to complete on December 15, 1999.

- **Focus on accomplishments**   Achieving goals and handing over deliverables is more important than the detailed tasks that led up to them. Publicize successes, such as effective practices, shortcuts, clever solutions, and so on.

- **Document lessons learned**   By publicizing effective techniques or ill-advised approaches, other team members can be more productive.

- **Report the status of significant issues and risks**   Describe the progress made toward resolving issues and managing risks during the last status period. Identify issues that have been closed and risks that have been successfully resolved. Also, document the risks that were avoided by implementing plans to circumvent those risks or because the work packages that were at risk have been delivered without issue.

Part Three:
Carrying Out a
Project

On Time! On Track! On Target! Managing Your Projects Successfully with Microsoft Project

■ **Create and distribute status reports on schedule**   If a status report isn't important enough for you to send it out on time, your readers might not consider it important enough to read.

Project Name		Project Status Report
To:	[Recipients]	
From:	[Project Manager]	
Date:	mm/dd/yyyy	
Re:	Project Status as of mm/dd/yyyy	

Executive Summary

Accomplishments for period	• Major accomplishments and activities (no more than 6 items) • Use management terminology and no technical jargon
Major issues	• Limit to issues that require executive action
Major risks	• Limit to risks that require executive action
Plans for next period	• High-level activities and deliverables planned for next period

Budget

- Include a summary table that shows budgeted and actual values by major tasks or phases.
- Explain the reasons for significant cost variances.

Schedule

- Include a summary schedule that shows planned and actual dates by major tasks or phases.
- Explain the reasons for significant delays or early deliveries.

Detailed Accomplishments and Activities

- List major deliverables completed
- List accomplishments

Accomplishments and Activities for Next Period

-
-

Page 1

Figure 14-4   By using a template for your project status report, you won't forget to include important information and readers can find the information they need more easily.

The file *Project Status Report.dot* in the *Templates* folder on the companion CD can serve as a foundation for your project status report.

Taming E-Mail

E-mail is usually a vital part of a project environment; it's fast and convenient to send messages when you have time and for others to read when they have time. However, e-mail has several shortcomings. Some of e-mail's failings are technical issues that you might work around but never truly control. However, the effectiveness of what you communicate in your e-mail is something that you *can* control. Some good e-mail messages do take time to write, but you can improve the effectiveness of your e-mail with a few simple guidelines:

- **Be concise and clear**   Everyone receives a lot of e-mail. Make your point quickly and simply, so the reader can easily understand your message and get on to something else. Because e-mail isn't interactive, taking the time to make your point in the *first* message can prevent a series of e-mail exchanges containing questions and answers.

- **Add informative subject lines**   Some e-mail doesn't need anything more than a subject line. For example, if you want feedback on a document you posted to the shared site, send an e-mail with the subject "Please provide feedback on the project plan by this Friday." Subjects like "For your information" don't tell recipients whether the messages are worth opening and make finding information difficult later.

- **Present your request and the deadline in the beginning**   Start your e-mail messages with what you want from readers and when you want it. Once you have their attention, you can fill them in with the details.

- **Don't assume your e-mail arrived or was read**   E-mail is lost, caught in spam filters, deleted by mistake, and other results that mean your message wasn't received. Follow up with a polite request if you don't receive a response by the deadline. If you prefer e-mail, follow up with another e-mail, but then switch to the telephone or a personal visit.

Best Practices

Poorly written project status reports can raise more questions than they answer. Here are some tips for producing status reports that truly inform your audience:

- If you include activities that are in progress, also include when they will be complete.

- Include the results of meetings, discussions, training sessions, and so on.

- Include specific, quantitative results. Use numbers rather than terms, such as few or numerous.

- Take the time to correct typographical errors and grammatical errors.

- Proofread the report for errors that Word doesn't catch.

- Include links to a project repository (see "The Project Notebook," page 178), so readers who want more information can locate it without calling you.

Part Three:
Carrying Out a
Project

On Time! On Track! On Target! Managing Your Projects Successfully with Microsoft Project

- **Avoid humor**   Without facial expressions to go by, readers can inter-pret your humor as insults.

- **Set a schedule for responding to e-mail and keep it**   Publicize your window for responding to e-mail and honor that response time.

> **Tip**   If you will be traveling or in meetings and won't be able to respond in your normal time frame, tell your team that as well. If your organization uses Microsoft Exchange Server for e-mail, the Microsoft Outlook Out of Office feature is ideal for reminding people of your schedule. On the Tools menu, select Out Of Office Assistant.

- **Check the spelling and grammar in your messages**   Proofread your messages carefully to find errors that Outlook didn't catch.

- **Set up a mechanism for handling low-priority e-mail**   To prevent hun-dreds of low-priority e-mail messages from swamping a project team, set up a distribution list or standard subject prefix to identify e-mail that is for readers' information, not action. People can filter this e-mail into different folders to delete or read at their leisure.

Here's an example of an effective e-mail:

From: Gretchen Rivas
To: Project Team
Subject: Action Required - Feedback on New Search Web Page

The search Web page is complete and available for your review at http://www.adatum.com/search_temp. This Web page includes the feedback from our initial review. We will finalize this Web page on Tuesday, so I need your feedback by 5:00 P.M. on Thursday, 3/16/2006. You can send me an e-mail or deliver a marked-up copy to my office.

Thanks, Gretchen

In Summary

Project management and communication are inseparable. Every project manager must tell people what they need to know, when they need to know it, and most important, in the way that helps them understand it. This chap-ter introduced the communication plan, which identifies who, what, when, and how for your project communications.

You also learned guidelines for good communication to ensure that you get your messages across and that you understand what other people are trying to tell you. The chapter explained techniques for conducting productive meetings, which help you achieve project objectives without wasting time or your project's budget. It described the information to include in project status reports and how to produce reports that your audiences will appreciate. And finally, it concluded with some guidelines on how to make the most of e-mail for project communication.

Part Four

Controlling Projects

In this part

Chapter Fifteen   **Managing Project Changes**. 256
Chapter Sixteen   **Modifying the Project Schedule**. 266
Chapter Seventeen **Balancing the Budget and Other Project Variables**. . 288
Chapter Eighteen   **Managing Risk** 296

Part Four:
Controlling
Projects

On Time! On Track! On Target! Managing Your Projects Successfully with Microsoft Project

Chapter Fifteen

Managing Project Changes

Change is one thing. Progress is another.

— *Bertrand Russell*

You're standing on a ski slope and your friend asks you to hold her ski poles while she unzips her jacket. No problem. You take the poles in your right hand. Then, she asks you to hold her gloves so she can scratch her nose. Those go in your left hand. It sure is warm, so you hold out your arms to hold her hat, backpack, and jacket. She cheerily says, "OK, I'm ready to go," and skis off as you stand there eyeing your load. There's no way you can ski down the hill. Change requests in projects often have the same sort of effect. Each one seems quite manageable, but at some point you realize they've made your project objectives completely impossible. To make matters worse, stakeholders are likely to forget the changes you obligingly added when the schedule runs long and the budget runs over.

Saying no to every change request is one option, but it's not realistic. People have new ideas or come up with a better approach once they understand the project a little better. Competing products introduce exciting new features, or components you're using are no longer available. You must accept that change is inevitable. The only sensible solution is to *manage* the changes that affect your project.

This chapter describes the basic steps for change management and also discusses who should be part of the *change review board*—the group that decides whether changes that are requested will be added to the project. You'll also learn about simple methods for tracking changes using Microsoft applications.

An Overview of the Change Management Process

Change management is the process of identifying and documenting potential changes, determining whether the changes are beneficial and necessary, analyzing the scope and impact of the changes, estimating the effort and cost of the changes, deciding whether to make the changes, and finally managing the changes after they're added to the project.

Boiled down to the basics, you need only two things to manage change:

- **The original goal**   As you learned in "An Overview of Project Planning" on page 48, you can't gauge progress unless you know where you started. Before you can manage changes, you must identify the items you want to control, usually referred to as *baseline documents*

Part Four:
Controlling
Projects

On Time! On Track! On Target! Managing Your Projects Successfully with Microsoft Project

(aka the project plan or project notebook), and the version that constitutes the baseline. Otherwise, you can't tell what the changes are (called *change requests* or CRs) and what was supposed to be there all along. For example, if you don't identify a set of requirements as the original to work from, you won't notice that a dozen new requirements crept in during design.

- **A process for tracking and managing changes** The change management process doesn't have to be complicated, although in large projects the basic steps can comprise many detailed procedures. But the process does have to identify the items that you control with the process, who is responsible for deciding whether changes are made, and some steps for getting change requests from the requesters through approval or rejection by the decision makers to ultimate action. The best change management process is one that balances the need for tracking and controlling changes with the need for some flexibility and responsiveness.

Figure 15-1 shows the basic components of change management. On the left side of the diagram are the steps to build the original project documents: the project plan, requirements, specifications, and so on. When the stakeholders approve the project documents, they become baseline documents under the control of change management. The right side of the diagram shows the steps for processing change requests, which, if approved, result in changes to the baseline documents.

Important   Your change management process has to be ready to go by the time stakeholders approve the project plan, because the plan is one of the items that you must control.

What Do You Control with the Change Management Process?

In project management, control documents include your project planning deliverables, such as the project scope and objectives, the project schedule, and the remaining sections of the project plan. As the project progresses, you add additional deliverables, such as requirements and specifications, schematics, design drawings, system architecture diagrams, style sheets—anything that you use to guide the results for the project.

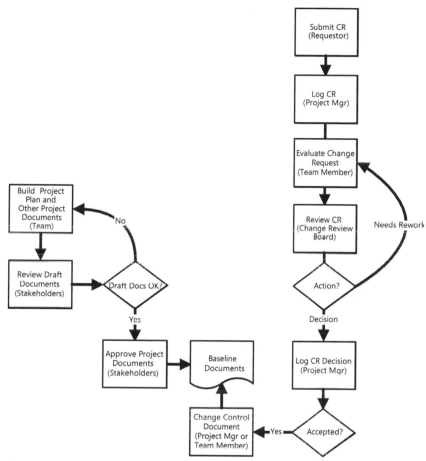

Figure 15-1   Change management is about deciding which changes will be made to items you control and tracking the progress of those changes.

When you first develop documents and other kinds of deliverables, you constantly make changes until you produce the final result that you submit to the stakeholders for approval. The important point is that these deliverables aren't control documents *until stakeholders sign off on them.* Until you reach that state, you can use features, such as Track Changes in Microsoft Word or a revision table within the file, to keep track of changes you make.

There are two possible outcomes when stakeholders review these draft deliverables. They can ask you to rework them to correct mistakes or fine-tune the content. For example, if stakeholders want you to pull the final date back in, you'll have to rework your project schedule to fast-track or

Part Four:
Controlling
Projects

On Time! On Track! On Target! Managing Your Projects Successfully with Microsoft Project

crash the project. The other possibility is the one you're waiting for—stakeholders approve the deliverables, which triggers several actions. Besides a big sigh of relief, you distribute the deliverables to team members who need them to do their project work, *and* you place the deliverables under control of the change management process.

Managing Change Requests

Now that you have control documents under the jurisdiction of change management, here's the basic approach to handling change requests:

1. *When a requestor submits a change request, you document the change request in a change request log* (see "Tracking Changes," page 262, for samples of a change request form and a change request log). A change request form is a great way to help people provide you with the detailed information you need to evaluate their requests. Every change request that's submitted is also added to the change request log. In this step, you document who submitted the request, the date it was submitted, and a brief description of the request.

   In addition, you choose the best person to evaluate the change request. For instance, if the customer requests an extension to a deck, you might assign the change request to the structural engineer, who can determine whether the design can handle the extra load or requires stronger supports. Add the person responsible for evaluating the request to the log.

   > **Tip**   For some change requests, the evaluation can require a serious commitment of time and money. The change request form in Figure 15-2 includes a signature block for approval to evaluate a change request. However, for small requests, your approval as project manager is enough.

2. *During the evaluation of the change request,* you'll work with the person assigned to evaluate the request to consider the effect on the project schedule, budget, objectives, quality, and other objectives. In addition, you should take into account whether the change request introduces any new risks to the project and how you would handle them.

   At this point, you write up a summary of the change request: its purpose, a brief description of the change, its effect on the project, risks, and your recommendation for whether the change review board should accept the request. You can include this information on the original change request. You submit change requests to the change review board to consider at its next meeting.

3. *The change review board considers the change requests you've submitted.* Most change review boards require that the requestor or someone who fully understands the change request be present to answer questions as the board deliberates the change request. If the change review board accepts the request, you document its decision in the change request log and take the steps necessary to add the change to your project.

If the change review board rejects a change request, you document the decision. The board might also ask you to do some more work on the change request. For example, the board members might want to see more detailed analysis of the impact of the change.

4. *For accepted change requests, you update the control documents and begin tracking the work that the change entails.* You might have to adjust the effort on an existing task in your project schedule or add new tasks. Of course, you must also assign the change to someone to perform. When the change is complete, you make a final update to the change request log to show the actual results of the change in hours, cost, and change to the project finish date.

Best Practices

You don't have to push *every* change request through *every* step of the change management process. Channeling even the most miniscule requests through the change management process could introduce weeks of delay before a change request receives approval. Change management is necessary but at the same time you have to keep things moving on projects. One solution to this dilemma is to set thresholds for who can approve changes to a project.

Some change requests are so bizarre you might not assign them to a team member to evaluate. You simply notify the requestor that his change is rejected. If people don't provide enough information, you can ask them to rework their requests and try again.

Changes that don't affect the schedule or budget don't have to go to the change review board. You can work out a plan with the project team and make the change, although you still track the change in the change request log.

However, when schedule, cost, quality, and other objectives are affected, change requests need to go through the change review board for approval. Even the change review board has its limits. For changes that affect the business case for the project, the customer and project sponsor must have a say in the decision. Alternatively, you can define an emergency change process to handle sudden yet substantial changes to business needs.

Part Four:
Controlling
Projects

On Time! On Track! On Target! Managing Your Projects Successfully with Microsoft Project

> **Note** For large projects, you might have several levels of change review boards. For instance, a major project with subprojects could have change review boards within each subproject with a top-level change review board for requests that affect the entire project scope.

Who Belongs on the Change Review Board?

Change review boards typically include the key stakeholders for the project. For example, the customer, representatives from all the groups involved in the project, and project team leads are likely candidates for the board. Functional managers for people working on the project might participate. And project managers are always a part of the board, because they submit the requests and have the most in-depth knowledge of the project.

Tracking Changes

Keeping track of change requests as they work their way through your process is crucial, but it doesn't require sophisticated tools. To satisfy the need for detailed information about each change request and an overall view of the status of all change requests, two separate documents are in order. A change request form is a document that people requesting changes can fill in and submit. These forms can store the details about the original change request as well as the analysis that you perform and the recommendation, as shown in Figure 15-2.

The Word template shown in Figure 15-2, *Change Request Form.dot*, is available in the *Templates* folder on the companion CD.

You can use different tools to set up a change request form. For example, a Word template is one solution. You can store the template in a shared folder for the project, so requesters can create a change request form and e-mail it or print it. If you manage a large project with a geographically distributed team, a Web page with an online form is another option. Depending on the technology that's available, you might also use a database with submittal forms, a Microsoft Windows SharePoint Services Web site, or other software solutions.

<Project Name> **Change Request Form**

Project manager:

Date:

Requestor:

To be filled in by requestor:

Business justification for change.

Describe the change and resulting deliverables.

To be filled in by project manager:

CR number:

Evaluation approval required: Yes No

Estimate to evaluate the change request:

Hours	Cost	Duration	Change to project end date

Approved by ______________ Date ______

Change request evaluation

Estimate impact to project:

Hours	Cost	Duration	Change to project end date

Describe recommendation and analysis.

Change request approved by ______________ Date ______

Figure 15-2 A change request form stores details about each change request.

A change request log can act as a repository for tracking the status of change requests submitted. As a change request moves from step to step in the change management process, be sure to update the log with its status. Figure 15-3 on the next page shows a simple change request log built with Microsoft Excel.

Part Four:
Controlling
Projects

On Time! On Track! On Target! Managing Your Projects Successfully with Microsoft Project

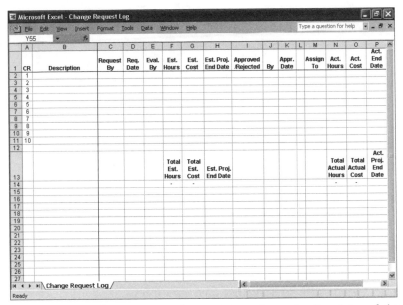

Figure 15-3   A change request log contains columns for the status of change requests, including who is responsible, status dates, and the estimated and actual impact of change requests on the project.

The Excel workbook shown in Figure 15-3, Change Request Log.xls, is available in the *Templates* folder on the companion CD.

Small changes come up all the time and if approved, they can add up to more than anyone expects. If you add the impact of change requests to your project schedule, you can see the result of those requests, but that doesn't make obvious the increase from your original plan. One way to keep an eye on the extent of change is to total the columns for hours and cost in your change request log.

Another way to manage small changes is to save them until you have enough to work on as a collection. Then you can see whether you have the time and budget to perform them. The full impact of all the changes is more obvious than the innocuous small requests. What's more, team members can be more productive by working on several small changes at once than to switch between their assigned tasks and change requests. However, this approach comes with a risk of rework if the parts of the project in which the changes lie are finalized while the change requests wait for their go-ahead.

In Summary

Change management is essential if you want to make good business decisions about the change requests that you receive during a project. Many people fear that the change management process can turn projects into slow-moving bureaucratic nightmares, but change management doesn't have to be that way. The first step is to decide the balance between managing change and allowing the flexibility to respond quickly. Then develop a process that specifies who approves changes and how you make approved changes part of your project plan.

Part Four:
Controlling
Projects

On Time! On Track! On Target! Managing Your Projects Successfully with Microsoft Project

Chapter Sixteen

Modifying the Project Schedule

The more alternatives, the more difficult the choice.

— *Abbe D'Allanival*

Getting the project schedule just the way stakeholders want it is like juggling chain saws. You have to pay attention to every detail or the results could be disastrous. One of the challenges is that you have so many alternatives from which to choose. Do you shorten the schedule and increase the cost? Do you sacrifice quality or reduce the scope? Do you look for more resources or look at how you can use the ones you already have more effectively?

Chapter 17, "Balancing the Budget and Other Project Variables," looks at the options you have from a business perspective. You can't look at what each alternative can do on its own. You must take into account the effects it has on every aspect of your project and, in many cases, other projects or business objectives at higher levels in your organization.

But you have to start somewhere. This chapter reviews different alternatives for optimizing your project schedule and how they affect duration, cost, scope, quality—and whether the people who work on your project ever get to go home. Each section explains how to apply these alternatives to your project schedule using Microsoft Project features.

Tip   This chapter is meant to introduce you to Microsoft Project features that can help you adjust your schedule. These features include options and all kinds of handy behaviors to tweak your schedule just so. To get to the nitty-gritty details of Project features, look at the book by Teresa Stover, *Microsoft Office Project 2003 Inside Out* (Microsoft Press, 2003).

Simplifying Solution Hunting

Setting up views and selecting options can make your search for solutions easier. Here are some setup tasks to complete before you start looking for ways to improve your schedule.

Displaying Summary Tasks

Regardless of whether you're trying to shorten duration or cut costs, summary tasks make it easy to see if you're getting the results you want. The project summary task shows start and finish dates, total duration, work, and cost for your project. Summary tasks show similar fields for portions of your project. As you make changes, you can check these fields to see if you are obtaining the results you want.

Part Four:
Controlling
Projects

On Time! On Track! On Target! Managing Your Projects Successfully with Microsoft Project

Here are the steps for displaying summary tasks and the project summary task:

1. On the Tools menu, select Options.

2. In the Options dialog box, click the View tab, if necessary.

3. At the bottom of the View tab in the Outline Options For *<project name>* section, select the Show Summary Tasks check box and the Show Project Summary Task check box. The project name displayed in the section heading will be the name of the current project, because these settings apply only to the current project file.

4. Click OK.

Displaying the Critical Path and Baseline

You can apply different tables to your Task Sheet to see values for tasks, but the best way to spot the critical path or variances from your baseline schedule is with Gantt Chart views.

■ *The Tracking Gantt view* displays gray taskbars for your baseline schedule, blue taskbars for noncritical tasks in your current schedule, and red taskbars for critical path tasks in your current schedule.

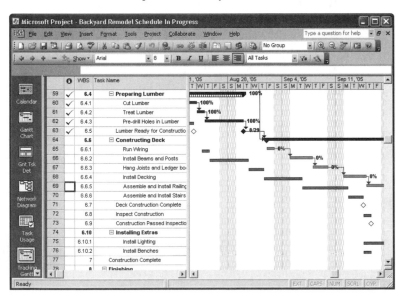

■ *The Detail Gantt view* displays noncritical path taskbars in blue, critical path taskbars in red, and tasks that are slipping past the baseline start date with a beige line to the left of the taskbar.

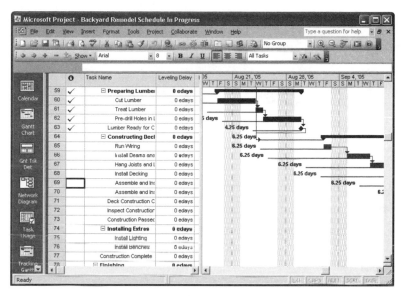

If you want to apply formatting to a Gantt Chart view, the Gantt Chart Wizard simplifies your job. On the Format menu, select Gantt Chart Wizard and step through the screens to choose the taskbar styles you want and the fields of information to display in the view.

Fast-Tracking a Project

Fast-tracking a project means overlapping tasks that were originally scheduled one after the other (see "The Fast-Track to an Early Finish," page 154). Fast-tracking is an effective way to shorten a project schedule without increasing cost. However, overlapping tasks can be risky if decisions made during the overlap affect work that's already been completed. You can simply add a little bit of overlap between two tasks or create two completely parallel tracks in your project. For example, if you can round up a second construction crew, you can build two houses at the same time instead of scheduling each type of construction worker to move from one house to the next.

To shorten your schedule, you want to overlap tasks on the critical path. Applying a filter to show only critical path tasks makes it easy to look for fast-tracking candidates. On the Formatting toolbar, in the Filter list, choose Critical. Project displays your critical path tasks as solid red bars and summary tasks as narrower black bars, as shown in Figure 16-1 on the next page.

Part Four:
Controlling
Projects

On Time! On Track! On Target! Managing Your Projects Successfully with Microsoft Project

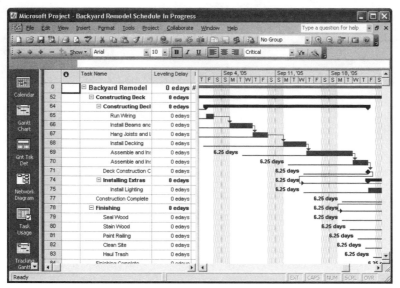

Figure 16-1   Filtering your task list for critical path tasks simplifies your search for ways to shorten the schedule.

Tip   After you overlap tasks, on the Formatting toolbar in the Filter list, choose the All Tasks filter to display all tasks, critical and noncritical alike.

Overlapping Tasks

You can shorten the critical path for your project by starting the next critical path task before its predecessor on the critical path is complete. Lag is the term for a delay after the end of one task before another task begins. In Project, you create partial overlaps by applying a *negative* lag to the dependency between the two tasks. Here are the steps:

1.   To edit the task dependency between two tasks, double-click the link line in the Gantt Chart view.

2.   In the Task Dependency dialog box, type a negative number of hours, days, or other time period, for instance, **−2d**.

3.   Click OK to add the overlap, as illustrated in the bottom window in Figure 16-2. The top window shows the original relationship between tasks.

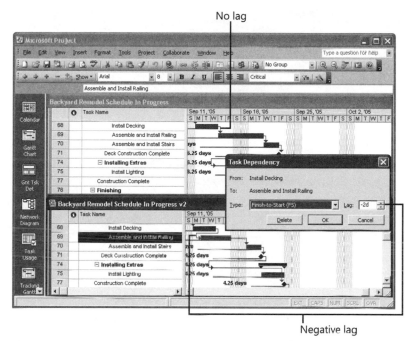

Figure 16-2 By typing a negative number in the Lag box, you start the successor task before the predecessor finishes.

Tip To edit a task dependency starting in the Task Sheet, double-click the name of the successor task in the Task Sheet. In the Task Information dialog box, click the Predecessors tab to display the predecessor tasks. To overlap the task with a predecessor, in the predecessor's Lag cell, type the negative value and click OK.

Running Tasks in Parallel

Running tasks in parallel shortens your critical path more than a partial overlap, but the task must use different resources and the risks must be acceptable. To run tasks in parallel, you add and remove links. Here are the steps:

1. To prevent the successor task from disappearing when you delete its predecessor, add the link between the successor and its new predecessor first. You can drag from the new predecessor to the successor to create the link. When the pointer changes to a chain icon, release the mouse button.

Part Four:
Controlling
Projects

On Time! On Track! On Target! Managing Your Projects Successfully with Microsoft Project

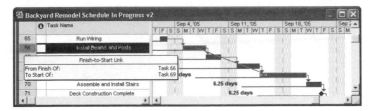

2. To delete the dependency between the old predecessor and the successor task, double-click the task dependency link line in the Gantt Chart pane and, in the Task Dependency dialog box, click Delete. For example, in Figure 16-3, the link between the Install Decking task and the Assemble and Install Railing task has been deleted. Assemble and Install Railing now occurs in parallel with Hang Joists and Ledger Board and Install Decking.

3. Add a new link between the old predecessor and another task to ensure that the work package still drives at least one project deliverable. For example, in the bottom window in Figure 16-3, Install Decking is now a predecessor to the Deck Construction Complete milestone.

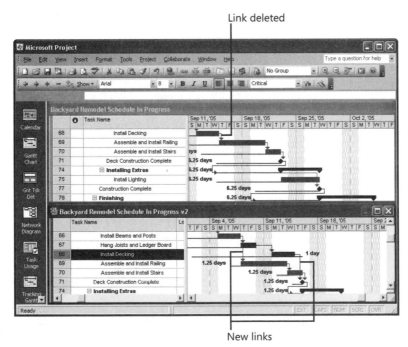

Figure 16-3   To run tasks in parallel, you must remove the old link between tasks and add new links.

Splitting Long Tasks into Short Ones

By splitting a task with a long duration into several shorter tasks, you might be able to improve your schedule and reduce cost. Instead of the same person performing the entire task, you might be able to assign different resources to the shorter tasks, so you can overlap the tasks. And if you can assign less expensive people to some of the shorter tasks, you can reduce the overall cost. Figure 16-4 demonstrates breaking up a long task to achieve both of these benefits. The original task in the top window takes 30 days and costs $24,000. By splitting the task into work that a designer and drafter can do, as illustrated in the bottom window, the new duration is 25 days and the cost is $18,000.

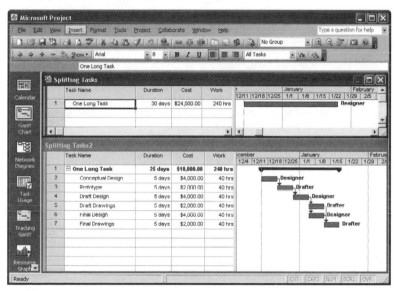

Figure 16-4   By breaking up long tasks into several shorter ones, you might be able to reduce the duration and the cost of the work.

To change a long task into several shorter ones, the easiest approach is to treat the original long task as a summary task and create the shorter tasks as subordinate tasks. Here are the steps:

1. Insert a blank row below the long task by clicking the Task Name cell immediately *below* the long task in the Task Sheet.

2. Press Insert as many times as needed to create blank rows for each shorter subordinate task.

Part Four:
Controlling
Projects

On Time! On Track! On Target! Managing Your Projects Successfully with Microsoft Project

3. The insertion point appears in the Task Name cell for the first blank task below the summary task, so you can type the name for the first subordinate task.

4. Press Enter to save the name.

5. Select the task you just created and, on the Formatting toolbar, click the Indent button (a green arrow pointing to the right, which is shown in Figure 7-4 on page 98.)

6. After the first subordinate task is indented, add the remaining subordinate tasks by pressing the Down Arrow and typing the task names.

7. Link the subordinate tasks based on the dependencies between the smaller packages of work and assign resources to the smaller tasks.

8. To remove the resource assigned to the summary task, double-click the summary task to open the Task Information dialog box.

Important   If you don't remove the resource assigned to the summary task, your summary task will double up on hours and cost—some from the resource assigned to the summary task and some from the resources assigned to the subordinate tasks.

---

9. Click the Resource tab.

10. Click the cell with the original resource name in it and press Delete to remove the resource assignment from the summary task.

11. Click OK to close the dialog box.

Scheduling Around Other Tasks

Training classes, meetings, and other events typically occur on specific days, so you can't use task dependencies to schedule them with other kinds of work tasks. If you don't do anything to schedule work package tasks around events, the people assigned to both are overallocated for those days. In practice, people often have to work longer or harder to make up for events they attend, so doing nothing might be acceptable. But if you want to do something about the double shifts, the best way to schedule work around an event is with a task calendar. You can set up a calendar that shows the event days as nonworking days. Then, if you assign that calendar to the work package tasks, Project won't schedule work on those days.

Although scheduling around tasks increases the duration of the schedule, it shows the reality of project work better, which means you have a better chance of meeting your finish date.

Warning   Creating task calendars and other techniques, such as adding splits to tasks, are best reserved for the execution phase of a project. Task calendars and splits don't adjust automatically to changes in a project schedule, and the schedule changes too much during planning to make these techniques worthwhile.

Here are the steps for assigning a task calendar to a task:

1. On the Tools menu, click Change Working Time.

2. In the Change Working Time dialog box, click New.

3. In the Create New Base Calendar dialog box, name the calendar (for example, Training Class) and click OK.

4. Specify the nonworking days for the class or meeting.

5. Click OK to close the dialog box.

6. To assign the calendar to a task, in the Gantt Chart, double-click the task to open the Task Information dialog box.

7. Click the Advanced tab.

8. In the Calendar list, choose the calendar you just created.

9. Click OK.

Shortening Lag Time

If tasks on the critical path include lag time between them, reducing that lag time in Project to shorten the critical path is amazingly easy. It won't cost any more; resources don't have to work harder; and risk is nil. The difficulty with this approach is that the lag time is often due to a dependency on other groups. For example, you might have a lag time to indicate the delay until stakeholders meet to approve documents. Or a vendor requires two months between your equipment order and delivery.

If stakeholders want you to shorten the schedule and other options are hard to find, ask the stakeholders if they can hold an interim meeting to reduce the delay. You can also negotiate with other groups to reduce lag times, for instance, by paying extra for expediting delivery.

Part Four:
Controlling
Projects

On Time! On Track! On Target! Managing Your Projects Successfully with Microsoft Project

If you convince groups to reduce lag, here are the steps for making the change in Project:

1. Double-click the link line between two tasks in the Gantt Chart view.

2. In the Task Dependency dialog box, in the Lag box, change the number of hours, days, or other time period to the new lag time you obtained. For example, if the lag has decreased from 30 days to 20, type **20**.

3. Click OK.

Adjusting Resource Allocation

Best Practices

If stakeholders decide to reduce the scope of the project either to shorten the schedule or reduce the budget, you might think that the solution is simply to delete the tasks for the scope you're removing. But that's not as good an idea as it seems. You probably know that decisions that go one way on Monday are as likely to go the other way by Friday. If you delete the tasks, you might have to add them back. The other reason deleting tasks is misguided is that those tasks contribute to the baseline you set for the schedule. If you delete baselined tasks, Project deletes all the fields for those tasks, and you'll find a sudden change in your baseline values, which stakeholders are sure to notice and question.

The preferable approach is to keep the tasks in the schedule but eliminate their scheduled fields (see "How Project Calculates Values and Variance," page 191). The baseline values for the tasks remain, so the total baseline values don't change. However, the new estimated values for the completed project do reflect the reduced scope so you can identify how much the cut helped. For the tasks that you are eliminating, set the Work and Cost fields to zero. To prevent the tasks from affecting the schedule, delete any task dependencies they have.

Changing the percentage that you allocate resources to tasks can reduce the schedule duration, but it might increase the cost or decrease quality. In Project, you can take two approaches to modifying the allocation of people to tasks. Increasing the units that resources are assigned to a task increases the number of hours they work on that task each day, which should mean that the task takes fewer days to complete. Increasing units is easy in Project, but in the real world, it only works for so long. People get tired of working long hours, and they begin to make mistakes. And if they don't earn overtime pay, morale decreases even faster still. A second approach is to contour resource assignments, which turns out to be a more realistic model of the time that people spend on tasks than all or nothing. This section describes how to do both.

Changing Units

Modifying resource assignments can be a game of hide and seek with Project if you don't understand how the program calculates resource assignment fields. If you create a task with the Task Type set to Fixed Units, you can type a task name and duration, choose a resource, and click OK. Project sets the units to 100% and calculates the work. If you want to change units (or make other modifications), assignments often seem less cooperative. This section explains how Project calculates the fields for resource assignments, so you can change units or other values and get the results you want.

Resource calculations depend on the relationships among task duration, work, and units. You can calculate any one of the values as long as the other two fields are set:

Duration = Work / Units

Work = Duration × Units

Units = Work / Duration

But how do you know which one Project calculates? Hidden inside the program is a bias for which value it changes. Project tries to change duration before changing work, and it tries to change work before changing units. Because stakeholders almost always want a project finished sooner, duration is always a good guess at the value you want to change. Besides, the work that a task requires doesn't change that often (unless it increases as you learn more about what is required), and the allocation of resources tends to stay the same as well.

Most of the time, deciding what to do is easy. If you specify duration and units, Project uses them to calculate work. If you specify work and units, Project uses them to calculate a new duration. You can even leave units blank and specify a value for work; Project simply sets the units to 100% and then calculates a new duration.

Sometimes, you want to change values for a task assignment in a way that conflicts with Project's bias. In these situations, the Task Type field tells Project which field to keep fixed when you assign resources. For example, a Task Type of Fixed Duration tells Project to change work or units. For fixed-work tasks, Project keeps the value for work the same and instead recalculates duration or units.

Armed with this newfound knowledge, you can now change units on a task with ease. Here are the steps:

1. If necessary, display the Task Form in the bottom pane of the Gantt Chart view. (If the Gantt Chart view shows only one pane, double-click the small rectangle immediately below the vertical scroll bar.

Part Four:
Controlling
Projects

On Time! On Track! On Target! Managing Your Projects Successfully with Microsoft Project

Then, on the View menu, choose More Views. In the More Views dialog box, double-click Task Form.)

2. In the top pane of the Gantt Chart view, select the task you want to modify.

3. In the Task Form, in the Task Type list, choose the task type for the field you want to keep. For example, if you want the number of work hours to stay the same and the duration to change, choose Fixed Work.

4. In the section of the Task Form that shows resource assignments, select the person's Units cell, and change the value to the new percentage that the person is available. For example, if someone was assigned at 50%, type **100%** to change it to full time.

5. Click OK. Project recalculates the task duration.

6. To keep your tasks consistent, change the Task Type back to Fixed Units.

In the top window in Figure 16-5, the crew member works half-time (50%) for 8 days to complete 32 hours of work. In the bottom window, by setting the Task Type to Fixed Work and changing the units to 100%, the crew member performs 32 hours of work in only 4 days.

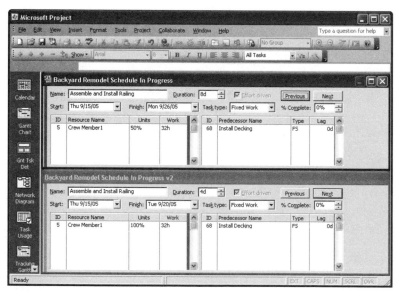

Figure 16-5 Change the Task Type to tell Project which field you want to keep the same value.

Adjusting Work Contours

The Work Contour feature in Project changes the allocation of resources over the course of their assignments. For example, you can apply the Bell work contour, which starts someone's assignment slowly, increases to a higher allocation in the middle, and then tapers off the assignment at the end, as demonstrated in Figure 16-6. Contouring tasks can help you optimize your schedule by modeling assigned time more realistically. For example, the work that people have to do on a task often dwindles at the end, so you might be able to start a new assignment before the previous one is complete without overallocating anyone.

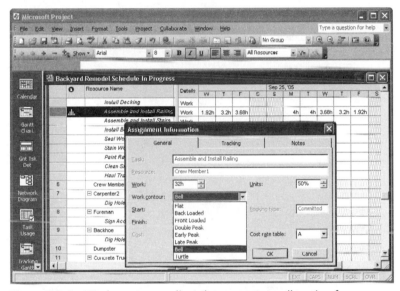

Figure 16-6 Work contours adjust the percentage allocation for resources over the duration of their assignment.

Here are the steps for applying a work contour to a resource assignment:

1. On the View menu, choose either Task Usage or Resource Usage. These are the only two views that show detailed assignment information.

2. For the resource whose assignment you want to contour, double-click the name of the task to contour.

3. In the Assignment Information dialog box, in the Work Contour list, choose the contour that you want. For example, Back Loaded adds

Part Four:
Controlling
Projects

On Time! On Track! On Target! Managing Your Projects Successfully with Microsoft Project

more time at the end of the assignment, which is similar to a crunch at the end. Front Loaded adds more time up front.

4. Click OK to contour the hours.

Assigning Overtime

Asking people to work longer hours is another strategy for shortening a project schedule. By working beyond the normal day, they can complete tasks in fewer days. If people earn a salary and don't earn any extra for working longer hours, you might reduce project costs as well. However, this sort of overtime abuse won't work for long. Employees get tired of long hours. Morale decreases and employee turnover increases—both of which negatively affect your project. If people are paid overtime rates, your project costs go up as well. In addition, you have to consider whether people could do more beneficial work with that time.

You can assign resources to work overtime in several ways. Here are some of the techniques you can use:

■ The easiest way to assign overtime is in the Resource Sheet by increasing the person's Max. Units field to a percentage greater than 100%. For example, setting Max. Units to 125% represents a 10-hour workday (assuming a standard workday of 8 hours). One problem with this approach is that the person is set up to work overtime for the entire project, which might be more than he is willing to do.

■ A more realistic approach is to define the period during which someone will work overtime. To do this, in the Resource Sheet view, double-click the resource you want to set up for overtime. In the Resource Information dialog box, in the Resource Availability section, specify the start and end date for the overtime and the units, as shown in Figure 16-7.

Note If you assign percentages in the Resource Availability section, the resource's availability for all other time periods remains at the Max. Units value you specify in the Resource Sheet.

■ If you want to assign overtime day by day, you can modify the working hours in a resource's calendar (see "Scheduling Around Nonworking Time," page 152). For example, you could specify the work hours for one Monday to start at 7:00 A.M. and end at 7:00 P.M.

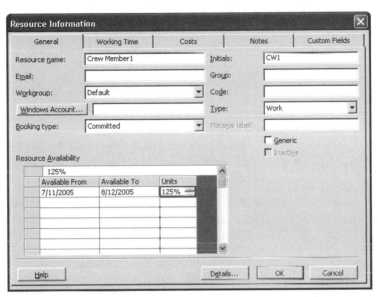

Figure 16-7 You can specify a resource's availability at different times.

Substituting Resources

Whether you have to replace a resource who can't work on your project anymore or you're looking to assign less expensive resources to cut costs, you can replace resources in assignments.

If you know the resource that you want to replace, you can simply choose a new resource in the Task Form. In the Resource Name section, select the name of the resource you want to replace and then, in the Resource Name list, select the new resource you want to assign. Project changes the resource assigned, but keeps the units, work, and duration the same. If you selected a person with more or less experience or who works faster or slower, you should consider changing the values in the Work and Duration fields to reflect the new person's productivity. In the background,

Overtime Hours Paid at an Overtime Rate

Project doesn't automatically assign hours that people work as overtime hours. If people receive premium pay for overtime hours, you must set up a few things before Project can calculate the cost accurately. In the Resource Sheet, be sure to fill in the Ovt. Rate cell with the amount that the person is paid for overtime. For example, resources with a standard rate (Std. Rate) of $50 an hour might receive $60 an hour for overtime.

Then, for each assignment, you must specify the number of overtime hours. Display the Task Form (on the View menu, select More Views and then double-click Task Form). Right-click the Task Form pane and select Resource Work on the shortcut menu. In the resource assignment table, Project displays the Units, Work, and Ovt. Work fields. The Work field represents the total work hours for the assignment, both regular and over-time work. All you have to do is type the number of overtime hours for the assignment in the Ovt. Work field.

Part Four:
Controlling
Projects

On Time! On Track! On Target! Managing Your Projects Successfully with Microsoft Project

Project recalculates the cost with the new resource's Std. Rate in the Resource Sheet.

To substitute a resource with someone similar, the Assign Resources dialog box provides several features for finding suitable replacements (see "Using the Assign Resources Dialog Box," page 148). Here are the steps for replacing a resource using the Assign Resources dialog box:

1. In the Gantt Chart view, select the task in which you want to replace a resource. (Otherwise, if the Task Form is active, the Assign Resources icon on the Standard toolbar is dimmed.)

2. On the Standard toolbar, click the Assign Resources icon (or on the Tools menu, choose Assign Resources).

3. In the Assign Resources dialog box (shown in Figure 16-8), select a resource name and click Remove to remove the resource from the task. The check mark to the left of the resource name disappears.

4. To add a resource, select the Units field for the resource and type the units for the resource assignment. If you want the person to work full time, type **100%**. Click Assign. Project adds a check mark to the left of the resource name and moves the assigned resource above all the unassigned resources in the list, as shown in Figure 16-8.

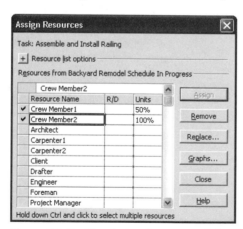

Figure 16-8 The Assign Resources dialog box shows all assigned resources at the top of the list of names and adds a check mark to the left of the assigned resources.

Tip If you want to replace an assigned resource, select the resource and then click Replace. The Replace Resource dialog box opens. In the Units field for the resource you want to use as a replacement, type the allocation you want and click OK.

Adding Resources to Tasks to Shorten Duration

Crashing is the term for adding more resources to a project to shorten its duration (see "A Crash Course on Project Crashing," page 156). Adding people is the strategy that many stakeholders and inexperienced project managers think of first, but adding more people might also increase the schedule rather than decrease it. Because of this, crashing is usually a last resort. If you must, in Project, adding resources to shorten duration is easy. Here are the steps:

1. In the Task Form, make sure that the Task Type is set to Fixed Units and that the Effort Driven check box is selected.

2. In the first blank Resource Name field, choose a resource to add. To assign a resource with units other than 100%, in the Units field, type the allocation percentage for the assignment.

3. If you want to add additional resources, repeat step 2.

4. When you've added all the resources you want, click OK. Project reduces the duration and calculates the work for each

Adding Resources Without Shortening Duration

Sometimes, you want to add resources while keeping the task duration the same. For example, adding resources to a meeting doesn't shorten its duration. In fact, more attendees can make meetings take longer unless you facilitate the session (see "Running Meetings Well," page 242). The trick to adding resources to a task and keeping the duration the same lies with the Effort Driven check box in the Task Form.

Project automatically selects the Effort Driven check box, which keeps the *total* work constant for a task as you add or remove people from the task. When effort-driven scheduling is turned on, Project changes the task duration and redistributes the total work to the new set of assigned resources. (Effort-driven scheduling applies only when you add or remove resources from a task, not when you modify values for resources already assigned to the task.)

If you clear the Effort Driven check box and add resources, Project adds the resources with the units you specified. The duration stays the same, so the total work for the task increases. For example, if a one-hour meeting starts with five attendees, the total work is five hours. However, if you add three more people, the meeting is still one hour long, but the total work increases to eight hours.

Part Four:
Controlling
Projects

On Time! On Track! On Target! Managing Your Projects Successfully with Microsoft Project

resource based on its units, as illustrated in the bottom window in Figure 16-9.

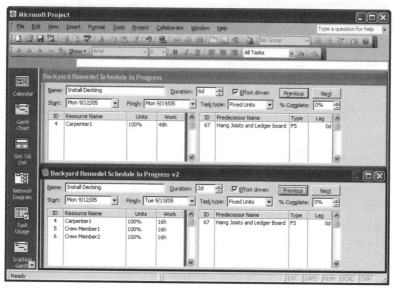

Figure 16-9   Project uses the units for each resource to reallocate the work hours.

Modifying Baselines

The typical approach to baselines in project management is to save one when the stakeholders approve the project plan and compare project performance to that baseline from then on. However, one of the reasons you might be reading this chapter is because something significant has happened to your project, and you've had to adjust the schedule in response. The original baseline is still important, but it might not be as helpful for measuring performance now that you've fast-tracked some tasks, crashed a few others, and removed some scope as well. In situations such as these, you can save a new baseline after you make major revisions to your Project schedule (requires Microsoft Project 2003).

Saving Additional Baselines

In Project, you can tell if you have an initial baseline saved in the Save Baseline dialog box. On the Tools menu, point to Tracking, and then click Save Baseline. A saved baseline displays text such as *(last saved on Fri 12/2/05)* after the baseline name. Because the Variance table displays value for only the first baseline in the list (named Baseline), saving additional baselines requires a couple of steps:

1. On the Tools menu, point to Tracking, and then select Save Baseline.

2. In the Save Baseline dialog box, make sure that the Save Baseline option is selected.

3. In the Save Baseline list, choose the first baseline name *without* a last saved on date, such as Baseline 2.

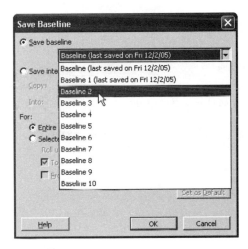

4. Under the For heading, select the Entire Project option.

5. Click OK. Project stores the current scheduled values in baseline fields, such as Baseline 2 Cost.

6. Before you do anything else, open the Save Baseline dialog box once more (see step 1).

7. In the Save Baseline list, choose Baseline and click OK to store the same baseline values in Baseline. By doing this, values you see in the Variance table compare the scheduled values to your current baseline.

8. A message box appears warning that you are about to overwrite a baseline that you've already saved. Click Yes.

Clearing a Baseline

If you decide that you want to remove a baseline that you've saved, do the following:

1. On the Tools menu, point to Tracking, and then click Clear Baseline.

Part Four:
Controlling
Projects

On Time! On Track! On Target! Managing Your Projects Successfully with Microsoft Project

2. In the Clear Baseline dialog box, make sure that the Clear Baseline option is selected.

3. In the Clear Baseline list, choose the baseline name you want to remove.

4. Under the For heading, select the Entire Project option.

5. Click OK. Project removes the values in the fields for the baseline you selected.

Viewing Multiple Baselines

If you want to see several baselines, the Multiple Baselines Gantt view shows taskbars in different colors for Baseline, Baseline 1, and Baseline 2, as shown in Figure 16-10. On the View menu, select More Views. In the More Views dialog box, double-click Multiple Baselines Gantt.

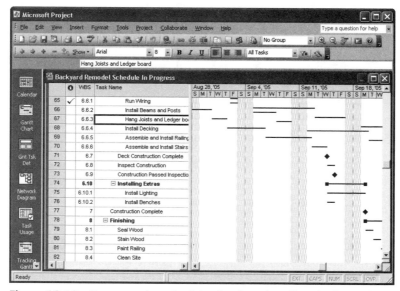

Figure 16-10   Compare the schedules for three baselines in the Multiple Baselines Gantt view.

Tip   If you want to modify the Multiple Baselines Gantt view to show different baselines, such as Baseline 4, right-click the Gantt Chart and choose Bar Styles on the shortcut menu. In the Bar Styles dialog box, you can replace the baseline start and finish date fields with the fields for the baseline you want to display.

In Summary

Tweaking a project schedule to deliver the combination of scope, schedule, and budget is a balancing act. Depending on which measures are more important, you can choose different techniques for modifying the schedule. Some techniques focus on rearranging tasks, whereas others look at reassigning resources. This chapter explained the alternatives and showed how to apply them using features in Project.

Part Four:
Controlling
Projects

On Time! On Track! On Target! Managing Your Projects Successfully with Microsoft Project

Chapter Seventeen

Balancing the Budget and Other Project Variables

There is such a choice of difficulties that I am myself at a loss how to determine.

— *James Wolfe*

To be a project manager, you had better be able to juggle. Your aim is to balance the project's objectives and scope with the constraints of time, money, scope, quality, and the realities of change requests, risks, and the ebb and flow of day-to-day progress. At the same time, you must temper the moods of your project team—from organizational inertia, when you need to plead for seemingly every bit of work, to a kind of euphoria in which team members become so absorbed in their work that time and money seem not to matter at all.

Regardless of the unfortunate circumstances that arise—a key resource's unexpected three-week Tahitian honeymoon, the pay rate of the person you find as a replacement, or the radical scope change when the customer wants clogs, not blogs—you must find a way to remedy the situation. Sometimes, you can adjust your project plan to complete the project within the original constraints. At other times, an infusion of additional funds or additional time is required. More likely, you'll juggle *all* variables of your project to achieve as much as you can while sacrificing as little as possible. The options from which you can choose are as numerous as your project objectives and as varied as the personalities of your team members. Balancing all the factors is a talent that takes time to develop, so this chapter introduces some of the strategies you can use to bring a project back into balance.

Cost, Scope, Quality, and Schedule

Although managing a project successfully is an art, the foundation is pure math. Cost is a function of project scope, desired level of quality, and schedule. In other words, how *much* depends on how *many*, how *good*, and how *long*. If you change one of these factors, something else has to give. So, you must evaluate your choices to decide which solution best fits the priorities for your particular project. For example, if quality is the key to differentiating a product from the competition, taking more time and increasing the budget might be the preferred choice. However, if getting that same product to market before the competition is critical, reducing the product features (scope) or accepting a slightly higher level of errors (quality) might be better.

As the project manager, you might be asked to compile recommendations for stakeholders to consider for getting a project back on track. If your budget is running out and that's all you have to spend, should you sacrifice scope, schedule, or quality? Will adding resources shorten the schedule or simply increase cost? And how will these changes affect the risks you take for the project? Following the money is one way to remain objective

Part Four:
Controlling
Projects

On Time! On Track! On Target! Managing Your Projects Successfully with Microsoft Project

through these complicated decisions. Go back to the benefits and monetary results you and the stakeholders forecast for the capital budget analysis (see "Understanding Capital Budgets," page 162).

Balancing Acts

The good news is that you can bring a project back into balance in any number of ways. Of course, that's the bad news as well. With so many options, how do you separate optimal solutions from the also-rans?

You can pare down the options by starting with the ones within the realm of your authority, that is, what the project sponsor gave you authority over in the project charter (see "The Project Charter: Publicizing a Project," page 25). If your course correction doesn't affect anything or anyone outside of your project team, you can push on without having to ask permission.

If internal changes aren't enough, you can expand your options to those that require stakeholder permission, such as increasing the schedule, increasing the budget, reducing scope, or modifying the business objectives. And if your organization manages a portfolio of projects, the final step is to see whether your project is important enough to warrant pulling resources from other projects.

Best Practices

When you ask stakeholders to decide what to do, it's a good idea to come with options that you recommend and be prepared to answer their questions. They'll want to know what other solutions you looked at and why those won't work. And they'll want to know why you recommend the options you provide. Chapter 12, "Evaluating Project Performance," describes how you determine how far the project is off track. Chapter 9, "Building a Project Schedule," and Chapter 16, "Modifying the Project Schedule," describe techniques to improve project performance.

Unless the problems that derailed your project are obvious when you check project status, review your project plan and the assumptions within it. If something has changed that skewed your project plan—the objectives, scope, schedule, and budget no longer align—you can see how much ground you'll be able to regain by optimizing the remainder of the project. By determining the sources of problems and trying different solutions before you go to the stakeholders, you're more likely to receive the support you request.

Reassigning Resources

Changing which resources do what and where resources come from can help you improve project performance. Depending on the resource strategy you choose, you might need stakeholder permission or the go-ahead from the project sponsor. Here are several ways to improve performance with resource changes:

■ *Reassigning resources to the critical path* shortens the schedule with no change to labor cost (see "A Crash Course on Project Crashing," page 156). In fact, if the project pays for overhead charges or the rent on extra office space, a shorter schedule could reduce overall costs as well. If you have the right kind of resources to spare working on non-critical path tasks, you can move them to the critical path and shorten the remaining duration. Sounds great, but this approach comes with a lot of caveats. You've probably heard the saying "Too many cooks can spoil the broth." Adding more people can backfire. For example, when tasks aren't interrelated, you can assign more people to them, such as different houses in a development, but only so many surgeons can work at the same operating table.

The other challenge with shortening the critical path is that the critical path can change. As you reassign resources from one task to another, the changes in duration can add tasks to the critical path that weren't on it before. Moreover, reassigning resources takes time and effort, so the decrease in duration you can achieve should be worth your attention.

Note   Suppose you can crash the project, but you don't have the resources within your team to do it. Depending on the resources you need, the solution might be as simple as hiring other resources or as difficult as prying specialized resources away from another project.

■ *Using less expensive resources* can reduce costs, but the effect on the schedule depends on the resources. Perhaps a vendor is anxious to add your company's name to its client list and is willing to work at a discount. However, you usually get what you pay for. Resources that cost less are typically less experienced, so the trade-off is lower cost versus a longer schedule—and you might have to accept lower quality as well.

■ *Working overtime* is another way to shorten the schedule, often at the expense of cost and possibly quality. You use the resources you have, so no groveling is required. If resources aren't paid overtime, you seem to obtain a shorter schedule at no extra cost. But that works for only so long. Eventually, your people burn out, and the quality of their work might suffer. On the other hand, if you must pay overtime, the cost increases. Furthermore, salaried employees who work overtime hours carry an opportunity cost (see Chapter 10, "Working with a Budget").

Part Four:
Controlling
Projects

On Time! On Track! On Target! Managing Your Projects Successfully with Microsoft Project

- *Outsourcing* some or all of the work can sometimes reduce cost and duration. Specialists or vendors might be able to complete work faster or at a lower cost. For example, if you have trouble hanging a picture straight, a professional carpenter is probably faster, less expensive, and better than you are for framing a house. One disadvantage to outsourcing is an increase in risk, because you have less control over the outsourced work. In addition, setting up outsourcing takes time and effort. If the subcontractor you choose turns out to be less experienced than you expected, chances are you won't have time to switch to another vendor without slipping the schedule.

> **Tip** Sometimes, you can negotiate better rates if you commit to a volume of work with the same vendor. Furthermore, negotiating fixed fees removes some of your risk of cost overruns.

- *Working with customer resources* is another option, particularly if the project objectives are very important to the customer. For example, in the backyard remodel project, the homeowners might decide to do some of the work to keep the budget within their means. Of course, this approach works only if the customer has resources with the right skills.

- *Increasing productivity* with faster or more experienced resources is an attractive strategy. For example, a more experienced engineer, even one whose hourly rate is higher, might accomplish work in significantly less time and with less direction. An experienced engineer might work more quickly and introduce fewer errors, so testing takes less time as well. The difficulty is that more productive resources cost more and are in higher demand.

Optimizing the Schedule

When the project schedule runs off course, project managers tend to revisit their original estimates. In fact, stakeholders have been known to apply pressure to improve estimates so that the project comes in on time and within budget. The problem with this approach is that estimates tend to be optimistic, which could be why the project needs rework. If you succumb to revising your original estimates, you might be telling stakeholders what they want to hear—at least until the project is over and the results are only too obvious. Instead of playing games with numbers, you can try the following techniques to improve your project schedule:

■ *Fast-tracking a project* shortens the schedule by overlapping tasks that normally run in sequence (see "The Fast-Track to an Early Finish," page 154). As long as tasks don't use the same resources, you can reduce duration without increasing cost by paying closer attention to when work can occur. Unfortunately, fast-tracking can increase risk, because you start some tasks before the ones they depend on are complete.

■ *Breaking a project into phases* is another way to control costs. This approach often complements a decision to reduce or alter the scope of a project, because scope removed in the first phase can be added back in later when more money is available. The risk is that the later phases never receive funding or approval.

Prioritizing Cost-Related Changes

Some cost changes have little effect on your project. For example, if your project includes a contingency fund, it can cover some additional work hours or the extended rental on a backhoe. More expensive or more influential budget changes can affect a project's goals and its financial health. However, for changes that are critical to achieving the project's benefits, adding money to pay for those changes might be more advantageous than sticking to the budget.

Project managers often have authority to approve additional costs up to a preset limit (for instance, increases that total less than 5 percent of the overall budget). Typically, stakeholders decide whether to approve changes when the cost increase on the project is significant. The project charter (see "The Project Charter: Publicizing a Project," page 25) usually specifies the extent of a project manager's financial authority.

■ *Progressively increasing scope and quality* is another option and is often called incremental or iterative development. With this strategy, the project takes the quick and dirty route, and delivers a rough product that does most of the job. Then work continues to add the rest of the scope and improve quality until all the project objectives are met. Because customers sometimes can't articulate what they want, this approach has an added advantage of giving the customer something to look at. The feedback you get about the first delivery can help the project produce results closer to what the customer has in mind.

Business Decisions

When everything you try isn't enough to correct your project's course, you have to reconsider the balance between cost, scope, quality, and schedule. And that means that you have to get stakeholders involved. Here are some guidelines when considering a change to project variables:

■ *Reducing scope* might be necessary when all other methods for controlling the project fail. The best way to reduce scope is to

Part Four:
Controlling
Projects

On Time! On Track! On Target! Managing Your Projects Successfully with Microsoft Project

eliminate the least important requirements first. For example, if the homeowners for the backyard remodel want lighting, the lights around the deck and stairs are important for safety, but the aesthetic spotlights that shine on the trees can probably be eliminated. As project manager, you can recommend the scope items that can be eliminated based on your overall understanding of the project's objectives. However, when deep cuts are needed, additional interviews to understand what the customer really needs are in order.

- *Changing financial goals*, such as ROI, might be an option, for instance, if your organization is willing to sacrifice some profit to beat the competition to market, to increase market share, or to achieve other strategic business objectives.

- *Increasing the duration of the schedule* might be acceptable from a business standpoint, but increased duration often comes with increased cost. If stakeholders decide to increase the schedule, you must evaluate the financial measures to ensure that they are still acceptable as well.

Important   Sacrificing quality is rarely a good idea. The phrase "Close enough for government work," conveys that feeling of resignation from results that are functional but less than what they could be. Reduced quality often ends up costing more in rework, repairs, team morale, and irretrievably damaged reputations.

In Summary

Money is important, but it isn't the only project characteristic that counts. As circumstances change, you must continually weigh cost against schedule, scope, quality, and risk to make sure the project achieves its goals within the constraints placed upon it. You can recover from some changes by fine-tuning your project. Although fine-tuning takes time, you can make the changes you need without obtaining permission from anyone else. For more dramatic changes, you have to work with project stakeholders and, sometimes, top management to choose the right approach.

Part Four:
Controlling
Projects

On Time! On Track! On Target! Managing Your Projects Successfully with Microsoft Project

Chapter Eighteen

Managing Risk

The pessimist sees difficulty in every opportunity. The optimist sees the opportunity in every difficulty.

— *Winston Churchill*

Projects are often tied to opportunities, everything from bringing a new product to market to improving your home for more enjoyment or resale. But opportunities invite risks—large and small—and risks can threaten a project's budget, schedule, and the quality of its results. Some risks are more likely to occur than others, and some risks have a greater effect, in terms of time and money. *Risk management* is about identifying risks, estimating the effect each risk could have, reducing the chances that risks will happen, and planning actions to take in response if they do. Like cutting costs by foregoing insurance coverage, you can choose to go without managing risk. But if risks occur, the risk planning you do and the risk responses you put into action are indispensable for keeping a project on schedule, its budget on track, and its stakeholders happy.

In this chapter, you'll learn some practices for managing risks. As you'll see, risk management is not a one-time task. It is a way of project management life that you begin during project initiation and then repeat continuously until the project is complete. Risk-management processes help you systematically track risks, assess their potential impact, and develop and evaluate plans to handle them. You'll learn more about each of these processes in the sections that follow. But first, you'll learn about some of the advantages that risk-management practices provide.

The Benefits of Managing Risk

Projects—like life—are grounded in uncertainty. Risks that come to fruition can undo carefully laid plans because dealing with unexpected or difficult conditions requires more time, more energy, and more money than you'd expect. Learning how to manage risk helps reduce the number of times you're caught off guard, and when you are, lessens the effect of what went wrong.

Risk management can help a project team accomplish its goals with less trouble and anxiety. Sure, discussion of risk and uncertainty might dampen the mood of the team members at the start, when their eyes are bright with enthusiasm. But the potential effect of many risks increases over time, so identifying risks early is well worth a small and short-lived letdown. You and the team will be ready to monitor and deal with risks before they take on a life of their own.

Consider risk management as an approach to avoiding issues that could have a detrimental (or catastrophic) effect on your project. It can increase your and other participants' understanding of the project. For example, risk

Part Four:
Controlling
Projects

On Time! On Track! On Target! Managing Your Projects Successfully with Microsoft Project

management provides a catalyst for measuring less risky solutions that offer the same level of quality or results. You can make stakeholders and managers aware of risks that they had not yet considered. And you can help everyone appreciate the implications of decisions that introduce a higher level of risk. In short, a realistic assessment of risks helps set expectations for project performance. Identifying and analyzing risks has a number of other benefits as well, such as

- Providing clarity of project objectives

- Resulting in better schedule and cost estimates

- Helping you and the team proceed with confidence knowing that risks are recognized and shared

- Documenting the need for contingency in the budget and schedule, and provide the information needed for allocating a contingency allowance

The Risk-Management Plan

Risk management—like budget and schedule planning—involves some guess work. You can't, for example, identify or anticipate every risk a project might face. In risk management, these risks are called *unknown unknowns*—events you simply can't foresee with unknown impact to your project. For instance, if you don't realize that life exists beyond our solar system, you can't anticipate the destruction of your construction project by the Galactic Department of Transportation. So, you start by identifying risks that you know might happen (called *known unknowns*), such as a stretch of bad weather that keeps you from pouring concrete. You define each risk that might occur and assess its effect on, say, the project's budget, schedule, scope, or resources. Then you develop plans for how to handle those risks and who will handle them if they should occur.

Risks can pop up at any point in a project's life. Some risks are present before work on a project begins. You might be handed a project whose scope and objectives are unclear. Financial assumptions might be too optimistic; resources once committed to the project might have taken new jobs, with new responsibilities and goals; organizational conflicts and department politics could threaten to divide the loyalties and the motivation of the project team. During project planning, you consider these risks as you build estimates, assign resources, and make other decisions.

Here are some of the factors that introduce risk:

- **Vague timing of future activities and events**   There's less certainty (and hence more risk) when a contractor says, "Yeah, I think I can fit you in come June. Probably take me a couple of weeks," instead of "I'll be there the morning of the 15th. I'll be finished on the 21st because I start another job the next day."

- **Stakeholders aren't involved**   Suppose your design team has come up with creative new packaging. The trouble is the materials are no longer available from any of your preferred suppliers, which you would have known if the procurement group had been involved. Identifying all the stakeholders for a project and including them in discussions can prevent surprise issues.

- **Options are limited**   Watch out for work that depends on people with rare combinations of skills or materials that are available from only a small number of sources.

- **Experience is limited**   Perhaps resources in key roles are new to the team or this is your first time working with a client. Responding to risks introduced by a lack of experience requires instinct as much as a well-crafted plan.

- **Unpredictable external events**   Risks like these fall into the category of environmental factors, for example:

  - ❏ A regulatory agency or city department changes permitting requirements or cancels your contract after the mayor's new budget is passed.

  - ❏ A rock slide closes the interstate to traffic, which means the supplies you're waiting for must be rerouted, delaying completion of some critical tasks.

Tip   Events that appear to be small risks are as important to evaluate as larger ones. Risks can crop up within the details of specific tasks such as the hours allocated or the estimated costs. As isolated events, these risks are easy to manage, but small-scale risks that mount up task-by-task can have a significant effect on schedule, budget, and, ultimately, on project scope and quality.

The good news is that risk-management processes don't need to be complex. A small set of documents will do, starting with a *risk-management plan*, which you prepare along with the project's communication plan and other

Part Four:
Controlling
Projects

On Time! On Track! On Target! Managing Your Projects Successfully with Microsoft Project

planning documents. It can be quite simple on small projects—a list of risks, an estimate of their impact, and a summary of actions you'll take if they occur. For more complex projects, your risk-management plan might include a separate information sheet or risk assessment form for each risk you've identified, as illustrated by the risk information sample form in Figure 18-1. Later, as you monitor and respond to risks that occur, you track what goes on risk-wise in a risk log. Simply having systematic procedures in place makes it easier to jump to action and make good decisions when risks occur.

Risk Information Sheet

ID 1.	Risk: County government regulations		
Priority: 1	Descr: Recently, the county government has been requiring more documentation and input from environmental experts before issuing permits. And, they have stopped permits or delayed them for smaller environmental issues. The construction site is close to a wetlands area, so we could have problems with permitting.		
Prob: High			
Impact: High			
Origin: Architect	Class: Business		Assigned to: Tim
Priority: 1	Response Options: M,A		Primary Response: Mitigate

Response Strategy
Hire an environmental expert to evaluate the property and estimate the chance of permit trouble before design begins.

Actions
1. Hire environmental expert
2. Provide conceptual sketches to expert
3. Talk to contact in county planning department to get inside scoop

Contingency Plan	
Identify constraints on construction that would stop permit and develop design that avoids those constraints.	
Status	Date

Approved	Date	Reason

Figure 18-1 In more complex projects, you might use a form to document each identified risk.

The form in Figure 18-1, *OnTime_Risk_Information_Sheet.doc*, is available in the *Sample Documents* folder on the companion CD.

For any size project, putting together a simple risk-management plan helps team members think about what they will do about risk *before* they need to do it. A plan forges a common understanding of the nature of each risk and sets out the steps to control and reduce a risk's probability and impact. A risk-management document typically includes the following sections:

- **Identified risks**   Include a list of *all* risks you've identified for the project with brief descriptions. You reserve your assessment of significance and decisions about risk response for other sections of the document.

- **Risk assessment**   Estimate the likelihood of the risk occurring and the potential impact to the project. Team members and stakeholders must agree on which issues pose the greatest threat, because you usually can't manage every risk you face. To limit the number of risks to a manageable number, the assessment section includes a prioritized list of risks.

- **Risk response**   Formulate the strategies you plan to use to avoid some risks completely, reduce the probability that risks occur, and lessen the impact if they do occur. This section identifies which risks you will respond to and which ones you will accept. Moreover, you can identify the money (and time) you keep in reserve to implement your risk responses.

- **Monitoring plan and metrics**   List the processes you plan to use to monitor risks and the metrics you use to evaluate risks.

- **Risk triggers**   Make a list of the risk triggers, the events or circumstances that provide early warning of risks that are in danger of occurring. For instance, if one of your risks is that a critical resource is in short supply, missing a task deadline may indicate that the risk is coming to fruition—or has already occurred—and you must take action.

- **Risk documents**   Include the risk information sheet and risk log you plan to use to manage risks.

Part Four:
Controlling
Projects

On Time! On Track! On Target! Managing Your Projects Successfully with Microsoft Project

Identifying and Describing Risks

You can't manage risks with one-on-one conversations in the hallway. The processes you follow to identify and describe risks (and later to assess and plan how to respond to risks) need to be more systematic. Resistance to formal risk management is more common than you'd expect. Someone might say, "We know every project has risks. We could spend the duration of the project trying to define them all. Let's just deal with them as they come up." That approach, of course, earns the award as the first risk for your project.

Tip   The formality and sophistication of your risk-management processes depends on the size and complexity of the project; how many groups, departments, or organizations are involved; and the expectation and needs of stakeholders. Yes, more formal risk-management processes require more time. However, you'll also realize greater benefits. For example, documenting your approach to managing risks on one project is great information to have when you're planning and making estimates for future projects.

From the beginning, you know at least some of the areas that present risks to manage: changes or additions to project scope, quality and performance benchmarks, controlling costs, and meeting the schedule. Begin by identifying risks you might encounter for each of these areas. For example, discussing task durations as you refine estimates often raises potential problems. Add those to your list of risks.

Tip   What better way is there to reduce and control schedule risks than by developing a realistic schedule in the first place—one with durations that take into account the possibility of risks occurring?

Think beyond your project when identifying risks. Meet with key project resources and ask them about risks they foresee. Ask experienced project managers to review your plan and talk to people who are experts in specific areas of the project. If you're working with a vendor for the first time, for example, talk to the vendor's other clients.

Be as specific as possible when identifying and describing risks. Identify the roles or resources whose work would be affected, the related tasks, and the deliverables and goals that might be jeopardized. Also, be as precise as possible in describing the consequences, such as the time added to the schedule or the extra cost if a risk occurs.

You might stop short of adding a risk when you see your lead engineer pull away on her new Kawasaki motorcycle without a helmet, but consider the risks that resources present. Which resources are booked to the maximum? Whose skills are vital to the completion of key tasks? Are hard-to-find resources assigned to the longest tasks on your critical path?

In a simple risk-management plan, the risk assessment includes a summary of the risks you've identified, the probability and impact, and background for your assessment. This information helps you prioritize the risks you monitor, because most projects have too many risks to watch them all. (You'll learn more about determining the ratings for probability and impact later in "Choosing the Risks You'll Manage" on page 305.) Table 18-1 illustrates a simple risk-assessment summary.

Table 18-1 A Simple Risk Assessment Summary

No.	Risk Event	Probability/ Impact	Assessment
1	Availability of appropriate conference facility	High / Very High	Most conferences are scheduled one to two years in advance, so it is very likely that the better quality conference facilities are already booked. In addition, a two-week window makes availability at the right time unlikely. To make a good impression on industry heavy hitters, it is imperative to have a high-quality facility.
12	Marketing initiative is late	Medium / Very High	A major marketing initiative will have management backing so it should not suffer for funds or resources as much as other projects. But it is still a project and prone to running late. If the marketing initiative runs late and comes after the conference, the impact is catastrophic.
2	Availability of appropriate lodging for several hundred executives	High / Medium	Because conference facilities are often connected with a hotel, it is very likely that the hotels with conference facilities have blocks of rooms reserved. However, the impact is not as great because there are usually multiple hotels nearby.

Note Microsoft Office Online (*http://www.microsoft.com/office*) offers templates related to project risk management, including a sample risk-management plan (in Microsoft Word), as well as a risk assessment questionnaire, and a risk identification questionnaire. Distribute the questionnaires to stakeholders and team members to identify risks and to collect information you need to assess and quantify the impact of the risks.

Part Four:
Controlling
Projects

On Time! On Track! On Target! Managing Your Projects Successfully with Microsoft Project

Assessing Risks

Assessing risks can be subjective. But for others, you'll have some details to work with. If you're managing a project to produce this year's hottest toy, a large percentage of initial revenue depends on seasonal sales. What are the prime risks to missing the release date? What happens to the revenue forecast if you miss the release date by 30 days or even one week? You can often quantify a specific risk (the late completion of a task or the decrease in manufacturing capacity), but you also need to understand the broader effects of the risk if it occurs—what other tasks depend on the task that is late, and what risks does that heighten or introduce?

Assessing risks boils down to two big questions:

- How likely is this risk to occur?

- How much damage might it do if it does?

The answers to these questions aren't easy to come by. Often, you have to rely on rough tools like your experience and the collective wisdom of the team. Sometimes, you can obtain harder evidence. Based on the information that you can gather and analyze, set up a scheme for classifying risks. You can go with low, medium, and high or work with numerical ratings (1 for low, 2 for medium, 3 for high). If you prefer to rank risks with more precision (at least as much as you can for events that are uncertain), you could divide these categories into narrower levels (adding low medium and high medium, for instance). Bottom line: you want a convention that lets you record the probability and impact of a risk consistently and that helps you evaluate the significance of risks given the number of risks and the size and complexity of the project.

Whether you go the analytical route or trust your gut, assessing risks in terms of time and money is essential. Without an estimate of the impact of a risk, how can you decide how much money and time to spend addressing it? For example, you can correlate thresholds of time and money to levels of impact. Less than $25,000 is low impact; $25,000 to $50,000 is medium impact; and anything over $50,000 is high impact. Similarly, you could assign the number of months of delay to represent low, medium, and high impact.

> **Warning**   Tasks that are difficult to estimate are red flags for risk. Work with the people assigned to those tasks to determine why the estimates are so uncertain. You can then determine how to manage the associated risks.

Choosing the Risks You'll Manage

You'll find risks under almost every stone that you, stakeholders, and the project team turn over. How can you possibly manage each of your specific project risks as well as those that result from factors largely out of your control? The answer is you can't. Risk management entails not only identifying the risks you might encounter, but also determining whether you should bother monitoring them at all. Clearly, you have to prioritize risks, and the probability, impact, and the cost (called the *risk value*) are your tools.

For risks with low probability and little impact, you might simply accept the consequences if the risk occurs. Or you might use some money from contingency funds (see "Setting Up Contingency Funds," page 309) to cover the cost. There's no reason to devise intricate response plans to risks that pose little danger to your project. They aren't likely to happen, and they don't hurt very much if they do. The ones to watch are those with a high probability of occurring and a significant effect.

Sorting by probability and ranking risks makes Microsoft Excel an ideal tool for evaluating probability and impact. After you add risks and their probability and impact to a worksheet, you can calculate risk value by multiplying probability and impact, as demonstrated in the Excel worksheet in Figure 18-2 on the next page. Risk value represents the consequences (the costs) of each risk should it occur.

For a visual indication of how many risks you should monitor, you can turn the tabular information into a chart in Excel, as shown in Figure 18-3 on the next page. For this chart, the legend correlates risk value with the duration of potential schedule delays. With a set of calculations such as these, you can prioritize risks and start developing plans for how to respond.

> **Tip**   Impact and probability of a risk event are not one-time measures. You must reevaluate risks and adjust these measures as work progresses.

Part Four:
Controlling
Projects

On Time! On Track! On Target! Managing Your Projects Successfully with Microsoft Project

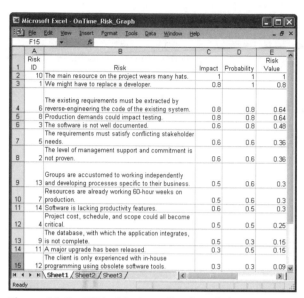

Figure 18-2 With risks in an Excel worksheet, you can calculate risk value and sort risks by probability and impact.

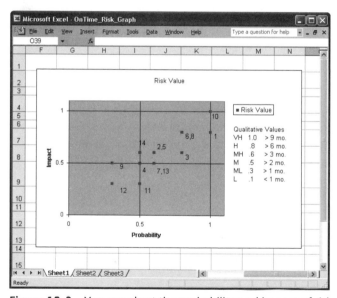

Figure 18-3 You can chart the probability and impact of risks (the risk value) to see how many fall in the quadrant of high probability and high impact.

The Excel workbook shown in Figure 18-3, *OnTime_Risk_Graph.xls*, is available in the *Sample Documents* folder on the companion CD.

Responding to Risks

After you have decided which risks are significant enough to manage, you need a response for each one. For example, if your project includes a helicopter delivery of a hot tub, you might consider an insurance policy to cover the damage if the hot tub falls on the house. Or, if your resources are completely booked, you might mitigate the risk of unavailable resources with a plan to line up subcontractors ahead of time. Identify the metrics you'll use to measure the success of the response, if you have to carry it out. For instance, the schedule variance is one measure you might use to see whether your resource response is working. Because risks have different probabilities and impact, responses must be appropriate for the magnitude of the risk. For example, a response that costs $100,000 is overkill if the price of delivering the project late is only $10,000.

In general, the best options are the ones that prevent a risk from occurring. But reducing impact or preventing impact from snowballing works, too. Here are some methods you can use to respond to risks to your project.

Best Practices

Similar projects share similar risks, which means you can learn about risks you're likely to encounter by studying what happened to other projects and by talking to people who were on those teams. If your organization doesn't record historical information about projects (see Chapter 21, "Archiving Historical Information"), show your manager the time and money that's at risk as an incentive to start.

When you hold a post-project review or lessons learned session (see Chapter 19, "Learning Lessons"), be sure to discuss the risks that occurred and the risk responses that worked—or not. In particular, talk about the risks that occurred that no one saw coming, so the next project manager and project team won't be blindsided.

- **Accept the risk**   If risks are negligible in probability or impact, the easiest option is to accept the consequences. Your hard disk might crash, but you'll be willing to accept the time it will take to restore your files from your company backups. You don't have to plan any other actions.

- **Avoid the risk**   If one portion of your project poses huge risks to completing the rest of the project, you might avoid the risk by eliminating the risky portion from the scope. Of course, this option works only if the scope change doesn't irreparably damage the business case for the project.

- **Limit the impact**   This is often called *risk mitigation*—taking steps to lessen whatever consequences a risk might pose. For example, if team members are unfamiliar with a new tool, but that tool must be used to

Part Four:
Controlling
Projects

On Time! On Track! On Target! Managing Your Projects Successfully with Microsoft Project

prepare project deliverables, sending the team to a training session mitigates that risk.

- **Transfer the risk**   This means that you put the majority of the burden of the risk on someone else. The most common example is purchasing insurance policies, which transfers risks to the insurance companies. You're not going to set aside project money to rebuild should a fire destroy your construction. Instead, you pay a small premium for fire insurance. However, your project still suffers a setback to the schedule.

  Asking vendors for fixed-price bids is another example of transferring risk. With a fixed-price bid, the subcontractor faces the risk of cost overruns if the work takes more time than allocated. (You might decide to share the risk by specifying the percentage of cost overruns that the subcontractor must absorb.)

- **Use contingency plans**   Contingency plans are alternative courses of action you can take if a risk occurs. They often rely on additional funds set aside to handle unanticipated costs. For instance, you might plan a conference for a reasonably priced hotel with a great conference room layout. Your contingency plan if that hotel is unavailable could be to choose another, more expensive hotel and increase the conference registration fee. The next section discusses how to gauge the size of a contingency fund and the processes for using one.

For any approach to risk response, you should evaluate your ability to implement a particular option. Here are some questions you can ask to help you decide whether a response is feasible:

- Do you have the resources for the response?

- How will the response affect resources on other tasks and other projects?

- Do you need to purchase or provide additional equipment? For example, would you need to purchase another computer or outfit another workstation to bring a new resource on board?

- How does the response affect performance expectations for the project?

- How quickly can you implement the response strategy?

Keep in mind that scope, schedule, budget, quality, and risk are interconnected. If a risk occurs, the response might entail scope changes or schedule changes. And those need to be tracked through your change management process (see Chapter 15, "Managing Project Changes").

Setting Up Contingency Funds

Living hand to mouth, without any budget or time set aside to handle unexpected events, is no way to run a project. Experienced project managers build some buffer into project schedules and establish contingency funds in their budgets as a way to respond to risks that occur. The question with contingency funds is "How much?"

You can determine an amount for a contingency fund in several ways, although the method is often part calculation and part negotiation with management. Some organizations use a percentage of project budget and duration to calculate contingency, basing the percentage on prior experience. Still another approach is to use a percentage of the target profit margin. In other words, project sponsors might agree to give up one percentage point of the expected return to cover the costs of uncertainty.

Most organizations ask project managers to estimate the cost of likely risk events. You can multiply the cost by the probability as a start for the amount of contingency funds you need to set aside. Here's an example:

- Design has run over budget on two of the last three projects, so you set the probability of cost overrun at 66 percent.

- The average overrun is 10 percent and your task cost is $20,000. You set the impact at $2,000.

- The risk value is the probability multiplied by the impact: 66% × $2,000, or $1,320.

However, you typically don't add the entire risk value to a contingency fund, because there's a low probability that *all* your risks will occur.

Tip Sometimes budgets are based on cost ranges instead of single numbers. Budgeting to a cost range is a type of basic contingency, so adding a contingency fund is redundant.

A contingency budget handles the *costs* of risks. As the project manager, you might be given a threshold for authorizing expenditures from the contingency fund. For amounts above that limit, you have to get approval of management, customers, or stakeholders.

You might also have what's sometimes referred to as a *management reserve*, which is money set aside by project sponsors and stakeholders to address risks and other situations that you didn't anticipate. This reserve, if it exists

Part Four:
Controlling
Projects

On Time! On Track! On Target! Managing Your Projects Successfully with Microsoft Project

at all, is usually a percentage of the total project budget. In addition to dealing with the occurrence of unknown risks, a management reserve can be used to fund significant change requests that happen to provide significant value. Project sponsors often control the management reserve.

Tip   Another component of contingency planning is to identify any nice-to-have requirements that everyone agrees can be abandoned, if necessary. The time and budget allocated to these requirements could be shifted to cover work related to key requirements if issues arise.

You can spread a contingency allowance over the phases of a project, with a percentage designated for each phase (with the unspent portion carried over to the next phase). Or you could spread the funds over major areas of responsibility (design, production, and testing, for example). Another approach is to hold the contingency allowance in a single pot and disperse it through a request and approval process.

Note   Publicize the conditions under which contingency funds are available. By doing so, you don't have to worry about team members relying on those funds to correct schedule and budget mistakes or stakeholders trying to grab their share before the contingency pot is gone.

Tracking Risks

The overall risk to a project varies as work progresses. Risk is high early on when uncertainty is at its peak. As the amount of work on the project is completed, the overall risk decreases. Your risk-management documentation should include a risk log that you use to track and update the status of each risk.

A risk log includes some of the same information as a risk-management plan, but in condensed form. Here are items to include in a risk log:

■ Monitored risks including a description of the risk, related tasks, and the planned response.

■ The person responsible for monitoring each risk. To evaluate the status of risks and the effectiveness of responses, you must assign someone who understands the task or the area of the project in which the risk might occur.

Because of the rise and fall in the probability and impact of risks, risk management is a continuous activity. Updating the risk log regularly is part and parcel to managing a project. In other words, don't wake up on day 83 of the project and decide it's as good a time as any to check risk status.

As you pass milestones in a project, you can close some risks. For example, if resource availability was a risk, but your project just obtained five more people because of another project's delay, you might close that risk. (Of course, the risk could return if the other project gets back on track.) Closing a risk may free up contingency funds you need for other risks.

On the other hand, you're likely to add risks as a project progresses. Perhaps a component that is vital to quality has turned out to be a tougher design problem than you thought. As you identify new risks and add them to the risk log, you assess the probability and impact, calculate risk value, and develop response strategies as you did for the risks identified at the beginning of the project.

Managing risk involves modifying your assessment and approach to active risks, looking ahead at future tasks to find ways to make up time and reduce costs, dipping into reserves when a clear need arises, and then repeating these steps periodically.

Here are some practices to keep in mind for conducting risk management as work on a project progresses:

- *Regularly update the risk log* so that it reflects the current status and performance of the project. Close risks that are no longer an issue and adjust the probability and impact of risks you're monitoring. Update the status of each risk that has occurred and document the steps you've taken in your response plans.

Tracking Risks In Project

If you use Microsoft Office Project Server 2003 and Windows SharePoint Services, you can track risks in a Microsoft Project schedule. On the Collaboration menu, choose Risk. You can enter risk information like the following:

- The probability that a risk will occur (as a percentage)

- The impact of a risk (using a value from 1 to 10)

- The cost impact should the risk happen

- The type of risk

- A description of the risk

- Your mitigation plan

- Your contingency plan

- The condition or conditions that trigger the contingency plan

If you're set up to track risks in Project, the program also helps you manage risks. For example, you can associate risks with specific tasks, documents (such as your mitigation plan), or other risks. It's a good idea to associate risks with specific tasks, whether or not you use Project.

Part Four:
Controlling
Projects

On Time! On Track! On Target! Managing Your Projects Successfully with Microsoft Project

> **Note** Some project managers refer to risks that occur as issues and log them in an issue tracking log. Other project managers use the term *issues* to refer to small obstacles that arise and track risks, both potential and real, in a risk log. Either approach is fine as long as you identify the difference up front.

- *Ask team members about risks in project status meetings.* Besides keeping the risk log current, this helps educate the project team about your risk-management procedures.

- *Follow your risk-management processes* for each new risk. Assign someone to assess each risk and develop a response plan.

- *Report risk status* with other project status. The way you update and report risk status depends on the size and scope of a project, the budget, and way you communicate. You might include a section in your regular status report. You also need formal risk review meetings, in which stakeholders discuss options for addressing risks, learn about the status and success of responses, and approve contingency funds if their say-so is required.

In Summary

You've successfully established an approach to managing risks when the processes you use can be repeated, measured, and demonstrated with pride to stakeholders. You don't have time to monitor every risk, so risk management includes prioritizing risks and monitoring only the most significant ones. By planning ahead, you can prevent some risks completely and limit the consequences of others. Risk changes throughout the life of a project, so risk management is an ongoing activity. You monitor risks and keep people informed about project risks in status reports, project status meetings, and regular risk review meetings.

Part Five
Closing Projects

In this part

Chapter Nineteen   **Learning Lessons**. 314
Chapter Twenty   **Managing Project Completion**. 330
Chapter Twenty-One   **Archiving Historical Information** 340

Part Five:
Closing Projects

On Time! On Track! On Target! Managing Your Projects Successfully with Microsoft Project

Chapter Nineteen

Learning Lessons

The essence of success is that it is never necessary to think of a new idea oneself. It is far better to wait until somebody else does it, and then to copy him in every detail, except his mistakes.

— *Aubrey Menen*

"I hope you've learned your lesson!" Unless you were different from most children, you probably heard that admonishment more than once while growing up. Unfortunately, that statement has made many people think of lessons as negative and mistakes as something to hide. As an adult, not repeating the mistakes of the past is an important part of improving performance for the projects you manage.

Improving performance isn't just about avoiding past mistakes. Progress comes from continually building on the successes of others. After the Wright brothers got the first airplane airborne, the path to today's jumbo jets was nothing more than a lot of enhancements.

This chapter focuses on how you learn from past performance to improve future results, which covers more about psychology than it does project management. Few people like to admit mistakes. Some don't like to advertise their success—either for fear of boasting or in a misguided attempt to keep the glory to themselves. Others keep quiet about successes because they think they're insignificant. You'll learn some techniques to draw out the successes that people have achieved as well as effective yet gentle ways to identify the mistakes that you don't want to repeat. More important, you'll learn how to leverage your lessons learned—by documenting them and publicizing them so that everyone else in your organization can put them into practice.

The Importance of Lessons Learned

The only real mistake is the one from which we learn nothing.

— *John Powell*

Maintaining information about past projects and making a point of reviewing that information *before* beginning new projects is the most effective way to improve project performance. Nothing is as disheartening as making the same mistakes you made once before. And why should anyone else have to suffer the frustration of repeating a mistake when you've already paid that price? Remembering what did work and repeating those successes is just as important. Best practices are effective because they help people move forward instead of reinventing what someone else already discovered. Here are some of the ways you can put lessons learned—positive and negative—to use:

■ **Apply proven effective techniques**   If you've used a document template to produce a document, you already know how reuse can speed up and increase the accuracy of your work. Proven practices,

Part Five:
Closing Projects

On Time! On Track! On Target! Managing Your Projects Successfully with Microsoft Project

processes, and documents work the same way for projects. Successful strategies, powerful approaches, timesaving techniques, shortcuts, checklists, and well-designed documents help future project teams start where past teams left off. For example, suppose you discover that the usually recalcitrant sales team calls you back when you leave messages that tell it which sales won't go through until it resolves an issue with you. By sharing this nugget with other team members and project managers, you can improve the performance of more projects than your own, increase the results of the entire organization, and spread joy to people around you.

Although every project is unique, many projects share tasks, types of resources, typical costs, and potential risks. If a completed project is similar to the one you're managing, you can reuse that project's documents as templates to save time and increase accuracy. Unlike in publishing and academic circles, plagiarism is a virtue for managing projects.

- **Eliminate the costs of past mistakes**   Mistakes can be costly in so many ways: overspent budgets, delays, missed deadlines, poor quality, reduced scope, unmet objectives, and damaged reputations, to name a few. Your organization has paid for past mistakes. It would just as soon not pay for them again. By reviewing the mistakes that others have made and taking steps to prevent them, you can avoid a second round of tuition.

- **Build better estimates**   Every project struggles with the unceasing optimism of the people who estimate project time, money, and other resource requirements. You can build more realistic estimates for your projects by evaluating actual values from completed projects. For example, if past projects underestimated the time and resources needed, you can increase your future estimates. If those projects ran into problems, you can estimate a shorter schedule and lower costs, because you've learned how to prevent similar problems.

Tip   Past performance is equally helpful if you're being pressured to set unrealistic dates or budgets. By showing stakeholders historical data, you have a better chance of convincing them that your estimates are realistic.

- **Educate project managers and team members**   Educating team members can make your job as project manager easier. Using lessons from past projects, you can show team members why you ask them to perform the tasks you do. They'll realize that you're trying to help rather than annoy. And, they'll work more autonomously so you have more time to keep projects on track.

Part Five:
Closing Projects

On Time! On Track! On Target! Managing Your Projects Successfully with Microsoft Project

Best Practices

Some people don't take anything on faith. Past performance can help you convince others that your plans will work, whether you're trying to build a schedule that the team can meet or prove the benefits of project management to your company's executives. For example, if previous projects couldn't meet the deadlines and budget you're being asked to accept, you can push for more realistic numbers. Or you could show that the time spent on quality assurance and control actually saves money instead of costing extra.

Lessons learned can also demonstrate how project management helps improve performance—or how the lack of project management hurts. Folks who are new to projects might not understand the value of project management practices. Lessons learned provide real-life examples that can be persuasive. For instance, suppose you've had trouble with scope creep in the past. If documented lessons learned identify the lack of change management as the culprit, you'll have an easier time convincing your executives to support a change management system. Knowing how much scope creep cost other projects or how much money a preliminary change management process has saved can be even more compelling to cost-conscious executives. Chapter 21, "Archiving Historical Information," discusses how to store project performance data for situations like these.

Important Project management grows more popular every year, so organizations continually require more project managers and more project-savvy workers. Unless you want to work overtime to manage an ever-increasing stable of projects, you can use lessons from past projects to teach others how to manage projects of their own.

Collecting Lessons Learned

Status updates, code reviews, and other project meetings can be convenient opportunities for gathering suggestions for what to do and what not to do in the future. But scheduling meetings regularly and specifically for identifying lessons learned is a better idea. Extracting lessons learned from reticent team members requires a delicate balance of honesty and tact. Getting the attendees into a productive mind-set and laying out the ground rules for these meetings takes some extra care.

There's enough work to do on projects that no one has time to attend unnecessary meetings. If people think a meeting is about finding fault, they'd just as soon do laundry or see the dentist for a root canal. What's more, poorly run meetings drive people into a daze; they fidget, then daydream, doodle, and eventually stop attending other meetings you schedule.

Tip You can initially present these lessons learned meetings as informal project reviews. You collect valuable information for future projects and educate team members on better project processes at the same time.

The following sections provide some suggestions for getting the most out of lessons learned sessions.

Meeting Participants and What They Do

Lessons learned sessions can be quiet—too quiet, if no one wants to expose his mistakes or worries that others might make fun of his discoveries. To the contrary, a troubled project could lead to chaotic sessions of finger pointing, as everyone tries to place the spotlight on someone else. Effective project reviews and lessons learned meetings don't just happen. They need a few participants to play special roles and the other attendees to interact in productive ways. The following sections describe each type of participant and how they contribute to running a worthwhile lessons learned meeting.

Tip   Sometimes, the same person can play multiple roles, depending on the size of your project, the number of meeting participants, and perhaps the openness you expect during the meeting. For example, the project manager could also act as facilitator, or a team member could double as the scribe. If you think that team members might be reticent about discussing lessons learned with a manager in the room, you can set up a meeting without managers to be run by an impartial facilitator.

Project Manager

Project managers initiate lessons learned meetings, so most of the meeting preparation falls into their hands. Here are the meeting responsibilities that a project manager usually performs:

- *Preparing for the meeting,* the project manager puts together any materials to be used during the meeting, such as project status, issues list, or items that team members have identified since the previous meeting. The project manager can set up the meeting or delegate those tasks to the meeting facilitator. Setting up a lessons learned meeting includes:

  - ❏ Planning the agenda

  - ❏ Estimating the length of the meeting

  - ❏ Scheduling the meeting date, time, and location

  - ❏ Distributing the meeting materials (at least a few days prior to the meeting)

Part Five:
Closing Projects

On Time! On Track! On Target! Managing Your Projects Successfully with Microsoft Project

■ *During the meeting,* the project manager kicks off the session with an overview of the project status; for example, the phase or milestone that prompted the lessons learned meeting, and the materials distributed before the meeting. The project manager also helps control the meeting interactions, participates in the discussions, and takes notes about accomplishments, problems, action items assigned, and decisions made.

Tip Because of project managers' thorough knowledge of their projects, they are likely to catch important points that the facilitator or scribe might miss.

■ *After the meeting is over,* the project manager works with the facilitator to write a lessons learned report (see "Documenting Lessons Learned" on page 325) and distributes the report to attendees and appropriate stakeholders (according to the communication plan described in Chapter 14, "Communicating Information"). For example, you probably don't want external stakeholders to see your lessons learned unless the lessons affect them directly. The project manager also tracks any action items to ensure that the people responsible complete them.

Lessons Learned Facilitator

The facilitator can assist the project manager by setting up the meeting or can focus only on ensuring a productive session. Here are the tasks that a facilitator performs to run an effective meeting:

■ Describe the goals of the meeting, such as identifying lessons learned for the project design phase

■ Explain the ground rules for the meeting (see "Ground Rules" on page 321) and the responsibilities of the participants

■ Control the meeting interaction

■ Keep the meeting focused on the agenda topics and progressing according to the set schedule

■ Suggest methods for setting priorities, promoting discussion, and making decisions

- Help the group resolve interaction issues, discussion logjams, and meeting conflicts
- Support discussions by making notes on a flip chart or white board

Scribe

The project manager and the facilitator are typically too busy with their other responsibilities to take thorough notes. Appoint someone who is familiar with the project to take notes about discussions, accomplishments, problems, action items, and decisions.

> **Tip** A person who is fast on a keyboard or has legible handwriting is important, but familiarity with the project is more so. Outsiders might not recognize acronyms and project-specific terminology, and they could struggle with which points are pertinent.

Team Members

Team members play simple roles, but they're not necessarily easy. Before the meeting, team members make notes about the lessons they've learned and review the materials that the project manager distributed. During the meeting, they share their discoveries and participate in the discussion. What's difficult about being a team member in these meetings is overcoming psychological obstacles and bad meeting habits, described in the next section.

Ground Rules

Surviving a meeting that spotlights some people's successes and other people's failures is a challenge. Egos and reputations are on the line. If you don't handle them with care, you won't learn as much as you had hoped. As the project manager, you have to manage more than your own personal interactions. If emotions run high, the productive discussions can quickly deteriorate to "That's the stupidest thing I've ever heard!", "What planet are you from?", or worse, a deafening silence.

Initiate Discussion with Open-Ended Questions

Like some parties, feedback sessions can take some effort to get started. Meeting attendees often hang back and let someone else be the first to talk. Ask the wrong kind of question, such as "Are things okay?" and your team members are likely to answer with "Yes." That is not the way to kick off discussion about lessons learned.

Open-ended questions (the ones that you can't answer with one word) are perfect for initiating discussions. For example, if you ask a team member "What worked well?" she might tell you about how she obtained a timely response from the sales team. To the contrary, if you ask "Are your tasks going well?" she might say "Yes." See "Accentuating the Positive" and "Analyzing Problems" on the next page for more examples of open-ended questions you can try.

Part Five:
Closing Projects

On Time! On Track! On Target! Managing Your Projects Successfully with Microsoft Project

Every good meeting needs ground rules, but lessons learned sessions need them more than most. Analyzing successes and failures is tough work, so repeating the rules is in order. Printing them on the agenda is a start. But the facilitator should review the rules at the beginning of the meeting and should jump in to redirect attendees if they go off track.

Accentuating the Positive

Rousing some initial discussion is much easier when you ask people about their successes: the tips, tricks, and other successful techniques they've discovered recently. People are more willing to talk about what they've done right. In fact, all but the quietest (or most secretive) team members enjoy sharing their successes.

Unless your meeting time is very limited or your attendees are unusually boastful, make a point of asking each person if they've found a technique they recommend. If your team members aren't jumping in with suggestions, here are some open-ended questions to help launch the exchange:

- Have you found techniques that save time (money, rework, patience, and so on)?
- What is your most exciting discovery on this project?
- Have you solved any tough problems recently? How did you solve them?
- What are the benefits of your approach?
- What do you recommend for future projects?

Analyzing Problems

The hardest part of collecting lessons learned is getting people to admit mistakes. Hiding mistakes is the worst response, but the one chosen most often. Although most people would agree that making mistakes is okay as long as you learn from them, convincing them to share their own gaffs is another matter. It's no surprise that team members don't want to be labeled as the one who triggered a cost overrun or a missed deadline. They worry that they'll lose their jobs or their chances for promotion. And sadly, in some work environments, their concerns are justified.

Your task as project manager and lessons learned detective depends on your organization's perception of mistakes. In organizations that recognize the value of learning from mistakes, your job is a little easier. Even in proactive environments, people are hesitant to admit mistakes. The most important step you can take to make people comfortable discussing failure is to focus on the problem, not the people. For example, if the discussion begins with "Mary didn't check the purchase orders and we received the wrong equipment," chances are that Mary will withdraw from the conversation, grow defensive, try to blame someone else, or choose one of many other unproductive responses. Instead, focus on the problem—we received the wrong equipment. Ask questions like "How can we improve our procurement process?" or "What can we change to ensure that we receive the right equipment next time?"

Here are a few open-ended questions to help identify problems in a non-blaming way:

- What would you do differently on the next project like this?

- What can we do better?

- How can we improve?

- What obstacles have you run into? What was your solution?

If you have the misfortune of working where the preferred approach is to find and punish scapegoats, don't expect to hear about mistakes right away. You must first earn team members' trust. And that could take longer than your project lasts. However, you can take steps to break down the barriers.

In a punitive environment, you have to show team members that it's safe to admit mistakes. You might need a process that doesn't publicize the raw notes of lessons learned meetings, only the recommendations for improvement that result. In addition, taking notes that don't include people's names might help attendees feel more comfortable about

Getting Better, Not Blamed

Focusing on improvement instead of blame can take getting used to. Personal and professional life is as rife with blame as projects are. And the same advice works in each of these environments. Talk about yourself instead of other people. Describe the problem you faced, how it affected you, and what you did about it. One way to frame a problem from your perspective is to begin your sentences with "I." For example, "I couldn't tell which servers were delivered." Admitting to mistakes that you've made or improvements you've discovered sets an example that your team members can follow.

The wrong approach is describing someone else's mistake. For example, if the answer to how to improve is "Make sure Mary checks the purchase orders," you'll be back where you started. You and the meeting facilitator have to help team members from reverting to old habits. If someone starts a sentence with "You" or someone's name, get ready to jump in and redirect the discussion.

Part Five:
Closing Projects

On Time! On Track! On Target! Managing Your Projects Successfully with Microsoft Project

talking. Use small problems and recommendations to demonstrate that they can report issues without repercussions.

Best Practices

Many organizations never get around to collecting lessons learned on projects, and the ones that do often save that task for the end. But project teams don't learn their lessons in the final days of a project. If you wait until then, many valuable lessons learned are already long forgotten.

Setting aside some time regularly to identify lessons learned is the best way to capture ideas while they're fresh. New techniques tend to become habit quickly. By scheduling lessons learned meetings at regular intervals, you can catch those tips while they still provide some excitement or stress relief.

Mistakes, on the other hand, have more staying power. The people who make them aren't likely to forget. However, you still want to catch that information quickly, so you can disseminate it to others and prevent those same mistakes from appearing again.

Important Some people don't like to say anything negative in public. At the beginning of the project, set up and publicize a method for team members to submit anonymous feedback, such as a written questionnaire. In the e-mail or memo announcing the lessons learned meeting, remind attendees that they can submit issues and suggestions via this alternative. You can rework the suggestions you receive into less threatening topics for the face-to-face session.

The Importance of an Agenda

Distribute an agenda for the lessons learned meeting a few days before it occurs. An agenda tells the attendees what they should be prepared to discuss and provides the first reminder of the meeting ground rules.

An agenda is even more important once the meeting begins. By following the agenda, you can be sure to cover all the important points, give each topic its fair share of meeting time, bring wayward discussions back to the topic at hand, and otherwise rein in meetings run amok. Figure 19-1 shows an example of an agenda for a lessons learned meeting.

A Word template, *Lessons Learned Agenda.dot*, is available in the *Templates* folder on the companion CD.

| <Project Name> | Lessons Learned Agenda |

Purpose of lessons learned meeting:

Date:

Start and end times:

Location:

Project manager:

Meeting facilitator:

Scribe:

Attendees:

Ground rules   Start and end on time

Follow the agenda

Everyone participates

One speaker at a time

Be constructive

Agenda items	Time allotted
1. Facilitator: Introduce meeting attendees.	
2. Facilitator: Review goals, responsibilities, and ground rules.	
3. Project manager: Present project, phase, or milestone summary.	
4. Identify accomplishments and successful techniques. Identify items that worked well Discuss.	
5. Identify problem areas. Identify items that worked well. Discuss.	
6. Identify action items.	

Page 1 of 2

Figure 19-1 Distribute an agenda before the meeting so attendees can prepare to discuss their lessons learned.

Documenting Lessons Learned

Lessons don't realize their full potential unless everyone knows about them. Without some way to share lessons learned, other project managers and team members will make the same mistakes you made, solve the problems you've already solved, and rediscover the same effective techniques you're already using.

Part Five:
Closing Projects

On Time! On Track! On Target! Managing Your Projects Successfully with Microsoft Project

A lessons learned report is one way to publicize recent successes and problems that have been resolved. It describes what went well on a project and what could be improved. The report describes the corrective items that resolved previous problems or action items proposed to fix problems the next time they arise. Lessons learned reports go into the project notebook to become part of the historical archive for a project (see "Information to Store about Projects," page 343). Figure 19-2 shows an example of a lessons learned report for the backyard remodel project.

Backyard Remodel Project | **Lessons Learned Report**

Meeting date: 9/30/2005
Project manager: Janice Galvin
Meeting facilitator: David So
Scribe: Terry Earls
Attendees: Entire project team

Purpose of lessons learned meeting: To identify successes and problems that occurred through the end of the design phase of the project.

Project Summary

Describe the status of the project, project phase, or milestone that this meeting encompasses.

- The backyard remodel project design phase is complete. The client approved the design and, with some consternation, the budget. The project manager submitted the architectural and engineering drawings to the county and received the construction permit on 9/23/2005

Successes

Identify all the items and techniques that worked well.

- *The engineer developed a software program* that converts the original components in the structural design to a bill of materials that uses stock lengths. This saved the project 5 percent on framing materials and should save 60 percent of the labor cost for cutting lumber.

- *The project manager researched construction loans and reviewed loan options with the client.* Because the project manager found construction loans with better terms than the ones that the client found, we were able to increase the budget by 5 percent.

Problems

Identify problems.

- *The client expected us to stay within budget.* We anticipated that a 25 percent increase would be acceptable, but the client insisted that we limit the increase to 5 percent. By meeting with the client early and reviewing loan options (see success above), we were able to satisfy the client's request.

- *The county construction permit took more time than we anticipated.* Late summer is a busy time for the county building department, because many projects are trying to push construction through before the weather turns cold.

- *Moving the hippopotamus that had taken up residence in the mud hole required more time and approvals than we anticipated.* We had to prepare a plan for the move to ensure that we did not endanger the animal further. The crowd of environmental protesters slowed down the survey team. In addition, finding a good home for the hippopotamus was challenging. We prepared a list of zoos in need of animals in case this situation arises again.

Action Items

Describe the solutions suggested to resolve identified problems.

- Janice: Store the list of zoos in the lessons learned database.

Page 1 of 1

Figure 19-2 Distribute a lessons learned report after a meeting so others can take advantage of what you've discovered.

A Word template, *Lessons Learned Report.dot*, is available in the *Templates* folder on the companion CD. The sample lessons learned report, *Backyard Remodel Lessons Learned.doc*, is available in the *Backyard Remodel Project* folder on the companion CD.

The problem with lessons learned reports is that they are quickly forgotten. A repository of lessons learned for all projects is a useful tool for project managers looking for solutions to pressing problems. The format that a repository takes depends on your organization and the technology that's available. For instance, a small company might develop a Microsoft Excel workbook to track lessons, as illustrated in Figure 19-3, whereas a large organization might use a Microsoft Access database or a Microsoft Windows SharePoint Services Web site.

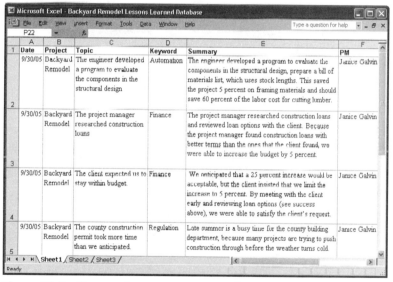

Figure 19-3   You can share successes as well as actions you'd rather not repeat by storing lessons learned from all projects in a repository available to all project managers and team members.

A sample lessons learned workbook, *Backyard Remodel Lessons Learned Database.xls*, is available in the *Backyard Remodel Project* folder on the companion CD.

Part Five:
Closing Projects

On Time! On Track! On Target! Managing Your Projects Successfully with Microsoft Project

In Summary

Learning from the past is the easiest way to improve performance in the future. Documenting lessons learned isn't difficult. But identifying lessons can be. Whether you're trying to identify what people did well or the mistakes that you can leverage, you must make people feel comfortable about sharing what they know. Running meetings that emphasize improvement rather than blame is the best approach. Written questionnaires are also effective, particularly in more difficult work environments.

Part Five:
Closing Projects

On Time! On Track! On Target! Managing Your Projects Successfully with Microsoft Project

Chapter Twenty

Managing Project Completion

All love affairs end. Eventually, the girl is gonna put curlers in her hair.

— Al McGuire

When the solution deliverables in a project are complete, you might *think* the project is done. But you still have a few *project management* tasks to finish. Although the closeout phase of a project is short, don't make the mistake of thinking it isn't important. The key accomplishment during closeout is receiving formal acceptance that the project is complete from the project customer. After all, if the customer *doesn't* consider the project a done deal, you aren't really in the closeout phase.

Another critical task in closing a project is ensuring that the transition to whatever should happen next runs smoothly. For example, with the backyard remodel project, you might provide the homeowners with the maintenance recommendations for the wood deck and the stone patio, and a quick review of how the electrical wiring works. If a project results in a new product, the closeout phase might include handing information over to manufacturing, operations, marketing, and other groups so they have what they need to build, sell, and support the product.

As long as you've been producing project reports *during* the project, generating closeout reports at the *end* of the project isn't a big deal, and the final results that the closeout reports show are valuable. Most important, the closeout reports provide the information you need to convince the customer that the project achieved its objectives. But closeout reports also act as educational tools for other project managers and project teams working on projects in the future.

This chapter summarizes the reporting you perform at the end of a project and references other sections in this book that describe project reporting in detail. See "Project Status Reports" on page 249 for information on how to gather and report during *and* at the end of the project. Chapter 19, "Learning Lessons," talks about documenting successes and needed improvements. Chapter 21, "Archiving Historical Information," describes techniques for storing your project information so you and others can find it in the future. This chapter also discusses how to obtain formal acceptance from the customer and how to handle the transition to life after the project is over.

Project Closeout Reports

Project closeout reports are like status reports, only more robust, because they sum up the final status of the project. The information they contain varies depending on the size of the project, what measures you've tracked during the project (see Chapter 12, "Evaluating Project Performance"), and

Part Five:
Closing Projects

On Time! On Track! On Target! Managing Your Projects Successfully with Microsoft Project

the deliverables and success criteria that the project is supposed to fulfill. For example, for the backyard remodel project, a constructed deck, a signed certificate of use from the county government, and a signed check for payment are good indications that the project is complete. The closeout report might identify those completed milestones along with a summary of the duration of the project, the final cost, and other information, as illustrated in Figure 20-1. Closeout reports for large projects typically include more information.

Backyard Remodel Project	**Closeout Report**

Project manager: Janice Galvin

Project Summary

The backyard remodel project is complete. The deck and patio have been built; the county inspected the construction and issued a certificate of use; and the customer has accepted and paid for the work. The final cost was 10% over budget, and the project finished two weeks late.

Cost

Estimated cost	$50,000
Final cost	$55,000
Variance	$5,000
Variance %	10%

Schedule

Estimated finish date	09/26/05
Actual finish date	10/10/05
Variance	2 weeks

Quality and Customer Satisfaction

The customer is very happy with the quality of the construction and particularly pleased with how thoroughly the crew cleaned up the yard at the end of construction.

Issues

None that have not been resolved.

Risks

Finding a home for the hippopotamus that had moved into the mud hole required some research and time. We didn't anticipate this risk, because a hippopotamus is an unlikely animal to find in a residential backyard.

Lessons Learned

The workload at the county building department delayed the permit for construction. In the future, we will check with the county to see how long it anticipates the permit process will take when that phase of the project is planned to occur.

Page 1 of 1

Figure 20-1   A closeout report includes key results for the project and can include useful information to improve future project performance.

The file shown in Figure 20-1, *Backyard Remodel Closeout.doc,* is available in the *Backyard Remodel Project* folder on the companion CD.

Quantitative Results

Closeout reports include quantitative measures of project performance ranging from standard approaches, such as variance between estimated and actual finish dates, to project-specific measures like the reduction in telephone calls to customer support. Here are some typical quantitative results that appear in closeout reports:

- **Cost**   Customers usually want to know the final cost of the entire project, the cost for each major phase, and other cost-related results, so it's no surprise that closeout reports contain final cost. They also show the variance between the final cost and the estimated cost both in dollars and as a percentage; they might include other cost-related results, such as profitability or ROI (see "Financial Measures," page 17). For large projects, you might break down reported costs in other ways, such as capital expense, labor costs, material costs, or cost of contractors versus employees.

- **Schedule**   Schedule results include the actual delivery date for the entire project and the variance between the final dates for key milestones compared to the forecast completion dates.

- **Effort**   The amount of effort required to complete the project can be valuable for resource planning on future projects. Although cost measures indirectly tell you how many hours team members devoted to the project, knowing the actual number of hours that people worked and when they worked them can help you assign resources more effectively in the future.

- **Completed scope**   Document the deliverables that the project produced. A section for completed scope is particularly important if the project didn't fully deliver the items in the original scope or if the project scope expanded or shrank significantly due to change requests.

- **Changes**   Summarize the significant changes from the original scope or specifications. (The complete list of changes is available in the project archive as explained in Chapter 21.)

- **Quality**   If the success criteria for the project include quality metrics, be sure to include the quality results in the closeout report. Without

Part Five:
Closing Projects

On Time! On Track! On Target! Managing Your Projects Successfully with Microsoft Project

quality metrics to meet, you might include other types of quality-related results, such as the best practices that the team applied or the number of hours of rework on deliverables.

Qualitative Information

Qualitative results are as important as quantitative ones. For example, if the project ran over budget or took longer than anticipated, the closeout report should explain the reasons. Here are some of the other items you might include in a project closeout report:

- **Explanation of variances** If variance in cost, schedule, or other measures is significant, identify the reasons for the difference and provide recommendations for preventing it on future projects.

- **Issues** Document the issues that arose during the project, the actions that successfully resolved those issues, and recommendations for preventing the issues in the future.

> **Important** Organizations often struggle with project organizational structure regardless of whether the company uses functional departments, a matrix organization, or a project-based resource pool. Include any issues that arose with the project organization structure and how those issues were resolved.

- **Risks** Document the risks that occurred during the project, the risk response chosen, and whether it was successful. In particular, highlight any risks that arose that *weren't* identified in the risk management plan.

> **Tip** Also consider documenting close calls—risks that didn't come to fruition, but were close to coming true, such as a resource shortage that was averted because team members worked double shifts for two weeks to meet a deliverable deadline.

- **Lessons learned** Although you might produce a separate lessons learned report and store lessons in a database for everyone to share, you can include the most significant lessons learned in the closeout report.

Obtaining Customer Acceptance

If only it were as easy to obtain customer acceptance as saying "Hey, we're done!" and the customer responding with "OK, great!" The risk with this friendly (and improbable) exchange is that the customer might come back a few months later complaining that the results aren't really what the company had in mind or that someone just noticed that a deliverable was missing. The best way to close a project and make sure it stays closed is to get the customer (and other stakeholders) to sign off on the project when it is complete.

Signing a document makes people think about the implication of their agreement, regardless of whether the document is a formal acceptance of a project, the final project payment check, or the deed to the ranch. As with the sign-off on the project plan you produced some time ago, a meeting to sign off on customer acceptance emphasizes the significance of the event. If a face to face meeting with the project sponsor, customer, and other stakeholders isn't feasible, hold a conference call to verbally accept the project and send the project acceptance form to the customer and sponsor to sign (and return to you to store in your project notebook). The project acceptance form doesn't have to be complicated, as the template in Figure 20-2 on the next page shows.

The template file shown in Figure 20-2, *Project Acceptance Sign-Off.dot*, is available in the *Templates* folder on the companion CD.

For most projects, customer acceptance isn't a yes or no response. The deliverables and success criteria you documented in the project plan switch from being direction for the project team to standards that the project customer uses to determine whether the project is complete.

Deliverables are usually tangible, so customers can verify that they received them or not. Success criteria, on the other hand, can take some time to verify. For example, suppose you just completed a software project and one of the acceptance criteria is system availability of greater than 99.99%. Determining whether the system meets this criterion requires setting up a realistic test environment, determining the exact measurement process, running the system with test cases for a period of time, and processing the resulting data to calculate the availability. If the system doesn't pass the test, the project goes back into the execution phase until the problems are resolved and you run another test.

Part Five:
Closing Projects

On Time! On Track! On Target! Managing Your Projects Successfully with Microsoft Project

<Project Name>   **Final Project Acceptance**

Project name:

Project manager:

Customer name:

Project checklist

- Deliverables accepted and signed off   ☐
- Success criteria met   ☐
- Closeout reports produced   ☐
- Project notebook archived   ☐
- Lessons learned session completed   ☐

Approved by

_____

Customer name

_____

Title

_____

Date

_____

Project sponsor

_____

Title

_____

Date

Page 1 of 1

Figure 20-2   The most important part of the project acceptance form is the signature block, but you can also include a checklist to indicate the project deliverables that are complete.

Good success criteria aren't open to interpretation. What if the customer requires that the same software system must have no critical or major defects and no more than 10 serious defects? Defects that corrupt data, computer systems that come to an abrupt halt, and anything that generates flames and smoke are typically recognized as critical. However, without clearly defined success criteria, the customer might categorize defects differently than everyone else. For instance, your customer might consider a crowded dialog box as a major defect because it could lead to data entry errors. Your team considers the same defect as cosmetic. By diligently

defining success criteria up front, reviewing and obtaining acceptance on plans
and prototypes throughout the project,
and reviewing deliverables and preliminary test results, obtaining agreement
that you have met the project's acceptance criteria is much easier.

Project Transitions

At the end of a project, you must handle
two types of transitions: one for the team
that worked on the project and the other
for the team that picks up where the
project leaves off. Because projects are
temporary, the members of the project
team move on at the end of a project. Particularly with long projects, team members are bound to have some emotional
reaction to leaving the project they
worked on—sometimes relief, but in
many cases, sadness or fear. Your job as
project manager is to ensure that people's transitions proceed smoothly so
that your project finishes without incident, and your team members are reasonably comfortable about the change. In most cases, you can complete this
task by communicating the status of team members' availability to their
managers who then plan the transitions. The other transition is handing off
information about the project to the people who take over the next steps—
whatever they are. Fortunately, this transition is usually easier and less emo-
tionally charged.

Transitioning Resources

The people and equipment that you assign to your project go on to something else after your project is complete. What resources do after they finish
working for you might not seem like your responsibility, but planning these
transitions is in everyone's best interest. When you work with your team
members and their managers to plan their reassignments, you ensure that
they finish the work they're supposed to do for your project. At the same
time, you gain respect from the people and their managers as someone who
is considerate of others and pays attention to detail. Furthermore, you

Best Practices

Achieving objectives and handing over deliverables is not the same as satisfying the customer.
Sometimes, customers can't describe what they
want, but they know when they see it—or know
that what they're looking at *isn't* what they want.
As well, you might have met the success criteria,
but the process wasn't pretty to watch. Because
everyone is different, success in your eyes might
not impress the customer.

Organizations survey customers to find out what
they think, because it's better to learn about and
correct a problem than to have customers complain to everyone they meet. Surveying the
sponsor, customer, and other stakeholders to
determine their satisfaction with results tells you
much more than the signature on an acceptance
form. Furthermore, you can ask them what they
liked and what they thought could be improved
to add to your lessons learned database. Include
the survey results in the closeout report.

Part Five:
Closing Projects

On Time! On Track! On Target! Managing Your Projects Successfully with Microsoft Project

might win points with the functional managers who have the team members lined up for their next assignments.

To plan resource transition you need to know how long and how much you need the resources. If resources go back to their functional groups, their managers will appreciate knowing when their people are available, so they can line up additional work without worrying about overloading or benching them.

Knowing whether resources can start working on something else while cleaning up their assignments for you is important, because assignments usually overlap. Assignments don't require the same level of intensity or time from start to finish, so it's common for people to start ramping up on a new assignment as work on the old one slowly trails off. Contractors and consultants appreciate knowing when they'll be done so they can start lining up new work without worrying about a gap between assignments, having to postpone another client, or working two full-time contracts simultaneously.

Handing Off Information

Although projects end, some part of them usually continues. Whether your project is a backyard remodel that the homeowner is going to maintain, a product that the sales team now has to sell, or a service that the technicians have to install and support, someone else needs to know what you did and what the status is. For example, construction projects typically hand over as-built drawings, which show how the resulting structure was built regardless of what the architect originally drew. As-built drawings might show a power line that was relocated because of a large buried rock or a framing detail that changed.

The information that you hand off depends on the project. Here are a few of the items you might want to provide to the team that takes over:

- The location of the archived project documents in case the team needs more information
- The closeout report
- Any tasks that are incomplete, their status, and why they weren't completed
- Unresolved issues

- Test results
- Final specifications, as-built drawings, and product documentation

Closing Out Contracts

If you've had anything to do with contracts—negotiating, signing, or clos-ing—you know that they mean paperwork. If your project involved a con-tract with the project customer, closing the contract offers the same degree of difficulty as obtaining customer acceptance. If the customer is happy and accepts the project as complete, ending the contract might be as simple as exchanging signed acceptance forms. In contrast, closing contracts can be difficult if parties disagree about whether the contractual terms have been met. Resolving these disagreements is best done without the lawyers involved—at least until a stalemate is obvious.

> **Tip** Most organizations don't close the financial books on a project until a few months after the final project delivery. By keeping the project open in the accounting system, additional charges, such as warranty repairs or sup-port, are easy to add as project expenses. However, it's a good idea to close the project to additional labor hours so that people don't inadvertently charge time to your project.

Closing contracts also represents closure for the contracts you set up with vendors. You must review every contract for the project, whether for con-tract employees, subcontractors, service agreements, and so on, to deter-mine the steps to close them. Then you diligently perform those steps.

In Summary

Closing a project is a combination of recording what happened during the project and tying up loose ends. Closeout reports document project perfor-mance and significant accomplishments. More important, these reports often include the information you need to obtain acceptance from the project customer that the project is, in fact, complete. Finally, when every-one agrees that the project is over, the last task is to close any contracts that the project required, whether with the project customer or with vendors.

Part Five:
Closing Projects

On Time! On Track! On Target! Managing Your Projects Successfully with Microsoft Project

Chapter Twenty-One

Archiving Historical Information

Insanity: doing the same thing over and over again and expecting different results.

— *Albert Einstein*

If an organization wants to improve performance on projects in the future, it must learn from the projects in its past. Whether a project was a spectacular success or a dismal failure, there's valuable information in the documents from completed projects about what to do or what *not* to do the next time. Unfortunately, many project managers file away project documentation as soon as a project is complete and don't think to look at it when another project begins. If you're breaking ground as the first project manager in a company, project documentation for past projects are probably as rare as lips on chickens, because no one realized that projects need documents like charters, plans, budgets, and status reports.

This chapter begins by explaining how project history can help future performance. It describes the project information to store in a historical database. You'll also learn about a few ways to archive project information depending on the technology available in your organization.

Why Chronicle Project History?

The distance between insanity and genius is measured only by success.

— *Bruce Feirstein*

Maintaining information about past projects and making a point of reviewing that information before beginning new projects is the most effective way to improve project performance. As you learned in Chapter 19, "Learning Lessons," nothing is as disheartening as making the same mistakes you made once before. By reviewing past projects during planning, project managers and everyone else on the project team can avoid past mistakes and the embarrassment and frustration of repeating them. Chapter 19 also explains why remembering what did work and repeating those successes is just as important. Instead of reinventing what someone else has already discovered, you can use the experience of others to make your project more successful.

Save Documents for Reuse

Besides helping to prevent mistakes and putting proven best practices to work, a project archive contains existing documents that you can use as the basis for building your project documentation. If your organization doesn't have templates for project plans, budgets, work breakdown structures, and the like, modifying a document from a similar (and successful) project that's already complete is a big timesaver. Although every project is unique,

Part Five:
Closing Projects

On Time! On Track! On Target! Managing Your Projects Successfully with Microsoft Project

Best Practices

If you notice the same features repeating frequently from one project to the next, consider taking a few minutes to create a template from one of those projects. Existing documents that have worked well in the past are great candidates for templates. You can take advantage of a document's layout, headings, and even text that tends to stay the same from project to project (such as the project deliverables that your company typically provides). The only step that might take more than a minute is replacing project-specific text with either sample text or instructions about the kind of content to include.

For example, suppose you want to create a template from an existing project plan built in Microsoft Word. The following steps describe how to save a document as a template and how to turn a template into a new document.

Saving a Word Document as a Template

1. With the document open in Word, on the File menu, select Save As.

2. In the Save As dialog box, from the Save As Type list box, select Document template. Word automatically selects the folder for templates specified in Word options. (To see the location of your template folders, on the Tools menu, select Options and then click the File Locations tab.)

3. In the File Name box, type a name like Project Plan Template and click Save.

Creating a New Document from a Template

1. To create a new project plan from the template, on the File menu, select New.

2. In the New Document task pane, below Templates, click the On My Computer link. Select the template you want to use and click OK. Word creates a new document, named something like Document1, but based on the template.

similar projects are likely to include similar objectives and types of resources, familiar tasks, standard costs, and potential risks.

Save Project Performance for Future Estimates

Schedules and budgets with actual numbers from completed projects are an invaluable resource for estimates you must produce for new projects. Every project struggles against the indestructible optimism of the people who estimate what the projects will require. You can circumvent the optimism of previous projects by reviewing how long similar projects in the past took and what they cost.

Likewise, historical data comes in handy, accounting for potential problems and changes that can increase time and cost. For example, if previous projects had problems that you now know how to prevent, you can make stakeholders happy with a shorter schedule and lower costs. If similar projects had to address the same change requests, you're better off including them in your plan at the beginning.

Important If you're being pressured to set unrealistic dates or budgets, retrieve numbers from comparable projects. You'll have a better chance of convincing stakeholders that your estimates are realistic, although stakeholders might stick to their original goals because of other factors. For example, an accounting system might have to be ready before the beginning of the next fiscal year, because the customer doesn't want to duplicate transactions in two systems. In such situations, you'll have to consider other tactics, such as fast-tracking (see "The Fast-Track to an Early Finish," page 154) or crashing the project (see "A Crash Course on Project Crashing," page 156).

Information to Store about Projects

If you have trouble getting enough time to plan a project, chances are good you won't have much time to study the project after it's finished. Fortunately, the project notebook you assemble during the life of a project contains much of the historical information you need. For example, the project notebook table of contents in Figure 21-1 on the next page lists information you typically gather while managing a project.

3. Save the file with a new name, such as Backyard Remodel Project Plan, and you're ready to start filling in your new project document.

Saving a Project Schedule as a Template

Creating a template for a Project file (not to mention templates for other Microsoft programs) works almost identically to the steps for creating a Word template.

1. With the schedule open in Project, on the File menu, select Save As.

2. In the Save As dialog box, from the Save As Type list box, select Template. Project automatically selects the folder for templates specified in Project options. (To see the location of your template folders, on the Tools menu, select Options and then click the Save tab.)

3. In the File Name box, type a name like *Project Plan Template* and click Save.

> **Note** The information that you gather and store in a project notebook depends on the project type, the size of the project, and the maturity of your project management practices. For example, on the Backyard Remodel Project, the project notebook doesn't need a section for testing, because the building inspections ensure the quality of the construction. And it doesn't need a section on training unless you intend to hold a class to teach your kids how to use the swings, your husband the grill, and the dog to keep his toenails off the redwood. However, the blueprints and as-built drawings for the remodel would go in the section on requirements.

After you add the final documents for a project to the project notebook (see Chapter 20, "Managing Project Completion," for details on project close-out reports, transition information, and other closure reports), the project is ready to join the archive of other completed projects. If you work strictly electronically, archiving a project could be as simple as moving the

Part Five:
Closing Projects

On Time! On Track! On Target! Managing Your Projects Successfully with Microsoft Project

electronic project folders to a new location for completed projects (and backing up all the files). If you also keep physical notebooks with hard copies of project documents, you'll have to store those on book shelves reserved for project archives.

Project Notebook Contents and Locations

Project Notebook Contents and Locations _____ 1

Business Case _____ 2

Problem Statement _____ 2

Mission Statement _____ 2

Project Contact List _____ 3

Project Plan–Original_____ 3

Project Schedule _____ 3

Project Variance Reports _____ 3

Requirements _____ 4

Detail Design Specifications _____ 4

Deliverable Acceptance Log and Forms _____ 4

Training_____ 4

Testing_____ 5

Change Request Log and Documents_____ 5

Risk Management Logs _____ 5

Issues Log _____ 6

Correspondence _____ 6

Meetings–Agendas and Minutes_____ 6

Status Reports_____ 6

Project Performance Measures _____ 7

Project Close-Out _____ 7

Lessons Learned_____ 7

Figure 21-1   A project notebook is a comprehensive dossier of project plans and actual performance.

The *Templates* folder on the companion CD contains *Project Notebook Contents.dot*, a Word template for keeping track of project documents and their electronic and hard-copy locations.

Shelf after shelf of identical three-ring binders is a daunting sight when you're trying to find a completed project to use as a guide. Navigating from folder to folder on the computer that holds files for completed projects and opening files with promising names can be equally tedious and time-consuming. Maintaining a file or small database of basic information about completed projects is one way to simplify finding similar projects.

The spreadsheet shown in Figure 21-2 is simplistic, but it's easy to maintain. You can filter the results by values in the Keywords column. For example, if you're working on a new project for marketing and want to find potential stakeholders, you can filter the Keywords column for "marketing" and start researching documents for marketing projects.

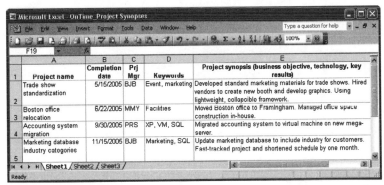

Figure 21-2   A file with brief descriptions of completed projects makes it easier to find projects similar to the one you're working on.

You can find the Excel spreadsheet file for project summaries, *OnTime_Project_Synopses.xls*, in the *Sample Files* folder on the companion CD.

Ways to Build a Project Archive

Customers, managers, team members, and project managers each require different types of project information. By organizing project documentation and storing it where it's easy to access, everyone can find the information they need when they need it.

Although you might still keep paper-based project notebooks (which might require one to dozens of binders), technology improves upon hard-copy storage, making it possible for people involved with a project to quickly find

Part Five:
Closing Projects

On Time! On Track! On Target! Managing Your Projects Successfully with Microsoft Project

the information they need. If your organization is modest, you don't need to acquire tons of technology. Basic features included with your computer's operating system can satisfy your electronic storage need. But you can put other technology to work if it's available. The best solution for a project archive is one that supports the size and quantity of projects you have and works within the limitations of your IT staff and budget. For instance, if you are the president, primary project manager, bookkeeper, and systems administrator, you can use shared folders. The following sections describe a few options for storing project information.

A project archive doesn't do much good if no one knows about it. Project managers get the most mileage from project archives, so make sure they know where completed projects are stored. But anyone involved with projects can find helpful documents and information in an archive. You can notify everyone on your project team about the project archive resource when you kick off your project. Or if you prepare a welcome packet for new team members, be sure to include the location of the archive and a brief description of what it holds.

Tip   If your company already has project management procedures and perhaps a centralized project office that manages the portfolio of projects, you're in luck. You don't have to worry about how to build a project archive. All you have to do is follow existing procedures to submit your completed project to the archive.

However, if you want to start a project archive in your organization, start small. You can work with existing tools to determine what you need to store. Then, as the organization's needs and project sophistication grow, you'll have the information you need to propose a tool like Microsoft Project Server.

Shared Folder

Storing project documents on a shared network drive is a simple solution for accessing project documentation. You create a folder structure for projects on a drive that everyone can access. Team members connect to the network drive and review or work on the documents they need. Figure 21-3 shows a simple example of a shared folder for projects.

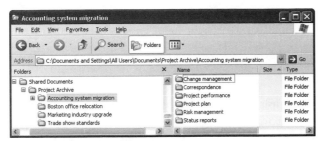

Figure 21-3   A shared folder on a network drive is a convenient place to store folders for archived projects.

The big disadvantage of shared folders is that change management is difficult to control. Unless you have an IT staff to set up the appropriate shared folder permissions, anyone can copy, modify, or even delete project documents.

Shared Workspace

Microsoft Windows SharePoint Services is another solution for storing project documents. During project execution, you can use a SharePoint Services Web site as a repository for documents and a place for communicating with team members. When the project is complete, you can keep the site as an archive of the project. For example, the project team that worked on this book used this method to communicate between several people and sites across the United States. All someone needs to reach the site is a Web browser and permissions to access its contents. If you use Microsoft Office 2003 programs, you can access documents directly from Word, Excel, Project, and other applications.

Note   If your organization has a document management system, you can use it to archive project documents—as long as the people who work with the project archive can access the document management system.

Microsoft Enterprise Project Management Software

Microsoft Enterprise Project Management software is an option for organizations that manage many projects and want a tool to help manage their project portfolios, past and present. Microsoft Enterprise Project Management software uses a project database to hold information about project schedules and resources and employs SharePoint Services Web sites to

Part Five:
Closing Projects

On Time! On Track! On Target! Managing Your Projects Successfully with Microsoft Project

provide shared workspaces for document libraries, risk tracking, and issue management.

In Summary

Creating an archive for completed projects helps project managers improve project performance by reusing successful practices and avoiding past errors. Project archives don't have to be a huge undertaking. The information you need is assembled during project closeout. And you can use technology that's readily available in the smallest organization. After you've set up a project archive, make sure that people involved with projects know that it's available.

Glossary

accrual method   When a project incurs actual costs for a resource as soon as the task starts, prorated as the task progresses, or after the task is complete.

activity   Work performed by resources to achieve a result. Also called a task.

actual cost   Cost that a project has actually incurred including labor, equipment, material, and indirect costs.

actual cost of work performed (ACWP)   Total cost incurred for work completed on a task or tasks through the project status date (or the current date if no status date is defined). ACWP is used in earned value analysis to identify whether a project is on schedule and within budget. ACWP is also called earned value.

actual duration   The length of time between when a task started and the present time.

actual finish date   The actual date that a task was completed.

actual start date   The actual date that a task started.

actual work   The work that resources have actually performed on a task.

allocation   The percentage of a resource's available working time that is assigned to a task.

assignment   The work a resource is supposed to perform on a task; the resource's time that is allocated to the task; and the date range when the resource is supposed to work on the task.

baseline   The original and stakeholder-approved plan for the schedule and cost for a project including any approved changes. Comparing the baseline to actual progress shows whether the project is on schedule and within budget.

baseline cost   The project costs in the baseline plan, used to calculate earned value measures and project cost performance.

budget at completion (BAC)   The estimated cost of the project at completion including actual costs to date and estimated costs from today until the finish date.

budgeted cost of work performed (BCWP)   The baseline cost for completed work, calculated by multiplying the percentage of work complete by the total baseline cost.

budgeted cost of work scheduled (BCWS)   The baseline cost for work scheduled to be complete by the status date or the current date regardless of how much work is complete.

calendar   The working, nonworking (holidays and vacations), and special working days (overtime) used to schedule when work occurs on tasks.

change control board   A group of project stakeholders who evaluate and approve or reject requested changes to project baselines.

change management   The process of receiving, evaluating, and approving or rejecting requested changes to project baselines. Sometimes, called change control.

change management plan   A document that describes the change management process for a project.

change order   A document authorizing a change for a project.

communication plan   A document that describes the information that stakeholders require and the methods and procedures for communicating that information.

constraint   A restriction on when a task can start or finish.

contingency plan   A plan that identifies alternative approaches to be used if the corresponding risk events occur.

contingency reserve   An amount of money, time, or both that is set aside for situations that can't be completely defined in advance, such as more time than originally planned to correct defects.

control   The process of comparing actual progress to the plan, analyzing the differences, evaluating alternatives, and taking corrective steps if necessary.

cost   Project costs for people, equipment, and materials.

cost performance index (CPI)   The ratio of budgeted costs to actual costs (BCWP/ACWP). To forecast the cost at completion, multiply the original cost baseline by CPI.

cost variance   The difference between the budgeted and actual costs of work performed. If the cost variance is positive, the project is under budget. In earned value analysis, cost variance is BCWP minus ACWP.

crashing   Trying to reduce the duration of a task or entire project for the least amount of money.

critical path   The tasks that determine the earliest possible finish date of a project. Each task in the critical path must be completed on time for the project to finish on schedule.

critical path method (CPM)   A technique for determining the sequence of tasks (critical path) in a project with the least amount of float and therefore the least scheduling flexibility.

deliverable   A tangible or measurable result for a project.

dependency   Relationship of the start or finish of one task to the start or finish of another task: finish-to-start, start-to-start, finish-to-finish, or start-to-finish.

duration   The length of working time between the start and finish of a task.

earned value analysis   A method of measuring project performance by comparing baseline costs to how much of the budget has been spent and how much should have been spent for the completed work. See budgeted cost of work performed, budgeted cost of work scheduled, and actual cost of work performed.

effort   The number of units of work to complete a task. Effort is not duration. For example, if two people work full time on a one-day task, the effort is two days.

effort-driven task   A task whose total work doesn't vary as resources are added or removed.

estimate at completion (EAC)   The forecast total cost at completion for a task or entire project.

fast-tracking   Shortening the duration of a project by overlapping tasks that would normally be run sequentially, such as design and construction.

finish date The date that a task is scheduled to be completed, based on the task's start date, duration, work calendars, and constraints.

fixed cost A cost for a task that does not depend on the task duration.

float The maximum delay for a task that doesn't delay the finish date of the project.

functional manager A department manager responsible for the people who work in that department. The project manager must work with functional managers to obtain and retain resources for a project.

Gantt chart A bar chart (named after Henry Gantt) that shows when tasks start and finish as well as the relationships between tasks.

lag The delay between the completion of a predecessor task and the start of a successor task.

lead The amount of overlap between the end of one task and the beginning of another. For example, a lead time of two days means that the second task can begin two days before the first task ends.

leveling Delaying tasks to eliminate resource overallocations caused by two or more tasks using the same resource at the same time.

link A dependency between tasks: finish-to-start, start-to-start, finish-to-finish, or start-to-finish.

management reserve An amount of money or time that is set aside to allow for events that are impossible to predict, such as choosing a new vendor for materials due to a factory mishap.

matrix organization An organization in which project managers and functional managers share responsibility for assigning resources to tasks and supervising their work.

milestone A significant event or accomplishment in a project, such as the completion of a phase or major deliverable.

network diagram A diagram that shows the dependencies between tasks. A network diagram shows tasks in chronological order from left to right.

outline A hierarchical representation of the tasks for a project. The Task Sheet in Project is an outline that represents the work breakdown structure (WBS) for a project.

overtime The amount of work assigned beyond a resource's regular working time. Overtime costs are calculated by multiplying the overtime hours by the resource's overtime rate.

percent complete The percentage of task duration completed, calculated by dividing the actual duration by the scheduled duration.

percent work complete The percentage of work completed, calculated by dividing the actual work by the estimated work.

PERT The Program Evaluation and Review Technique evaluates the probable duration of a project by calculating a weighted average of the best-case estimate, most likely case estimate, and worst-case estimate.

predecessor A task that controls the start or finish of another task. In Project, predecessor does not necessarily indicate a task that occurs earlier in a schedule.

project charter A document issued by an executive, project sponsor, or customer, announcing a project and delegating authority to the project manager.

project plan   A document that describes a project and the plan for completing it and achieving its objectives. The project plan guides the execution and control of the project.

quality assurance   A process for evaluating project performance in relation to the specified standard of quality.

quality control   Monitoring project performance for quality and identifying sources of unsatisfactory quality measures.

resource pool   A set of resources available to work on project tasks, whether used by only one project or shared by several projects.

risk management   The process of identifying what can go wrong, determining how to respond to risks should they occur, monitoring a project for risks that do occur, and taking steps to respond to the events that do occur.

schedule   The overall time line for a project including task dates, durations, relationships, costs, and resource assignments.

schedule performance index (SPI)   The ratio of work performed compared to the work scheduled (BCWP/BCWS).

scope   The extent of work that must be performed to complete a project.

slack   The amount of time a task can slip without affecting the finish date of the project. Also called float. Free slack is the amount of time a task can slip without delay-

ing another task. Total slack is the amount of time a task and its successors can slip without delaying the project finish date.

stakeholders   People interested in, involved in, or affected by a project, such as customers, management, and project team members.

standard rate   The rate charged by a resource for regular work hours.

start date   The date that a task is scheduled to start, based on its predecessors.

statement of work   A description of the work to be performed for a project, usually included in a contract.

successor   A task with a start or finish date that depends on another task. In Project, successor does not necessarily indicate a task that occurs later in a schedule.

summary task   A task that summarizes the dates, duration, and work of all its subordinate tasks.

task   A portion of work in a project with a start and finish date.

variance   The difference between the baseline and estimated dates, work, or cost in a project.

work   The time units required to complete a task. Work is different from task duration.

work breakdown structure (WBS)   A hierarchical diagram showing work broken down into smaller packages to facilitate estimating work and costs, and tracking progress.

work package   A task that represents actual work that resources do; it appears at the lowest level of the WBS.

About the Author

Bonnie Biafore began working at an engineering firm in New York City after graduating with a master of science in structural engineering. She ended up with an assignment to help select a computer-aided design system for the company and implement it to help develop engineering drawings. Little did she know that this was her first project management assignment. That she had no idea what she was doing was no doubt obvious to everyone else involved.

Nevertheless, several years and several assignments passed before Bonnie realized that she was *managing projects*. As it turns out, with training and experience, she became pretty good at it. Eventually, she started her own company, MonteVista Solutions, Inc., offering project management consulting and training services. She received her Project Management Professional Certification (PMP) from the Project Management Institute (PMI) in 2003.

Along the way, Bonnie began writing books about personal finance, investing, and project management. Her friendly writing style and irrepressible sense of humor help turn typically dry subjects that people have to read into something they want to read. Her book, the *NAIC Stock Selection Handbook*, won awards from both the Society of Technical Communication and APEX Awards for Publication Excellence. Bonnie writes regularly for Microsoft's Work Essentials Web site, other Web sites, and several magazines.

When not chained to her computer, she coordinates gourmet meals, plans her finances, and practices saying *no*, unsuccessfully, to additional work assignments. You can learn more at her Web site:

http://www.bonniebiafore.com

Index

Symbols

% Complete field, 204–5

A

Access, 199
accounting systems, 189
accrual method, 351
accuracy
 ensuring in communications, 238
 for project estimates, 128–29
 reporting time with, 188–90
achievable objectives, 81–82
acknowledging project team members, 38
acronyms
 RICA, 106–7
 use of, 27
activity, 351
actual cost, 351
actual cost of work performed (ACWP),
 200–204, 351
actual duration, 351
actual finish date, 351
actual start date, 351
actual work, 351
ACWP (actual cost of work performed),
 200–204, 351
advisers. See also project sponsors, project
 stakeholders
 asking project sponsors' advice, 32–33
 documenting project, 36
agendas
 creating meeting, 244
 lessons learned session meetings, 324
allocation, 351
analyzing project performance
 about, 185, 207
 calculating values and variance, 191
 data needed for, 185–88
 earned value analysis, 199–207
 filters for checking schedule progress,
 194
 finding over-budget costs, 197–98
 Gantt views for, 191–93
 identifying problems, 322–24
 including schedule-related tables in
 views, 193
 making checklist of views and filters for,
 193

project cost reports for, 198–99
 time and status data for tracking
 progress, 188–90
 tracking schedule progress, 190–91
 watching for upcoming risks, 188
APY (annual percentage yield), 20
archiving project information
 about, 341
 creating project archives, 345–47
 estimating from past performance,
 342–43
 reusing documents, 341–43
 selecting information to archive, 343–45
 storing data about risks, 307
Assign Resources dialog box
 assigning resources in, 148, 282
 replacing resources in, 282
assignments. See also project resources
 defined, 351
 notifying managers of changes in, 34
assumptions
 communications and, 237
 inspecting project, 55
 reviewing in scope statement, 77
audiences for communications, 225
authority
 gaining as project manager, 39
 having project sponsor lend, 32, 49–50
 project charter and establishment of, 49
 publicizing project manager's, 28
automated dependencies, 136–37
avoiding
 estimate problems, 124–27
 scope creep, 53, 77–79

B

BAC (budget at completion), 203–4, 351
backyard remodel project
 Backyard Remodel Schedule in
 Progress.mpp file, 190
 Backyard Remodel Schedule.mpp file,
 171
 Backyard Remodel Scope Statement.doc,
 77
 Cost table for, 196–97
 deliverables for, 82–83
 high-level tasks for, 91–92
 PERT durations for, 131

backyard remodel project, *continued*
  problem definition for, 63
  schedule for, 171
  scope statement for, 76
  WBS for, 88
balancing project variables. *See also* costs,
    project scope, quality
  about, 289–90, 294
  asking stakeholders for suggestions,
    289–90
  guidelines for changing project variables,
    293–94
  optimizing schedules, 292–93
  options for, 290
  prioritizing cost-related changes, 293
  reassigning resources, 290–92
ballpark estimates, 124–25
baseline cost, 351
baseline data
  budgets, 181
  clearing, 285–86
  defined, 351
  how Project calculates, 191
  saving additional baselines, 284–85
  saving values for baseline schedules,
    179–81
  viewing multiple baselines, 192, 286
baseline documents
  defined, 257
  illustrated, 258–59
BCWP (budgeted cost of work performed),
    200, 202–4, 351
BCWS (budgeted cost of work scheduled),
    200, 202–3, 351
blame, 322–24
body language, 240
bottom-up estimating, 129
brainstorming rules, 69
breaking up
  duration of task length, 273–74
  project into phases, 293
budget at completion (BAC), 203–4, 351
Budget report, 198
budgeted cost of work performed (BCWP),
    200, 202–4, 351
budgeted cost of work scheduled (BCWS),
    200–203, 351
budgets. *See also* capital budgets
  calculating costs in schedules, 165–67
  capital, 162–65
  contingency reserves, 127, 309–10, 352
  effects of over-budget projects, 165
  estimate accuracy and, 128–29

evaluating with earned value analysis,
    199–200
exporting costs from project schedule,
    170–74
finding costs over, 197–98
fixed costs for tasks, 167, 170
learning lessons from past, 316–17
planning and, 56
prioritizing cost-related changes, 293
specifying rates for work resources,
    167–68
time vs. money trade-offs in crashing,
    157–59
using baseline, 181
building project archives, 345–47
building work breakdown structure (WBS),
    89–93
  about, 89
  adding detail, 93–94
  developing teams for, 92
  filling in task levels, 91–92
  identifying high-level tasks, 89–90
  revising WBS, 92–93
  verifying design of, 93
burdened labor rates, 167, 169
business objectives, 79–80

C

calculating project estimates, 129–30, 131
calendars
  defined, 351
  setting working and nonworking days,
    152–53
  task, 153, 275
capital budgeting tool, 163–65
capital budgets
  about, 161, 162
  using, 163, 174
  working with capital budgeting tool,
    163–65
Cash Flow report, 198
Center for Business Practices, 8, 9–10
change control boards, 351
change control plans, 58
change management binder, 179
change management plan, 352
change management process. *See also*
    changes
  control documents in, 258–60
  defined, 257–58, 351
  illustrated, 259
  managing request changes, 260–61, 263
  role of change review boards, 261–62

change orders, 352
Change Request Form.dot file, 262–63
change request log, 263–64
change requests. *See* CRs
change review boards, 261–62
changes. *See also* change management
  process
  controlling in shared project documents,
    346–47
  handling small, 264
  inevitability of, 48
  managing requested, 260–61, 263
  monitoring with review boards, 262
  notifying managers of assignment, 34
  prioritizing cost-related, 293
  quantifying at project completion, 333
  resetting financial goals, 294
  scope creep and project, 53, 77–79
  tracking, 190, 262–64
charts. *See also* Gantt Charts
  calculating net present value with, 19
  project organization, 85, 109–11, 120
checking spelling
  e-mail, 252
  project status reports, 251
checklist for analyzing project
  performance, 193
clearing baselines, 285–86
closeout reports, 331–33
closure. *See* project completion
commitments for projects, 24–40
  functional managers' support, 33–34
  getting project sponsors', 32–33
  identifying project stakeholders, 29–35
  need for, 25
  obtaining and maintaining, 37–40
  project customers, 30–32
  publicizing project charters, 25–28
  reluctant stakeholders and, 30–31
  signed documents of, 177–78
  team members', 34–35
communication binder, 179
communication plans
  about, 222–23
  building, 232–33
  defined, 352
  identifying people's information needs,
    223–25
  illustrated, 223
communications. *See also* communication
  plans, e-mail communications,
  meetings
  about project, 221, 252–53

advantages of good, 221–22
art of, 225
benefits of good, 9
building plans for, 232–33
choosing what to communicate, 225–29
communication plans, 222–23
creating reminders for, 233–35
distributing project charters, 28
effective, 235–37
e-mail, 251–52
ensuring good, 237–38, 239
handing off information at project
  completion, 337–39
information for management
  stakeholders, 227–28
listening and, 239–40
maintaining with team members, 6–7,
  35, 38
methods for, 230–32
needed by functional managers, 229
planning, 57
project status reports, 249–50, 251
roles and responsibilities for, 210
skill required for project, 240
to team members, 229
types of project, 226–27
with stakeholders, 6–7
companion CD
  Backyard Remodel Closeout.doc,
    332–33
  Backyard Remodel Schedule in
    Progress.mpp file, 190
  Backyard Remodel Scope Statement.doc,
    77
  Change Request Form.dot file, 262–63
  communication plan, 223
  Issue Tracking Log.xls, 246
  Lessons Learned Agenda.dot, 324
  lessons learned meeting template, 212
  Lessons Learned Report.dot template,
    327
  lessons learned workbooks, 327
  OnTime_Project_Charter.doc, 49
  OnTime_Risk_Graph.xls, 306
  OnTime_Risk_Information_Sheet.doc,
    301
  PERT durations for backyard remodel
    project, 131
  problem statement, 50
  Project Acceptance Sign-Off.dot
    template, 335–36
  Project Notebook Contents.dot template,
    344
  project organization chart, 111

companion CD, *continued*
  Project Status Report.doc, 250
  Project_Synopses.xls file, 345
  responsibility matrix, 108
  sample resource pool, 120
  schedule for backyard remodeling
    project, 171
  stakeholder analysis document, 37–36
  template for work package, 102
  WBS for backyard remodel project, 88
complex task estimates, 131
conference calls, 231
conflicts
  between projects and corporate values,
    15
  resolving over project responsibility, 105
  reviewing assumptions for, 77
  winning over reluctant stakeholders,
    30–31
constraints
  date, 137–39
  defined, 352
  factoring into project objectives, 81–82
  in problem statements, 63
contingency plans, 308, 352
contingency reserves, 127, 309–10, 352
contouring resource assignments, 279–80
contracts, 339
controlling projects, 6
controls, 352
corporate values
  matching project strategies to, 15–16, 70
  projects conflicting with, 15
cost estimates, 161. *See also* project
    estimates
cost information
  entering resource, 117
  improving estimation accuracy, 128–29
  time vs. money in project crashing,
    157–59
Cost Overbudget filter, 218
cost performance index (CPI), 203, 352
Cost table, 195–97
cost variances (CV), 202, 352
cost/use field in Project, 166
costs
  about labor rates, 167
  calculating in schedules, 165–67
  defined, 352
  earned value analysis for tracking,
    199–200
  finding over-budget, 197–98
  fixed costs for tasks, 167, 170
  fixing defects, 187

  prioritizing changes to, 293
  project cost reports, 198–99
  quantifying project completion, 333
  quantifying qualitative benefits, 164
  specifying rates for work resources,
    167–68
  tracking and viewing costs and variances,
    195–97
CPI (cost performance index), 203, 352
CPM (critical path method), 352
crashing
  about, 156–57
  dangers of, 157
  defined, 352
  time vs. money in, 157–59
critical path
  defined, 352
  filtering task list to show, 269–70
  project crashing and, 157–59
  reassigning resources to, 290–91
  shortening, 270–71
critical path method (CPM), 352
CRs (change requests)
  defined, 257
  using, 260–61, 263
customers
  getting feedback on deliverables, 187
  identifying, 66
  obtaining project sign-off from, 335–37
  project support from, 30–32
  working with resources from, 292
Customize Fields dialog box, 118
CV (cost variance), 202

D

data
  analyzing quality in project progress, 187
  needed for performance analysis, 185–88
date constraints. *See also* project schedules
  honoring task dependencies rather than,
    138–39
  tips for using, 137–39
deadlines in project schedules, 139–40
decision making
  decision matrix as aid in, 70–72
  decision milestones, 141–42
  influence and authority linked with, 39
decision matrix, 70–72
Default Task Earned Value Method list
    (Options dialog box), 205
deliverables
  defined, 75, 83, 352
  developing high-level tasks from, 89–90

examples of, 82–83
getting customer feedback on, 187
identifying, 53–54
interim, 82, 83
milestones for external, 143
naming, 143–44
tangible and intangible, 82, 83
dependencies
allowing for lag and lead time, 135
automated, 136–37
creating in Project, 135–36
defined, 352
editing task, 271–72
honoring task, 138–39
identifying task, 134–35
milestones for external deliveries, 143
types of task, 133–34
Detail Gantt view, 268
developing mission statements, 65–67
clarifying project objectives, 65–66
identifying project customers, 66
outlining project strategies, 65, 67
refining drafts, 67–68
developing project plans, 79
developing scope statement, 77
diagrams
network, 353
work breakdown structure, 86, 87
disabling automated dependencies, 137
discounted cash flow. See net present value
documents. See also archiving project
information, templates
contents of project notebook, 178–79
control, 258–60
creating project schedule template,
342–43
electronic distribution of, 230
lessons learned report, 325–27
required for solving people problems,
217
saving as Word template, 342–43
sending and storing project, 231–32
shared folders for, 346–47
storing on SharePoint Services Web site,
347
template for risk-management plan, 303
duration
breaking up length of task's, 273–74
defined, 352
increasing schedule, 294
interpreting project estimate, 128
modifying task's, 277–78
shortening project, 283–84

E

EAC (estimate at completion), 203, 352
earned value analysis, 199–207
BCWS, ACWP, and BCWP measures in,
200–202
calculating in Project, 203
cost and budget evaluations with,
199–200
creating graph in Excel, 206–7
defined, 185, 199, 352
determining results on % Complete or
Physical % Complete, 204
performance evaluations with, 202–4
setting options for calculations in, 204–5
viewing earned value graph, 201–2
viewing table of earned value, 205–6
Earned Value Cost Indicators table, 205
earned value graph, 201–2
Earned Value report, 199, 206
Earned Value table, 205
effective communications, 235–37
efficiency
adjusting tasks for, 153–54
project management benefits for, 7–10
effort, 352
effort-driven scheduling, 283
effort-driven tasks, 352
electronic distribution of documents, 230
e-mail communications, 231–32
checking spelling, 252
guidelines for, 251–52
report distribution as, 232
employees. See also project teams
effect of projects conflicting with
corporate values, 15
performance rewards for, 189
enabling effort-driven scheduling, 283
Enterprise Project Management, 347
Enterprise Project Management tools, 199
estimate at completion (EAC), 203, 352
estimate to complete (ETC) measure, 204
estimates. See project estimates
ETC (estimate to complete) measure, 204
evaluating
estimates after milestones, 129
project strategies, 69–70
resources and skills needed, 56
events for milestones, 143
Excel
building responsibility matrix in, 107
calculating project estimates in, 130
capital budgeting tool template, 163

Excel, *continued*
  change request logs in, 263–64
  earned value graphs in, 206–7
  exporting Project cost information to, 199
  exporting task costs to workbook, 172–74
  filtering responsibility matrix in, 108–9
  importing resource information into Project, 114–15
  lessons learned workbooks, 327
  NPV function, 19
  saving export maps, 174
  sorting and ranking risks in, 305–6
  spreadsheet files for project summaries, 345
  XIRR function, 20, 21
  XNPV function, 19, 20
excellence, 213
executing projects
  evaluating progress when, 44
  steps required for, 177–82
expectations of stakeholders, 38
expenses, 169
export maps, 170
exporting costs from schedule, 170–74
  exporting task costs to Excel workbook, 172–74
  filtering tasks before, 171–72
  Project cost information to other software, 199

F

facilitating lessons learned sessions, 320–21
fast-track projects, 269–72
  about, 154, 269
  choosing tasks to fast-track, 154–55
  improving schedules with, 293
  overlapping tasks, 155–56, 270–71
  running tasks in parallel, 271–72
fast-tracking, 352
feasibility studies, 69
feedback
  initiating in lessons learned sessions, 321
  providing team members with, 212
filtering
  applying Project resource filters, 218
  filters for checking schedule progress, 194
  responsibility matrix, 108–9
  task list to show critical path, 269–70

tasks before exporting cost information, 171–72
financial results
  factors in prioritizing project's, 17–21
  including in project objectives, 16
  payback period for project's, 17–18
  project management benefits for, 7–8
  project objectives and, 79–80
finish date, 353
Finish No Later Than constraint, 138
finish-to-finish dependencies, 134
finish-to-start dependencies, 134, 136
fixed costs, 167, 170, 353
float, 353
follow up
  on communications, 231
  on meetings, 244
forming stage of teams, 213
fun, 212
functional managers
  defined, 353
  evaluating resources and skills needed, 56
  gaining support for projects, 33–34
  project information for, 229

G

Gantt Chart Wizard, 269
Gantt Charts
  creating dependencies using, 135
  defined, 353
  Detail Gantt view, 268
  generating from PERT durations and weightings, 132
  Multiple Baselines Gantt view, 192, 286
  Tracking Gantt view, 191–92, 268
  views showing critical path and baseline values, 268–69
go/no-go decisions, 128
goals
  assigning specific, 210–11
  changing financial, 294
government regulations
  as project objective, 80
  deliverables defined by, 83
Guide to the Project Management Body of Knowledge (Project Management Institute), 4

H

high estimates, 126
honesty in project management, 39, 212

I

identifying
 project problems, 43–45
 project strategies, 68–69
 risks, 302–3
import maps, 170
Import Wizard, 99–100
importing
 project organization information into
  Visio, 111
 project resource information into Project,
  114–15
 WBS text file into Project, 99–100
indirect costs, 169
initiating projects, 5
inspecting project assumptions, 55
interim deliverables, 82–83
internal rate of return (IRR), 20–21
interpersonal relationships with project
  managers, 34
IRR (internal rate of return), 20–21
Issue Tracking Log.xls template, 246

K

kickoff meetings, 245
known and unknown unknowns, 298

L

labor rates
 about, 167
 burdened, 167, 169
lag time
 about, 136
 allowing for, 135
 defined, 353
 shortening, 275–76
lead time, 135
 defined, 353
leadership, 39
legal regulations, 80
length of meetings, 244
lessons learned. See also lessons learned
  sessions
 collecting, 318–21, 334
 communicating, 229
 documenting, 325–27
 evaluating project's risks as, 307
 Excel workbooks for, 327
 importance of, 6, 48, 315–18
 learning about performance from, 215
 running sessions about, 318–21
 when to evaluate, 324
lessons learned facilitator, 320–21

lessons learned meeting template, 242
Lessons Learned Report.dot template, 327
lessons learned sessions
 agendas for, 324
 documenting findings of, 325–27
 ground rules for, 321–24
 running, 318–21
 when to schedule, 324
lessons learned workbooks, 327
leveling, 353
linking
 projects to corporate values, 15–16
 status reports to project notebooks, 251
 tasks to work packages, 101
links, 353
listening skills, 239–40
low estimates, 125–26

M

maintaining project schedules, 137–40
management. See functional managers,
  project management, project managers
management by walking around, 215
management meetings, 247–48
management reserves, 309, 353
managing project resources
 about, 209
 developing teams, 213–15
 evaluating people's performance, 215–19
 motivation and, 209–13
 reviewing performance against plans,
  217–18
 solving people problems, 216–17
material resources
 entering, 116
 entering rates and quantities for, 169
matrix organization, 353
measuring progress
 deliverables as means for, 83
 milestones for, 142
 WSB and, 89, 94
meetings. See also lessons learned sessions
 agendas for, 244
 communicating at, 230–31
 following up on, 244
 guidelines for, 241–44
 initiating discussions, 321
 kickoff, 245
 limiting time of, 244
 making most of, 240
 management, 247–48
 project status, 245–46
 running lessons learned sessions,
  318–21

Microsoft Access, 199
Microsoft Enterprise Project Management, 347
Microsoft Excel. *See* Excel
Microsoft Office Online, 299
Microsoft Office Project Server 2003, 311
Microsoft Outlook, 233–35
Microsoft Project Enterprise Project Management tools, 199
Microsoft Project Plan Import Export Template (Excel), 114
Microsoft Project. *See* Project
Microsoft SQL Server, 199
Microsoft Visio, 110–11
Microsoft Windows SharePoint Services Web site, 347
Microsoft Word. *See* Word
milestones, 140–43
  charting project progress with, 142
  creating, 143
  decision, 141–42
  defined, 353
  identifying, 53–54
  illustrated, 141
  naming, 143–44
  project start, 142
  reevaluating estimates after, 129
  types of, 141–43
mistakes
  communicating about, 238
  focusing on improvements vs. 322–24
  learning lessons from, 316–17
  when to identify lessons from, 324
modifying project schedules
  about, 267
  adding resources to tasks, 283
  assigning overtime, 280–81
  changing resource allocation units, 276–78
  clearing baselines, 285–86
  contouring tasks for project resources, 279–80
  cutting project duration with more resources, 283–84
  eliminating tasks from without deleting, 276
  fast-track projects, 269–72
  modifying baselines, 284–86
  saving additional baselines, 284–85
  scheduling around tasks, 274–75
  shortening lag time in, 275–76
  splitting long tasks into short ones, 273–74

  substituting resources, 281–83
  viewing multiple baselines, 192, 286
More Tables dialog box, 114, 205–6
motivating team members, 209–13
Multiple Baselines Gantt view, 192, 286
multitasking workers, 151

N

naming
  milestones and deliverables, 143–44
  resources, 115
  summary tasks, 91–92
  tasks, 91, 144–45
net present value
  defined, 18
  prioritizing projects using, 18–20
network diagrams, 353
newsletters for communications, 232
nonworking time, 152–53
norming stage of teams, 213–14
NPV function (Excel), 19

O

objectives. *See also* corporate values
  about project, 4, 52
  business, 79–80
  characteristics of realistic, 81–82
  clarifying, 62
  defined, 83
  delineating project success from, 79
  documenting stakeholders', 36–37
  financial results in, 16
  focusing project with, 62
  identifying project, 65–66
  project management, 4–7
  seeing if strategies achieve, 69–70
  types of, 79–80
Office Online, 299
Office Project Server 2003, 311
OLAP cubes, 199
ongoing operations, 4
OnTime_Problem_Statement.doc, 50
OnTime_Project_Charter.doc, 49
OnTime_Resource_Pool.mpp file, 120
OnTime_Responsibility_Matrix.xls file, 108
OnTime_Risk_Information_Sheet.doc, 301
opening Resource Information dialog box, 116
optimizing schedules, 292–93
Organization Chart template (Visio), 110
organizing project resources, 56

outline codes, 117–18
outlines
    defined, 353
    work breakdown structure, 86, 88
Outlook, 233–35
outsourcing work, 292
Overbudget Resources report, 198, 217–18
Overbudget Tasks report, 198
overlapping tasks, 155–56, 270–71
overtime
    assigning, 280–81
    defined, 353
    shortening schedules with, 291
overtime rate costs, 165–66
Ovt. Rate field in Resource Sheet view,
    165–67

P

padded estimates, 126–27
parallel tasks, 156
parametric models, 130
partial overlaps, 155–56, 270–71
part-time workers, 151
past performance. *See* lessons learned
payback period for projects, 17–18
percent complete, 353
percent work complete, 353
perfectionism and scope creep, 78–79
performance. *See* analyzing project
    performance, team performance
performing stage of teams, 213, 215
PERT (Program Evaluation and Review
    Technique)
    about, 130–31
    creating in Project, 131–33
    defined, 353
Physical % Complete field, 204–5
planning. *See also* communication plans,
    project plans, risk-management plans
    about, 5, 43, 58
    brainstorming and, 69
    budgetary, 56
    change and, 48, 58
    communication, 57
    developing risk-management plans, 57
    focusing effort with project plan, 46
    identifying deliverables and milestones,
        53–54
    identifying problems, 43–45
    inspecting project assumptions, 55
    mission statement, 52
    objectives, 52
    obtaining time for, 48

organizing resources, 56
overview of, 48
problem statement, 50
project schedules, 55–56
project strategy, 52
quality plans, 57
scope statement, 52–53
signing off on project plans, 46
stakeholder commitment to plans,
    45–46
steps in, 50–51
team member buy-in for, 46
work breakdown structure for, 55
predecessors
    creating dependencies with, 135–36
    defined, 133, 353
    editing dependencies between successor
        and, 271–72
prioritizing projects, 16–22
    about, 16
    balancing risks and opportunities, 21–22
    financial considerations in, 17–21
    internal rate of return, 20–21
    net present value and, 18–20
    payback period and, 17–18
problem statements
    about, 61, 72
    eliciting stakeholders' input on, 64
    identifying problem in, 61–62, 64
    including constraints in, 63
    planning and, 50
    project mission statements vs., 64
problems. *See also* problem statements
    defining by providing solutions, 62
    identifying project's, 43–45, 61–62, 64
productivity
    factoring into project schedules, 149–50
    increasing, 292
    people problems and, 216–17
Program Evaluation and Review Technique.
    See PERT
progressively increasing project scope, 293
Project. *See also* Task Sheet
    adding estimates to schedule, 130
    applying resource filters, 218
    applying schedule-related fields to views,
        193
    assigning resources, 112–19, 147–48
    automated dependencies, 136–37
    building WBS in, 95–98
    calculating baseline data, 191
    categorizing project resources, 117–18
    changing resource allocation units in,
        276–78

Project, *continued*
  creating hyperlinks to work packages,
    101
  dependencies for tasks, 135–36
  designating overtime rates, 281
  designating work resource rates, 167–68
  earned value measures calculated in, 203
  effort-driven scheduling, 283
  entering material resource rates and
    quantities, 169
  entering resource cost information, 117
  exporting cost data, 170–74, 199
  factoring productivity into schedules,
    149–50
  filters to check schedule progress, 194
  honoring task dependencies, 138–39
  importing resource information into,
    114–15
  importing WBS into, 99–100
  making performance analysis checklist,
    193
  milestones, 143
  modifying WBS in, 98–99
  PERT estimates, 131–33
  project cost reports, 198–99
  providing unique task names, 144–45
  resource calendars, 153
  resource pools, 119–20
  Resource Sheet view, 113–14
  reviewing schedule progress in, 191–93
  saving baseline values for schedule,
    179–81
  schedule templates, 342–43
  scheduling part-time workers and
    multitaskers, 151
  setting options for earned value
    calculations, 204–5
  specifying resources available, 119
  standard calendar, 152
  task calendars, 153, 275
  Task Sheet for assigning resources,
    145–46
  tracking risks in, 311
  types of task dependencies, 133–34
  values and variance calculated in, 191
  viewing costs and variances in Cost table,
    195–97
  Work Contour feature, 279–80
Project Acceptance Sign-Off.dot template,
  335–36
project archives. *See* archiving project
  information
project charters
  contents of, 27–28, 49

defined, 353
distributing, 28
function of, 26
preparation and signing of, 50
sample, 26–27
project completion
  about, 6, 331
  closing out contracts, 339
  collecting qualitative information at, 334
  customer sign-off at, 335–37
  handling transitions at, 337–39
  project closeout reports, 331–33
  quantifying results at, 333–34
project contingency funds, 127, 309–10,
  352
project cost reports, 198–99
project customers. *See* customers
project deliverables. *See* deliverables
project estimates
  basing on past performance, 316–17,
    342–43
  developing, 123–24
  improving accuracy of, 127–29
  interpreting duration of, 128
  methods of calculating, 129–30
  need for cost estimates, 161
  problems to avoid with, 124–27
  sensible practices for, 127–31
  statistical PERT, 130–33
  work estimates based on estimated
    scope, 125
project history. *See* archiving project
  information
project information
  communicating to team members, 229
  distributing different types of, 226
  for functional managers, 229
  tailoring to stakeholders, 227–28
  types of, 226–27
project management. *See also* project
  managers
  benefits of, 7–10
  executing project plan, 177–82
  honesty in, 39
  including tasks in WBS, 92
  objectives and processes in, 4–7
  project team's benefits from, 8–10
  scheduling vs., 5
  updating WBS with sticky notes, 95
  using responsibility matrix, 105–6
Project Management Institute, 4
project managers
  acknowledging team members, 38
  assigning goals, 210–11

building relationships with, 34
choosing what to communicate, 225–29
closing out contracts, 339
creating communication reminders, 233–35
criteria for selecting projects, 14–15
delineating communication roles, 210
eliciting stakeholders' input, 64
ensuring good communications, 237–39
establishing authority of, 28, 32, 39, 49–50
guidelines for meetings, 241–44
handling project completion tasks, 337–39
including name of in project charter, 28
managing team members, 112
motivating team members, 209–13
need for, 4
noting significant project variance, 249
obtaining planning time, 48
organizing project teams, 111–12
prioritizing cost-related changes, 293
project selection and, 3
promoting projects, 38
responding to risks, 307–8
reviewing team performance, 215–18
role in lessons learned sessions, 319–20
solving people problems, 216–17
tasks of, 181–82
tasks remaining at project completion, 331
teaching lessons learned, 317–18
too much or too little communications, 225
understanding financial measures, 17
working with functional managers, 33
working with project review boards, 22
project mission statements
about, 64, 72
defined, 64
example of, 68
planning and, 52
problem statements vs., 64
questions for developing, 65–67
reaffirming project importance with, 64–65
refining, 67–68
Project Notebook Contents.dot template, 344
project notebooks
contents of, 178–79
electronic alternatives for, 345–47
linking project status reports to, 251

selecting information to archive from, 343–45
project objectives. See objectives
project organization chart
about, 85, 120
illustrated, 110
purpose of, 109–11
project planning. See planning
project plans
defined, 354
focusing effort with, 46
function of, 79
getting approvals and commitments to, 177–78
project notebook for, 178–79
revising objectives in, 81
saving baseline values for, 179–81
signing off on, 46
stakeholder commitment to, 45–46
using baseline budget, 181
project resources. See also project organization chart, project teams, responsibility matrix
adding to tasks, 283
adjusting allocation of, 276–78
assigning to tasks, 123, 145–48
categorizing, 117–18
contouring tasks for, 279–80
creating resource in Project, 115–19
designating overtime rates for, 281
developing plan for, 111
entering cost information for, 117
estimating needs for, 123–24
importing information about, 114–15
methods for adding in Project, 113–15
naming, 115
outlining project responsibility, 105–6
outlining skills required, 56
putting together project teams, 111–12
rates and quantities of material resources, 169
reassigning, 290–92
scheduling part-time workers and multitaskers, 151
sharing, 119–20
shortening project duration with more, 283–84
specifying available, 119
specifying rates for work resources, 167–68
substituting, 281–83
transitioning at project completion, 337–38

project review boards, 22
project schedules. *See also* balancing project
    variables, crashing, project estimates,
    shortening project schedules, tasks
  about, 55–56, 123, 267
  adding milestones to, 140–43
  adjusting tasks for efficiency, 153–54
  assessing risks in, 304–5
  assigning overtime, 280–81, 291
  assigning resources to tasks, 123, 145–48
  calculating costs in, 165–67
  changing resource allocation units,
    276–78
  clearing baselines, 285–86
  creating template for, 342
  cutting lag time in, 275–76
  date constraints in, 137–39
  deadlines in, 139–40
  developing project estimates, 123–24
  developing resource plans, 111
  displaying summary tasks for, 267–68
  effort-driven, 283
  exporting costs from, 170–74
  factoring productivity into, 149–50
  fast-tracking projects, 154–55, 269–72
  filters for checking progress, 194
  Gantt Chart views for, 268–69
  honoring task dependencies in, 138–39
  learning lessons from past, 316–17
  maintaining, 137–40
  modifying baselines, 284–86
  optimizing, 292–93
  part-time and multitasking workers in,
    151
  project crashing, 156–59
  providing unique task names, 144–45
  quantifying project completion results,
    333
  reviewing progress in Project, 191–93
  saving baseline values for, 179–81,
    284–85
  scheduling around tasks, 274–75
  shortening, 154–56, 283–84, 291
  splitting long tasks into short ones,
    273–74
  substituting resources in, 281–83
  tracking progress in, 190–91
  types of task dependencies, 133–34
  viewing multiple baselines, 192, 286
  working and nonworking days in,
    152–53
project scope. *See also* balancing project
    variables
  defined, 354

eliminating tasks without deleting, 276
  progressively increasing, 293
  quantifying project completion results
    for, 333
  reducing, 293
  racking schedule progress with change
    in, 190
  work estimates based on estimated, 125
project selection
  accurate cost estimates and, 128–29
  project managers and, 3
project sponsors
  announcing, 25, 28
  asking advice of, 32–33
  communicating with, 224
  establishing project manager's authority,
    49–50
  ways of supporting projects, 32–33
Project Statistics dialog box, 190–91
project status meetings, 245–46
project status reports, 249–51
  adding risk status to, 312
  illustrated, 250
  linking to project notebooks, 251
project strategies
  about, 68, 72
  brainstorming to develop, 69
  choosing, 70–72
  evaluating, 69–70
  identifying, 68–69
  including constraints in, 63
  planning, 52
  stating in mission statement, 65, 67
project teams
  acknowledging each member, 38
  adding resource information for, 112–15
  communicating with, 6–7, 35, 38, 224
  developing, 213–15
  effect of low estimates on, 126
  gaining members' commitment to
    projects, 34–35
  identifying project chain of command,
    109–11
  perfectionism and scope creep, 78–79
  project management benefits for, 8–10
  putting together, 111–12
projects. *See also* analyzing project
    performance, project management
  assessing risks in, 304–5
  benefits of managing risks, 297–98
  breaking into phases, 293
  capturing lessons from, 6, 48
  characteristics of, 3–4
  choosing strategies for, 70–72

communications in, 221–22
conflicting with corporate values, 15
criteria for selecting, 14–15
defined, 3
defining success for, 79
describing risks of, 302–3
developing realistic objectives, 81–82
fast-tracking, 154–55, 269–72, 293
focusing business objectives, 62
identifying problems of, 43–45, 61–62,
    64
importance of planning, 43
inspecting assumptions of, 55, 77
kickoff meetings for, 245
linking to corporate values, 15–16
maintaining focus with scope statement,
    75–76
measuring progress in, 83, 142
need for commitment to, 25
objectives for, 4
organizing resources for, 56
planning overview for, 48
processes for managing, 4–6
project charters for, 25–28
promoting, 38
reaffirming importance of, 64–65
review boards for, 22
scope of, 4
selecting information to archive, 343–45
signing off on plans for, 46
stakeholders in, 35
statement of work, 54
Project_Synopsis.xls file, 345
promoting projects, 38

Q

qualitative information on project
    completion, 334
quality. *See also* balancing project variables
    as project objective, 80
    cost of fixing defects, 187
    data needed to analyze progress on, 187
    quantifying, 164, 333
    reductions in, 294
    scheduling reviews of, 187
quality assurance, 354
quality control, 354
quality plans, 57
quantifying
    project completion results, 333–34
    qualitative benefits, 164

R

reassigning project resources, 290–92
reducing
    project scope, 293
    quality in project, 294
refining project mission statements, 67–68
reminders for communications, 233–35
renaming tasks, 144–45
Replace Resource dialog box, 283
reports
    Budget, 198
    Cash Flow, 198
    Earned Value, 199, 206
    e-mail distribution of, 232
    lessons learned, 325–27
    Overbudget Resources, 198, 217–18
    Overbudget Tasks, 198
    project closeout, 331–33
    project cost, 198–99
    project status, 230, 249–51
resource calendars, 153
Resource Information dialog box
    applying outline codes to resources, 118
    creating resource rates in, 117
    opening, 116
    specifying resource availability, 119
resource outline codes, 117–18
resource pools, 119–20, 354
resource rates, 117, 195
Resource Sheet view
    adding resources in, 113–14
    categorizing resources in, 117
    cost/use field, 166
    illustrated, 116
    specifying work rates, 167–68
    Std. Rate and Ovt. Rate fields, 165–67
Resources/Assignments With Overtime
    filter, 218
responsibility matrix
    about, 35, 105, 120
    creating, 107–8
    filtering in Excel, 108–9
    illustrated, 107
    purpose of, 105–6
    RICA acronym for levels, 106–7
return on investment (ROI), 18
reviewing
    involving project sponsors in reviews, 32,
        50
    risks at project completion, 334
    scheduling quality reviews, 187
    scope statement's assumptions, 55, 77

revising work breakdown structure, 92–93
rewards
    employee performance and, 189
    handing out project pens, mugs, and
        products, 245
RICA acronym, 106–7
risk logs, 311–12
risk management, 354
risk management binder, 179
risk mitigation, 307
risk-assessment summary, 303
risk-management plans
    about, 299–301
    choosing risks to manage, 305–7
    contents of, 301
    dealing with known and unknown
        unknowns, 298
    developing, 57
    factors to cover in, 298–99
    illustrated, 300
    risk-assessment summary in, 303
risks. *See also* risk-management plans
    assessing, 304–5
    balancing opportunities with, 21–22
    benefits of managing, 297–98
    choosing ones to manage, 305–6, 307
    contingency funds for, 127, 309–10, 352
    evaluating for project strategies, 70
    factors introducing, 298–99
    identifying and describing, 302–3
    incorporating in performance analysis,
        188
    inherent nature of project, 297
    inspecting project assumptions for, 55
    known and unknown unknowns, 298
    responding to, 303–8
    reviewing at project completion, 334
    tracking, 310–12
ROI (return on investment), 18
running meetings, 226–28, 244

S

sample files. *See* companion CD
Sarbanes-Oxley Act, 3
Save Baseline dialog box, 285
saving
    additional baselines, 284–85
    document as Word template, 342–43
    export maps in Excel, 174
    values for baseline schedules, 179–81
schedule performance index (SPI), 203,
    354
Schedule table, 193

schedule variance (SV), 203
schedules. *See also* project schedules
    defined, 354
scheduling, 5
scope creep, 53
scope statements. *See also* project scope
    about, 52, 75–76
    as high-level view of project, 90
    avoiding scope creep, 53, 77–79
    backyard remodel project, 76
    defined, 83
    developing, 77
    example of, 53
    identifying high-level tasks from, 89–90
    illustrating in work breakdown structure,
        88
    reviewing assumptions of, 55, 77
scribe for lessons learned sessions, 321
selecting projects
    criteria for, 14–15
    linking projects to objectives, 15–16
    minimum return on investment and
        project funding, 18
    overview, 13
    project managers and process of, 3
    tips for, 13
    understanding project's financial
        measures, 17
SharePoint Services Web site, 347
sharing
    project documents in shared folder,
        346–47
    project resources, 119–20
    time-saving techniques, 315–16
    workspaces, 347
shortening project schedules, 154–56. *See
    also* fast-track projects
    additional resources per task, 283–84
    fast-tracks for projects, 154–55
    overtime and, 291
    project crashing, 156–59
    running tasks in parallel, 156
skills
    communication, 240
    listening, 239–40
slack, 354
Slipping Assignments filter, 218
Slipping Tasks report, 194
solutions
    defining problems by providing, 62
    solving people problems, 216–17
SPI (schedule performance index), 203,
    354
sponsorship of projects, 25, 28

spreadsheet files for project summaries, 345
SQL Server, 199
stakeholder analysis document, 37–36
stakeholders
    adding to responsibility matrix, 107–8
    asking for suggestions balancing project variables, 289–90
    communicating with, 6, 224–25, 227–28
    defined, 354
    documenting, 36
    eliciting input from, 64
    identifying, 29–35
    importance of, 28–29
    knowing expectations of, 38
    project support by, 21
    reaffirming project importance for, 64–65
    understanding project scope with cost estimates, 161
    working with reluctant, 30–31
standard calendar, 152
standard rate costs, 165–66
standard rates, 354
start dates, 354
start-to-finish dependencies, 134
start-to-start dependencies, 134
statement of work, 54, 354
status reports, 230
Std. Rate field in Resource Sheet view, 165–67
sticky notes, 95
storming stage of teams, 213–4
strategic planning. See planning, project strategies
success
    defining with objectives, 79
    publicizing project, 238
    talking about project, 322
success criteria, 53–54
successors
    creating dependencies with, 135–36
    defined, 133, 354
    editing dependencies between predecessors and, 271–72
Summary table, 193
Summary Task Information dialog box, 193
summary tasks
    adding subordinate tasks to, 97–98
    defined, 86, 354
    displaying on project schedules, 267–68
    filtering out before exporting cost information, 171–72
    illustrated, 87–88

naming, 91–92
recording for WBS, 95–96
removing resources from, 274
SV (schedule variance), 203

T
tables
    applying schedule-related fields to Project views, 193
    Cost, 195–97
    Earned Value Cost Indicators, 205
    Earned Value, 205
    Schedule, 193
    Summary, 193
    Variance, 193
    viewing earned value in, 205–6
tangible and intangible deliverables, 82–83
task calendars, 153, 275
Task Details Form, 180–81
Task Form, 147
Task Mapping dialog box, 172
Task Recurrence dialog box (Outlook), 234–35
Task Sheet
    assigning resources in, 145–46
    editing task dependency, 271
    illustrated, 146
    using Task Form vs., 147
    viewing WBS in, 86–87
tasks
    adding resources to, 283–84
    adding subordinate summary, 97
    adjusting for efficiency, 153–54
    assigning resources to, 123, 145–48, 195
    calculating estimates for complex, 131
    choosing to fast-track, 154–55
    deadlines added to, 139–40
    defined, 354
    dependencies for, 135–36
    determining size of WBS, 94
    eliminating from scope without deleting, 276
    filling in remaining WBS, 91–92
    high-level tasks for backyard remodel project, 91–92
    identifying correct dependencies for, 134–35
    identifying high-level WBS, 89–90
    lag and lead time for, 135
    linking to work packages, 101
    making into subtasks, 98
    modifying duration, work, and units for, 277–78

tasks, *continued*
  naming, 91–92, 144–45
  overlapping, 155–56, 270–71
  project manager's, 181–82
  reporting percentages complete for, 186
  risks associated with hard-to-estimate,
    305
  running in parallel, 156
  scheduling around, 274–75
  setting fixed costs for, 167, 170
  shortening duration with more
    resources, 283–84
  showing critical path with filtered,
    269–70
  showing only work packages, 171–72
  splitting long into short, 273–74
  summary, 86–87, 354
  types of dependencies, 133–34
TCPI (to complete performance index),
  204
team members. *See also* team performance
  communicating to, 229
  getting project estimates from, 127, 312
  knowledge of project manager's role, 210
  motivating, 209–13, 212
  providing feedback for, 212
  reaffirming project importance for, 65
  reviewing performance against plans,
    217–18
  role in lessons learned sessions, 321
  watching performance of, 215–16
team performance. *See also* analyzing
    project performance, lessons learned
  evaluating, 215–18, 219
  learning from past, 48, 215, 315–18
  project objectives and, 80
  reviewing people's actual vs. planned,
    217–18
  rewarding, 189
  watching team members', 215–16
teams. *See* project teams
technical objectives, 80
templates
  capital budgeting tool, 163–65
  change request form, 262
  creating project schedule, 342–43
  Issue Tracking Log.xls, 246
  Lessons Learned Agenda.dot, 324
  Lessons Learned Report, 327
  Project Acceptance Sign-Off, 335–36
  Project Notebook Contents, 344
  project status report, 249–50
  risk-management plan, 303
  work package, 102

time
  accuracy of reporting, 188–90
  data for tracking project progress, 189
  lag, 135–36
  lead, 135
  nonworking, 152–53
  obtaining for planning, 48
  tracking time in accounting systems, 189
  trade-offs with money when crashing
    budgets, 157–59
to complete performance index (TCPI),
  204
tools, 211
top-down estimating, 129
tracking
  changes, 190, 262–64
  costs and cost variances, 195–97
  risks, 310–12
  schedule progress, 190–91
  time with accounting systems, 189
Tracking Gantt view, 191–92, 268
transitions at project completion, 337–39

U

unit values for tasks, 277–78
unknown unknowns, 298

V

VAC (variance at completion) measure, 203
Variance table, 193
variances
  calculating on baseline values, 180, 191
  cost, 202
  defined, 354
  noting significant project, 249
  reviewing at project completion, 334
  tracking and viewing costs and, 195–97
  viewing cost, 195–97
viewing
  costs and cost variances, 195–97, 205–6
  schedule-related fields in views, 193
Visio, 110–11
Visio WBS Chart Wizard, 96

W

WBS. *See* work breakdown structure
Windows SharePoint Services, 311
Windows SharePoint Services Web site,
  347
Word
  building WBS in, 96
  Lessons Learned Agenda template, 324

Lessons Learned Report template, 327
saving document as template, 342–43
work, 354
work breakdown structure (WBS)
  adding right amount of detail to, 93–94
  benefits of, 88–89
  building, 89–93
  creating in Project, 95–98
  defined, 75, 85, 103, 354
  detailing work packages, 101–2
  determining size of tasks, 94
  diagram form for, 86–87
  high-level tasks for backyard remodel
    project, 91–92
  importing into Project, 99–100
  including project management tasks in,
    92
  modifying, 98–99
  outline form for, 86–88
  planning with, 55
  recording summary tasks and work
    packages for, 95–96
  revising structure of, 92–93
  summary tasks and work packages in, 86
  task names in, 91
  teams to develop, 92
  template for work package, 102

updating with sticky notes, 95
verifying design of, 93
Work Contour feature, 279–80
work estimates based on estimated project
  scope, 125
work packages
  about, 85
  adding detail to, 101–2
  creating hyperlinks to, 101
  data for analyzing progress on, 186–87
  defined, 86, 354
  filtering tasks to show only, 171–72
  illustrated, 87–88, 102
  naming, 91
  recording for WBS, 95–96
  template for, 102
work resources
  obtaining project times and status from,
    188–90
  specifying rates for, 167–68
work values for tasks, 277–78

X

XIRR function (Excel), 20–21
XNPV function (Excel), 19–20

Additional Resources for Business and Home Users

Published and Forthcoming Titles from Microsoft Press

Beyond Bullet Points: Using Microsoft® PowerPoint® to Create Presentations That Inform, Motivate, and Inspire
Cliff Atkinson • ISBN 0-7356-2052-0

Improve your presentations—and increase your impact—with 50 powerful, practical, and easy-to-apply techniques for Microsoft PowerPoint. With *Beyond Bullet Points*, you'll take your presentation skills to the next level—learning innovative ways to design and deliver your message. Organized into five sections, including Distill Your Ideas, Structure Your Story, Visualize Your Message, Create a Conversation, and Maintain Engagement—the book uses clear, concise language and just the right visuals to help you understand concepts and start getting better results.

Take Back Your Life! Special Edition: Using Microsoft Outlook® to Get Organized and Stay Organized
Sally McGhee • ISBN 0-7356-2215-9

Unrelenting e-mail. Conflicting commitments. Endless interruptions. In this book, productivity expert Sally McGhee shows you how to take control and reclaim something that you thought you'd lost forever—your work-life balance. Now you can benefit from Sally's popular and highly regarded corporate education programs, learning simple but powerful techniques for rebalancing your personal and professional commitments using the productivity features in Outlook. When you change your approach, you can change your results. So learn what thousands of Sally's clients worldwide have discovered about taking control of their everyday productivity—and start transforming your own life today!

On Time! On Track! On Target! Managing Your Projects Successfully with Microsoft Project
Bonnie Biafore • ISBN 0-7356-2256-6

This book focuses on the core skills you need to successfully manage any project, giving you a practical education in project management and how-to instruction for using Microsoft Office Project Professional 2003 and other Microsoft Office Professional Edition 2003 programs, such as Excel® 2003, Outlook 2003, and Word 2003. Learn the essentials of project management, including creating successful project plans, tracking and evaluating performance, and controlling project costs. Whether you're a beginner just learning how to manage projects or a project manager already working on a project, this book has something for you. Includes a companion CD with sample Project templates.

Design to Sell: Using Microsoft Publisher to Inform, Motivate, and Persuade
Roger C. Parker • ISBN 0-7356-2260-4

Design to Sell relates the basics of effective message creation and formatting to the specific capabilities built into Microsoft Publisher—the powerful page layout program found on hundreds of thousands of computers around the world. Many Microsoft Office users already have Publisher on their computers but don't use it because they don't think of themselves as writers or designers. Here is a one-stop guide to marketing that even those without big budgets or previous design or writing experience can use to create compelling, easy-to-read marketing materials. Each chapter has an interactive exercise as well as questions with answers on the author's Web site. Also on the Web site are downloadable worksheets and templates, book updates, more illustrations of the projects in the book, and additional before-and-after project makeovers.

Microsoft Windows® XP Networking and Security Inside Out: Also Covers Windows 2000
Ed Bott and Carl Siechert • ISBN 0-7356-2042-3

Configure and manage your PC network—and help combat privacy and security threats—from the inside out! Written by the authors of the immensely popular *Microsoft Windows XP Inside Out*, this book packs hundreds of timesaving solutions, troubleshooting tips, and work-arounds for networking and security topics—all in concise, fast-answer format.

Dig into the tools and techniques for configuring workgroup, domain, Internet, and remote networking, and all the network components and features in between. Get the answers you need to use Windows XP Service Pack 2 and other tools, tactics, and features to help defend your personal computer and network against spyware, pop-up ads, viruses, hackers, spam, denial-of-service attacks, and other threats. Learn how to help secure your Virtual Private Networks (VPNs), remote access, and wireless networking services, and take ultimate control with advanced solutions such as file encryption, port blocking, IPSec, group policies, and tamper-proofing tactics for the registry. Get up to date on hot topics such as peer-to-peer networks, public wireless access points, smart cards, handheld computers, wireless LANs, and more. Plus, the CD includes bonus resources that make it easy for you to share your new security and networking expertise with your colleagues, friends, and family.

For more information about Microsoft Press® books and other learning products,
visit: **www.microsoft.com/mspress** *and* **www.microsoft.com/learning**

Microsoft®
Press

What do you think of this book? We want to hear from you!

Do you have a few minutes to participate in a brief online survey? Microsoft is interested in hearing your feedback about this publication so that we can continually improve our books and learning resources for you.

To participate in our survey, please visit:

www.microsoft.com/learning/booksurvey

And enter this book's ISBN, 0-7356-2256-6. As a thank-you to survey participants in the United States and Canada, each month we'll randomly select five respondents to win one of five $100 gift certificates from a leading online merchant.* At the conclusion of the survey, you can enter the drawing by providing your e-mail address, which will be used for prize notification *only*.

Thanks in advance for your input. Your opinion counts!

Sincerely,

Microsoft Learning

Microsoft | Learning

Learn More. Go Further.